Windows 3.1
Made Easy

Windows 3.1
Made Easy

Tom Sheldon

Osborne **McGraw-Hill**

Berkeley New York St. Louis San Francisco
Auckland Bogotá Hamburg London Madrid
Mexico City Milan Montreal New Delhi Panama City
Paris São Paulo Singapore Sydney
Tokyo Toronto

Osborne **McGraw-Hill**
2600 Tenth Street
Berkeley, California 94710
U.S.A.

For information on translations or book distributors outside of the U.S.A.,
please write to Osborne **McGraw-Hill** at the above address.

Windows 3.1 Made Easy

1234567890 DOC 998765432

ISBN 0-07-881725-0

Contents

Acknowledgments

I would like to acknowledge all the users in the CompuServe Windows Beta Users forum and Windows Beta Developers forum. Over the course of a year, we discussed features, talked about problems, and came up with solutions. What a unique way to launch a product.

Frances Stack deserves mention for pushing this project forward and keeping it, and me, on schedule.

Last, but not least, I would like to thank Alexandra for taking care of me during the project, for copyediting, and for her work on several of the chapters.

Introduction

Welcome to *Windows 3.1 Made Easy*. This book is about the much anticipated Windows 3.1 graphical user interface. This version of Windows has been in beta testing for over a year at over 1500 sites. It is one of the most thoroughly tested software packages in history.

This book is designed to get you up and running with Windows, starting with an overview of the basic interface and leading you into advanced topics. Follow the simple installation and setup steps in your Windows manual, then use this book for step-by-step instruction. The examples in this book guide you through Windows features and give you ideas about how to use Windows tools and accessories in your everyday activities.

If you've used a previous version of Windows, you will learn about the new features of Windows 3.1. Some of these new features are part of Microsoft's "Information at your fingertips" strategy. As the name implies, computer systems now provide access to a wide variety of information in a wide variety of formats. The Windows graphical user interface provides easy access to large volumes of sound, graphics, and multimedia information, and provides a platform for the development of even more sophisticated applications.

Some of the new features of Windows 3.1 are listed here:

- *Enhanced performance and reliability* Windows 3.1 is improved in performance and is more capable of recovering from errors. For example, you can press (CTRL)-(ALT)-(DEL) to end an application that has "crashed" and still return to Windows where you can save your other documents.

- *TrueType fonts*   The addition of TrueType fonts provides what-you-see-is-what-you-get (WYSIWYG) capabilities to almost every Windows system. The high-resolution fonts you see on the screen will print without using special cartridges or upgrades.

- *Multimedia support*   Windows 3.1 supports a wide variety of sound boards as well as connection to external musical instruments and MIDI-controlled devices. You can create sounds and animation and include them in your documents.

- *Drag-and-drop functionality*   Drag-and-drop capabilities provide a new way to interact with the Windows graphical user interface using the mouse. Simply select an icon for a file or another object, drag it to an appropriate icon for the action you wish to take, and drop it on the icon. For example, select a file icon and drop it on a printer icon to print the file.

- *Object linking and embedding*   Object linking and embedding is a new feature that promotes "compound documents." A compound document is one created with elements from many different applications. Now one document can hold all the files (graphics, spreadsheets, and text) for a single project. Editing and updating of any linked element can take place in the compound document.

- *Common Features*   Many Windows options, such as Open, Save, and Print now include common dialog boxes. They look the same no matter what application you're in, so you don't have to relearn the dialog box features every time.

There are, of course, many other new features discussed throughout the chapters ahead. But now you need to get started with Windows. Chapter 1 is an overview of Windows, and in Chapter 2 you learn different ways to start Windows.

Chapter 3 starts your exploration of the Windows interface; you learn about working with Windows itself. Then, in following chapters, you learn about common features so you'll be prepared to use almost any Windows application.

The chapters continue with a discussion of customizing Windows, using Help, accessing files, and using the Windows applications. Finally, there is a chapter about games; after all your effort, you deserve to have some fun.

Windows Update Notes

I offer a set of update notes to keep you informed about the latest information about Windows. The notes contain the following information:

- Update information from Microsoft Technical Support and the Microsoft Knowledge Base information service

- Known bugs, problems, and solutions

- Software and hardware compatibility information

- System and hardware notes

- The latest tips, tricks, and techniques for using Windows and Windows applications

I also participate in various online forums where Windows users discuss hardware and software problems and solutions. This user information is often the most important when it comes to helping you run Windows, and is included in the notes.

The first set of notes will be available about two months after the Windows 3.1 release. I constantly update the notes to guarantee the set you receive has the latest information. To further guarantee the accuracy of the information, I print and assemble the notes in-house on an as-needed basis.

To order the notes, use the coupon in the back of this book. Send a check or money order for $10, made payable to Tom Sheldon. If you are a California resident, add 72 cents. The price covers shipping and handling costs. This is an offering of the author, not Osborne/McGraw-Hill.

1

Windows Overview

Welcome to the world of Microsoft Windows. Windows gives you a brand-new way to work with computers that is not only more exciting, but also helps you be more productive. Applications (software) written to work with Windows have a similar look and feel. That means you can easily switch from one manufacturer's program to another's without having to relearn basic functions like opening, editing, printing, and saving documents. In addition, Windows provides a Clipboard feature, so you can "cut" text and graphics images from one application and "paste" them into another.

This chapter presents a guided tour of Windows that helps you find your way around the screens as you get familiar with Windows terminology.

The Windows Desktop Metaphor

The designers of Windows wanted to create an interface that would be instantly familiar to almost everyone, so they employed a desktop metaphor. The entire computer screen is like a desktop, and windows are placed on this desktop in the same way you might arrange papers, calendars, notepads, calculators, and other workplace tools on your desk. The first window you see when you start Windows is shown in Figure 1-1.

Furthermore, when you do paperwork on your desktop, you might have several sheets of paper side by side or stacked on top of one another. In Windows, several windows can be open at once, so you can place documents side by side for comparison, or stack them so you can shuffle through your work during the day. The advantage of having several projects open at once is that you can get at your work quickly when a client calls with a question or when the boss walks in. And you can copy information from one window to another. Figure 1-2 shows a spreadsheet open in one window, a notepad in another, and a word processing document in still another.

Although several applications can be open at once, only one window is *active* and can respond to your immediate keyboard input. Clicking a window with the mouse makes it the active window, and its title bar is highlighted;

Figure 1-1. *The Program Manager window*

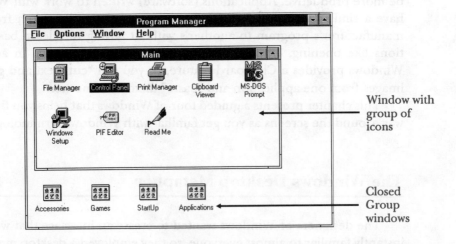

Window with group of icons

Closed Group windows

Figure 1-2. *Several windows can be open at once on the Windows desktop*

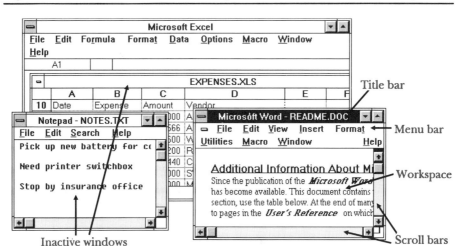

you can then start typing text or executing commands for that window. In Figure 1-2, the window titled "Microsoft Word - README.DOC" is the active window; notice its highlighted title bar. Any text you type or commands you execute will affect the active window, while the other windows wait patiently in the background until you make them active.

The *workspace* is the area of the window where you type text, draw, or otherwise work with data. When the information in the workspace is saved to disk and given a filename, that name appears in the title bar. In Figure 1-2, the file README.DOC is open in the Microsoft Word window. The title bar helps you distinguish between open windows. Suppose you need to run two copies of the same application at once, to compare and edit documents—the title bars allow you to see which document is in each window.

Some applications, like Microsoft Word for Windows, let you open multiple documents at once in separate windows, so you don't have to run more than one copy of the program.

Note

Mouse or Keyboard?

Before continuing, you'll want to get familiar with your mouse and keyboard. The Windows interface works best with a mouse, and although you don't need one to take advantage of Windows's features, it's highly recommended that you use a mouse.

Mouse Usage and Terminology

If your system has a mouse, a pointer in the shape of an arrow appears on the screen. In the following illustration, the mouse pointer points to a button in the upper-right corner of the window:

To move the pointer, move the mouse along your desk or tabletop. (If you run out of room while moving the mouse, you can pick up the mouse and reposition it.) Most mouse devices have two buttons, and some have three. With Windows, you use only the left and right buttons.

This book employs the following terms to describe the actions of the mouse:

Term	Action
Point	Move the onscreen pointer by moving the mouse. Point the tip of the arrow to an object on the screen, such as a button, icon, or character.
Click	Press and immediately release a mouse button.
Click and hold	Press and hold down the mouse button until you complete an action.
Drag	Point at an object on the screen; then click and hold while moving the mouse. The object moves with the mouse.
Double-click	Click a mouse button twice quickly. Double-clicking is the Windows/mouse equivalent of executing a command by pressing the (ENTER) key.

Keyboard Usage and Terminology

The keyboard can be used instead of the mouse to access menu items on windows. (The *menu bar* that appears on many windows is explained in "The Menu Bar and Pull-Down Menus," later in this chapter.) To access window menus with the keyboard, press the (ALT) key followed by another key related to the menu item you want. Most menu options are represented by an underlined letter or number that you press to activate the option.

For example, to open the File menu from the Program Manager menu bar,

Menu bar

you would press (ALT)-(F), because *F* is the underlined letter in the File option. This File menu will open,

and you can then type the letter of the menu option you want to select. Note that you don't have to press the (ALT) key again once the menu is open; just press the underlined letter of the option you want.

As you work with Windows menus using the keyboard, keep in mind:

- Once you become familiar with menu options and the keys that activate them, you can use the keystroke method to execute a command without looking at the menu.

- Some menu options may not be available for your current activity. These options will appear "grayed out," as are the Move and Copy commands in the File menu shown previously. (When you select text or graphics to move or copy, these menu options will become available.)

- Some menu options have *speed keys*—special keys or key-combinations that accomplish the same action as the menu option. In the previous illustration, the Move option, when available for use, can be executed by pressing (F7). You'll want to get familiar with these speed keys, since they often are the fastest way to execute a command. Even mouse users can benefit from learning them.

Types of Windows

It's important to understand the difference between the various types of windows that can appear on your Windows desktop. Typically, the Program Manager is the first window you see when Windows starts, as shown in Figure 1-1. From the Program Manager, you can open *application windows*. Programs such as Microsoft Word for Windows, Aldus Pagemaker, and Micrografx Designer run in application windows. Program Manager is itself an application window used to start your programs and organize the way you work.

Within an application window, you will sometimes see a type of "sub-window" called a *document window*. The Program Manager window shown in Figure 1-3 has two document windows, Main and Accessories. Note that the Main and Accessories windows are positioned inside the Program Manager window. They cannot be moved out of the Program Manager window onto the desktop.

Don't be confused by the term *document window*—this kind of window is not restricted to document files. In the Program Manager, document windows hold groups of icons and are usually referred to as *group windows*.

In applications, such as word processors, document windows hold documents. Figure 1-4 shows two document windows open in the Microsoft Word for Windows application window. The advantage of document windows is that only one copy of the application needs to be loaded in memory. Each document window then shares the menus and other features of the host application. Note that the document windows in Figure 1-4 do not have menu options of their own.

Figure 1-3. *The Main and Accessories document windows are part of the Program Manager window. They share Program Manager's menu commands, but cannot be moved outside of its window borders*

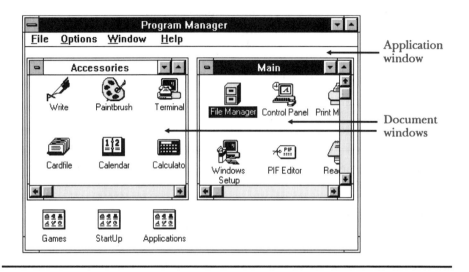

Figure 1-4. *In an application like Microsoft Word, one or more documents can be open at once, each in its own document window*

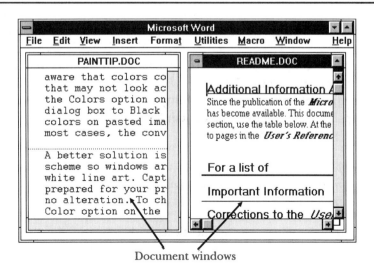

Windows as Icons

All windows can be temporarily removed from the screen when not in use by reducing them to icons on the desktop. This is called *minimizing* the window. The name of the application and any files loaded in its workspace appear under the icon, as shown here:

Notepad -   Paintbrush -   File Manager -
README.TXT   BOXES.BMP   [d:\draw*.*]

When a document window is minimized, it appears within the host application window. For example, here is the Program Manager window with all its group windows minimized to group icons:

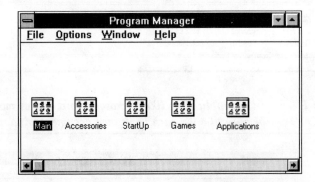

Double-clicking any of these icons opens the group to reveal the application or utility icons within. Use group windows in Program Manager to organize your applications into meaningful groups. For example, you might have a group called Newsletter that contains the programs and documents used to create a monthly newsletter.

An application remains in memory whether its window is open or minimized. Reducing the window to an icon does not exit the application—it's just a way to remove clutter from the screen so you can work with other windows.

Note

Keep in mind that applications with icons in the Program Manager window are not running, as those on the desktop are. As shown in Figure 1-5,

Figure 1-5. *Icons in Program Manager are used to start applications. Icons on the desktop represent applications already loaded in memory*

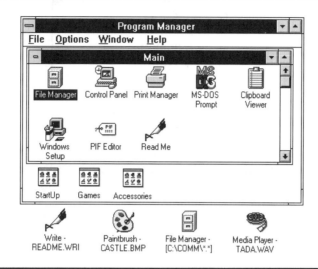

the icons in Program Manager are used to start an application; icons on the desktop represent applications that are already loaded in memory.

Window Elements

Now it's time to take a quick look at the individual elements of a window. Here you examine the Program Manager window, but most other windows have similar features.

The Control Menu

The button for opening the Control menu is located in the upper-left corner of every window. When you click the button, the Control menu shown here appears:

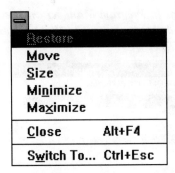

The Control menu has options for moving, sizing, minimizing, maximizing, and closing windows. The Control menu is really designed for keyboard users who need to access functions that mouse users would perform by pointing, clicking, and dragging.

The Menu Bar and Pull-Down Menus

When a window has a menu bar at the top, and you select an option from the bar, a *pull-down menu* appears. Here is the File menu for the Program Manager:

You can select options from menus by pointing and clicking with the mouse, or by using keyboard techniques described in "Keyboard Techniques and Speed Keys" in Chapter 3, "Using the Windows Interface."

1

Window Sizing Buttons

Click the button at the upper-right corner of a window to minimize it to an icon or maximize it to fill the whole screen. These Minimize and Maximize buttons are shown here:

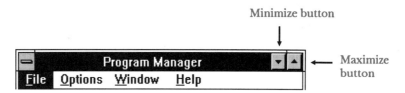

When a window has been maximized, the Maximize button is replaced by the Restore button, as shown here:

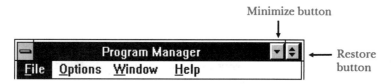

Click this button to restore the window to the size it was before being maximized.

Scroll Bars

Scroll bars appear on a window when all of its contents can't fit within the window. Most application windows have scroll bars, as shown in Figure 1-6. The scroll bars may appear on the right border for scrolling vertically, on the bottom border for scrolling horizontally, or both. Scroll bars can only be used with the mouse.

Borders

Borders define the limits of a window and also provide some functions. Mouse users can click and drag any window border or corner to *resize* the

Figure 1-6.   *Mouse users can use scroll bars to move vertically or horizontally*
through a document

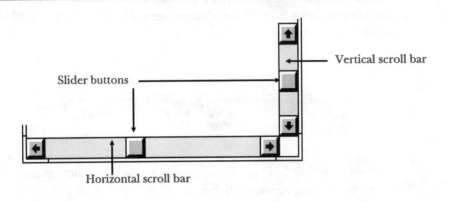

Slider buttons ────────────────────────→

Vertical scroll bar

Horizontal scroll bar

window. When you point to a border or corner, the mouse pointer changes
to a double-headed arrow, as shown on the right-hand border of this window:

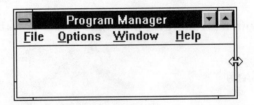

You then click and drag the pointer to resize the window.

The Title Bar

You've already learned about the title bar that appears at the top of a
window. One more thing to remember about the title bar is that, with a mouse,
you can use the title bar to move a window to another location. Just point to
the title bar, and then click and drag the window.

Dialog Boxes

Menu options that include an ellipsis (...) display *dialog boxes* when you select them. A dialog box is a related menu or list of options or settings that help the command to accomplish its task. You provide information or make choices in the dialog box before executing the command. For example, the Print Setup dialog box in Figure 1-7 is used before printing to choose a printer, the paper orientation, and the paper size.

Multitasking with Windows

You have seen how Windows lets you load and run several applications at the same time; this capability is called *multitasking*. Most of the time you'll probably work with one application while others wait in background windows until you need them. However, Windows also lets you have a background (nonactive) application working on one task while you are doing something else in the active window. For example, a background application can sort a mailing list or print a document as you write a letter in another window.

Figure 1-7. *A dialog box is used to choose options and specify settings for executing a command*

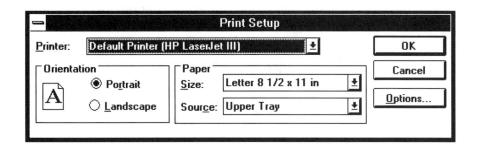

Multitasking may slow your system down a bit, but in some cases the trade-off for multitasking is beneficial. Consider that your computer spends a lot of its time idling while you type in your word processor. Thousands (or even millions) of potential processing cycles go to waste every time you pause to think or look at your notes. Multitasking lets your system use idle time by handling other tasks in the background. Every time you pause, Windows jumps to the background application and continues processing.

To multitask several applications, start each application in its own window. Execute a task like sorting or printing, and then go ahead and activate another window to work on something else. That's all you have to do.

Remember

For multitasking to work properly, applications must be written to run under Windows. DOS applications can only be multitasked when running in 386 enhanced mode, as discussed in Appendix A, "Windows Modes and Memory," and Appendix B, "Running Non-Windows Applications."

Cutting and Pasting with the Clipboard

The Windows Clipboard accessory lets you move text or graphics from one application to another. Think of the Clipboard as an invisible bulletin board where you temporarily place text or graphics until you're ready to use them, either in the same document or in another application window. For example, you might create a company logo in Paintbrush and then transfer it to WordPerfect to be printed at the top of a letter.

Almost all application windows have menu options for cutting and pasting information to and from the Clipboard, as shown here:

Edit	
Undo	Alt+BkSp
Cut	Shift+Del
Copy	Ctrl+Ins
Paste	Shift+Ins
Delete	Del

1

Cut, Copy, and Paste are Clipboard options, and are explained in the following table:

Clipboard Command	Function
Cut	Deletes the selected text or graphic and places it in the Clipboard, overwriting the current Clipboard contents.
Copy	Places a copy of the selected text or graphic in the Clipboard, overwriting the current Clipboard contents. The original is not removed as with the Cut command.
Paste	Copies the contents of the Clipboard to the current insertion point position in a window. The contents of the Clipboard remain intact.

Examining and Saving Clipboard Contents

Look again at Figure 1-1, and you'll see a Clipboard icon in Program Manager's Main group. When you need to examine the contents of the Clipboard, double-click this icon.

Each time you copy or cut text or graphics into the Clipboard, the existing contents of the Clipboard are overwritten. If you need to retain the contents of the Clipboard, you must save them to a disk file. This may be necessary when you want to reuse blocks of text or graphics from one session to another. You might even want to build a glossary of text blocks or a scrapbook of graphics images that you use often.

Windows Accessories and Games

The Program Manager contains two group windows called Accessories and Games. The Accessories window contains icons for starting various tools and utilities useful in your Windows work sessions. Here are a typical Accessories window and an explanation of the utilities it contains:

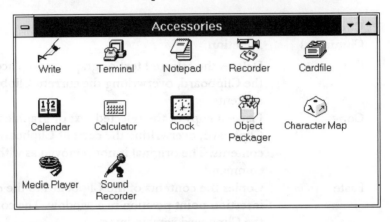

Utility	Function
Write	A word processor with character- and paragraph-formatting features
Paintbrush	A painting program for creating graphics images
Terminal	Lets you connect with other computers and data services over phone lines
Notepad	A small, easy-to-use note-writing utility
Recorder	Stores mouse movements and keystrokes so you can play them back later
Cardfile	Tracks names, addresses, phone numbers, and other types of information. Cardfile will even dial phone numbers
Calendar	Keeps track of your appointments
Clock	Displays a digital or analog clock
Packager	Lets you create packages of data in one application and paste them into another
Character Map	Used to insert symbols and special characters (foreign) into your text
Media Player	A utility for playing sound and multimedia devices
Sound Recorder	A utility for recording, editing, and playing back sounds

The Games window lets you access games for entertainment when you're not so busy. The Games group contains the card game Solitaire and the game Minesweeper.

Control Panel Options for Customizing Windows

The Main group window in the Program Manager contains an icon called Control Panel. When you select the Control Panel icon, the following window appears:

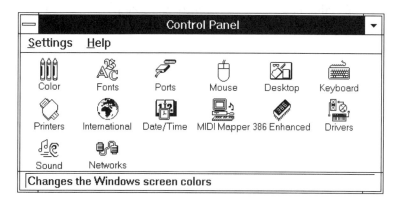

Each icon in this window opens a utility for customizing various elements within Windows, as described in the following table:

Utility	Function
Color	Sets the color scheme for Windows
Drivers	Installs special drivers
Fonts	Adds and removes screen and printer fonts
Ports	Sets the speed and protocols of your system's serial ports
MIDI Mapper	Controls MIDI-attached devices
Mouse	Controls the way the mouse operates

Desktop	Changes the appearance of the desktop, including its colors and patterns, and the alignment of icons inside windows
Networks	Controls the connection of Windows to a network
Printers	Adds, removes, and configures printers
International	Sets country codes, language type, currency formats, and number formats
Keyboard	Sets the repeat rate and speed delay of the keyboard
Date/Time	Sets the date and time
Sound	Assigns sounds to system events
386 Enhanced	Controls the way applications run in 386 enhanced mode

2

Starting Windows

In this chapter you learn how to start Windows and begin using it, so it's assumed you've already installed the program on your hard drive.

During installation, Windows determines the type of computer, display monitor, mouse, and printers your system has, and whether you are connected to a network. Based on this information, Windows then starts up in a specific mode. In most cases, the startup method determined during installation will be the best for your day-to-day activities. From time to time, however, you may want to start Windows in another mode, depending on the applications you want to run or the tasks you need to do.

This chapter explains the operating modes for Windows, and examines some other startup and operations issues.

Starting Windows

To start Windows, turn your computer on and wait for the DOS prompt to appear. This will be the drive C prompt unless your system startup configuration has been altered, or your computer is attached to a network.

You'll see the drive letter followed by a blinking cursor. Type **WIN** and press (ENTER) to start Windows.

As explained in Chapter 1, "Windows Overview," the Program Manager window is the first one you'll see (look again at Figure 1-1). Keep in mind that this book assumes you have just installed Windows.

What's Your Mode?

It's a good idea to begin by determining the *operating mode* in which Windows has started, and the way it uses computer memory. To view startup information about your Windows program, open the About Program Manager dialog box. To do so, first make sure that Program Manager is the active window. This should be the case if you have just started Windows. If it isn't, click the Program Manager window to activate it (or press (ALT)-(TAB) until the Program Manager title bar is highlighted).

To open the About Program Manager dialog box, do one of the following:

Mouse users: Click the Help menu option, and then click
                      About Program Manager.
Keyboard users: Press (ALT) to highlight the menu bar. Hold it
                      down and press (H) to select the Help menu, then
                      (A) to select the About option.

In this book, keypress combinations like the preceding one will be expressed like this: (ALT)-(H) (A).

Note

The About Program Manager dialog box that you see will be similar to that in Figure 2-1. It includes the Windows version number and operating mode, available RAM (random access memory), and available system resources (explained later in this chapter in the section "Analyzing the About Program Manager Dialog Box"). Note that the About Program Manager box in Figure 2-1 is for a system running Windows in 386 enhanced mode; your Windows program may be running in standard mode.

Standard Mode   Standard mode is the normal operating mode for Windows running on systems with Intel 80286 processors. If you have an 80386

Figure 2-1.   *The About Program Manager dialog box shows the Windows version number, operating mode, and other Windows operating information*

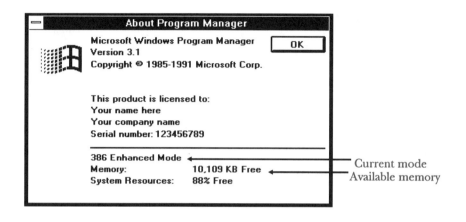

or 80486 system, you can also run this mode to get better performance, but you'll give up some of the features of 386 enhanced mode.

386 Enhanced Mode   386 enhanced mode is a multitasking mode that provides additional features for owners of Intel 80386 and 80486 systems—such as virtual memory, which treats disk storage as memory when you're running short on RAM. In addition, DOS applications can be multitasked and run in separate windows (instead of full-screen). Multitasking runs applications simultaneously, giving each a share of computer processing time.

Depending on the type of processor your system has, Windows starts in one of the two modes just described. Here are descriptions of system types and the modes they use:

- Intel 8088/8086-based systems will not run Windows 3.1. You can run Windows 3.0 on these systems.

- Intel 80286-based systems run Windows in standard mode only.

- Intel 80386/80486-based systems run Windows in 386 enhanced mode if 2MB of memory are available; otherwise, Windows runs in standard mode.

Tip

Although 386 enhanced mode provides additional features—such as virtual memory and the ability to multitask non-Windows (DOS) applications—using this mode may slow down your system. If you don't need these operating enhancements, use standard mode for better overall performance.

Windows normally starts in the mode it determines (during installation and setup) is best for your system. When you need to force Windows to start in another mode, use these startup command parameters:

WIN /S   If you have an 80386/80486 system and don't need the features of 386 enhanced mode, this command starts Windows in standard mode.

WIN /3   This command starts Windows in 386 enhanced mode.

Analyzing the About Program Manager Dialog Box

If your system contains an 80286 processor and has 1MB or more of RAM, you should see standard mode indicated in the About Program Manager dialog box. If your system has an 80386 or 80486 processor and has 2MB or more of RAM, 386 enhanced mode should be indicated.

The amount of RAM listed in the About Program Manager box indicates how much memory is available to your applications after DOS, Windows, and any startup applications are loaded. "System Resources" is not the same as available memory; rather, it designates the amount of RAM that Windows sets aside for its own use to track dialog boxes, buttons, messages, and menus. System resources may run low while available RAM remains high, usually because you're running too many applications at once. If this happens, you'll see "Out of memory" messages. Simply close applications you don't need and continue your work.

If you run out of RAM when starting applications, you might try running Windows in 386 enhanced mode to take advantage of virtual memory, if your system hardware allows. With this arrangement, your hard disk is used to make up for any lack of RAM. As you work with Windows, check the About

Program Manager dialog box periodically to determine if Windows is running efficiently, and to see if you need to add additional memory.

2

Appendix A provides a further discussion of modes and memory.

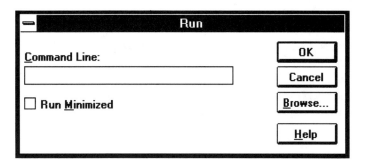

Tip

Running Programs in Windows

If you're anxious to run one of your Windows applications and you see its startup icon in the Program Manager, double-click it now with the mouse. You may need to first open the group window that holds the startup icon for the application, and then double-click the group icon and double-click the application startup icon.

If an icon is not available for the program you want to run, or if you don't have a mouse, you can use the Program Manager Run command to get the application started. Do one of the following:

Mouse users: Click the Program Manager File menu
                          option to open the File drop-down menu;
                          then click the Run option.
Keyboard users: Press (ALT)-(R) to open the Run dialog box.

The following dialog box will appear:

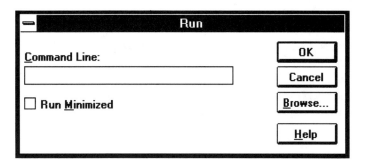

In the Command Line text box, type the path and name of the program you want to run. For example, to run Microsoft Word for DOS located in the

WORD directory on drive D, you would type **D:\WORD\WORD** in the Run
dialog box.

Starting Applications When Starting Windows

In the preceding section "What's Your Mode?," you saw how to add the
/S or /3 parameter to the Windows startup command to start Windows in
one of its two operating modes. You can also include the name of a program
that you want to load along with Windows. For example, to start Windows
and open Microsoft Word for Windows at the same time, enter the following
startup command (assuming Word is in the C:\WINWORD directory):

WIN C:\WINWORD\WINWORD

Because the Program Manager is designed to make program startup easy,
this command-line method is limited in its usefulness. However, if you use
only one application in Windows, you can add this type of startup command
to your computer's AUTOEXEC.BAT file to bypass the Program Manager
altogether. It might be handy for teachers in a classroom environment, for
example, to bypass Program Manager and get student users directly into the
application being taught.

Perhaps you need to start a particular application and also specify one of
the Windows run modes. To do this, type the mode parameter before the
application name and path. The following command starts Windows in
standard mode and immediately runs Word for Windows:

WIN /S C:\WINWORD\WINWORD

If you have specified the Word for Windows directory in the PATH command
of your AUTOEXEC.BAT file, you can omit the drive letter and path from
the startup command, as shown here:

WIN /S WINWORD

Tip

*You'll find an exercise for tailoring the AUTOEXEC.BAT file later in this chapter,
in the section "Starting Windows Automatically."*

Starting an Application from the StartUp Group

Another way to load an application when Windows starts is to include the application startup icon in the Program Manager StartUp group. The advantage of this method is that you can load more than one application at startup. These applications then rest on the desktop, ready for use.

In the following exercise, you copy the File Manager icon from the Main group to the StartUp group, using the Copy command on the Program Manager File menu. As you become more familiar with the programs and accessories you use most often, you can copy their program icons, as well, to the StartUp group. Note that this procedure copies the icon, leaving the original File Manager icon in the Main group.

1. If Windows is not loaded, type **WIN** at the DOS command line and press (ENTER).

2. At the Program Manager window, open the Main group window by double-clicking it with the mouse, or by pressing (ALT)-(W) and typing the number listed on the menu for the Main group.

3. Click the File Manager icon, or use the arrow keys to highlight it.

4. Press (ALT)-(F) (C) to select the Copy option from the File menu. The Copy Program Item dialog box appears, indicating the name and group of the currently selected icon (File Manager in the Main group).

5. To select the group where you want to copy the icon, click the down arrow in the To Group list box until StartUp appears, as shown here:

6. Click OK or press (ENTER) to complete the operation.

The next time Windows starts, File Manager will automatically load into memory. You can include other icons in the StartUp group with the same procedure.

Starting Windows Automatically

You can include the Windows startup command in your computer's AUTOEXEC.BAT file if you want Windows to start automatically every time you turn your computer on. The AUTOEXEC.BAT file is located in the root (\) directory of your C drive, and is explained fully in your DOS manual. To edit the file, use the Windows Notepad editor to add the WIN command as the last line in the file. Follow these steps:

1. Double-click the Accessories group, or press (ALT)-(W) to open the Windows menu and then type the number of the Accessories group.

2. When the group opens, double-click the Notepad icon, or highlight it using the arrow keys and press (ENTER).

3. When the Notepad window opens, press (ALT)-(F) (O) to open a file.

4. The Open dialog box appears with the File Name field highlighted. Type **AUTOEXEC.BAT** and press (ENTER).

5. When the file appears in the Notepad workspace, press (DOWN ARROW) until you reach the last line in the text. On a new line, type **WIN**. Follow this with any startup parameters, if desired—for example, to start in a specific mode or load an application.

6. Press (ALT)-(F) (S) to save the file, and answer Yes to the inquiry about writing over the existing file.

Other Startup Considerations

Here are some things to keep in mind if some of your programs don't run as expected, or if Windows runs short on memory.

Minimizing RAM Usage

2

You are less likely to have problems starting Windows or running its applications if you reduce the amount of RAM in use before you start the Windows program. This is especially true if you are also attempting to run non-Windows applications that require a set amount of memory.

The most likely cause of Windows startup problems is a conflict with programs that are loaded in memory before Windows starts. Memory-resident programs (TSRs) such as pop-up utilities, or special drivers that are loaded at the DOS command prompt should be started *after* running Windows, if possible. You may even need to disable or remove their startup commands from CONFIG.SYS or AUTOEXEC.BAT, using the Notepad editor as described earlier in "Starting Windows Automatically." If you still have problems starting Windows, refer to Appendix B, "Running Non-Windows Applications."

Tip

To disable other programs' startup commands in the AUTOEXEC.BAT or CONFIG.SYS files, insert the REM statement before the startup command instead of removing the startup command completely. Refer to your DOS manual for more details.

Running Non-Windows Applications

A non-Windows application (one not designed to work with any version of Windows) may be able to start within the Windows environment, but the application will take over the entire screen in standard mode. It will not have any of the typical Windows features such as pull-down menus and scroll bars; its operation will be exactly the same as if it were started from the DOS command line. If you are running 386 enhanced mode, non-Windows applications can run inside a window of their own. This is possible because 80386-based machines allow programs to run in their own protected partitions. Each partition is protected from problems other programs may be having in their partitions.

The benefit of running a non-Windows application under Windows is that you can easily switch from it to Windows and other applications, and even cut and paste information among them.

Since non-Windows applications were not written with Windows in mind, they are not capable of cooperatively sharing RAM with other applications that you run. Non-Windows applications tend to dominate memory. You will probably need to free up memory elsewhere in order to supply the non-Windows applications with more memory. For additional information on this subject, refer to Appendix B, "Running Non-Windows Applications."

Upgrading to Microsoft's DOS 5.0 or Digital Research's DR DOS 6.0 will help solve memory problems exhibited when running non-Windows applications.

Tip

Exiting Windows

When you're done using Windows, always remember to exit the program using the methods described in the following paragraphs. *Never* simply turn your system off while Windows is still running, because documents in windows left open could be corrupted or lost.

There are three ways to quit Windows, but before doing so, you need to make a change to one of the settings in the Program Manager, as explained next.

Saving Settings on Exit

In this and the next few chapters, you'll be making changes to the arrangement of groups and icons in Program Manager. To ensure that these changes are saved from one Windows session to the next, the Save Settings on Exit option must be turned on. To check the current status of this option, click the Options menu item in the Program Manager, or press (ALT)-(O). If a check mark does not appear in front of the Save Settings on Exit option, click it now (or press (S)) to turn this feature on. The Options pull-down menu should look like this:

2

Press (ALT)-(O) again to open the menu and ensure the option is checked.

With the Save Settings on Exit feature enabled, all changes you make to the arrangement of icons within group windows, as well as to the arrangement of group windows in the Program Manager, will be saved for your next Windows session. In addition, any menu options you enable with check marks will stay enabled for the next sessions. For example, the Save Settings on Exit option will remain enabled for all your Windows sessions until you turn it off.

Exit Methods

To exit Windows, first make sure the Program Manager is the active window by clicking its title bar, or press (ALT)-(TAB) until the title bar is highlighted. Then:

- To close Windows with the mouse, simply point to and double-click the Control menu button, as shown here:

- To close Windows with the keyboard, press (ALT)-(SPACEBAR) to open the Control menu, and then press (C) to select the Close option. Or,

- Use the speed key combination (ALT)-(F4). (Notice that this and the other speed keys are listed on menus.)

When you quit Windows, this dialog box appears:

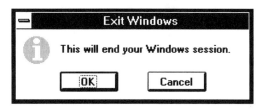

Normally, you would click OK or press (ENTER) to execute your quit command, but, so you can continue with the exercises in the next chapter, click the Cancel button or press (ESC).

3

Using the Windows Interface

This chapter presents a hands-on, step-by-step look at Windows. You see how to work with windows, menus, and control features, and how to get around in dialog boxes. If Windows is not already running on your computer, type **WIN** now to get it started.

Getting Around in Program Manager

You've already done some work in Program Manager—the first window you see when Windows starts. A picture of the default Program Manager screen is shown in Figure 3-1. Inside the Program Manager window are *groups* that may also be open as windows or minimized as icons. In Figure 3-1, the Main group is open as a window, and its program icons are visible. The StartUp, Accessories, and Games groups are minimized as icons at the bottom of the Program Manager window.

The exercises in this section help you master the techniques for navigating in Program Manager with both the mouse and the keyboard.

Figure 3-1. *The Program Manager as it appears the first time Windows is started, with the Main group open*

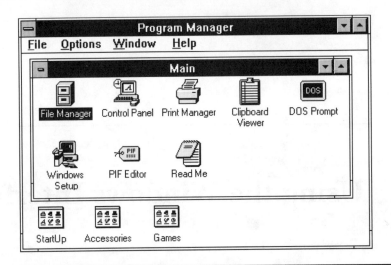

Mouse Techniques

Windows is designed to take full advantage of a mouse or other pointing device (such as a trackball). As you move the mouse device, a pointer moves on the Windows desktop. The pointer itself changes shape as you move it over different areas of the screen. It converts to an I beam (the *insertion point*) when you're editing text, and it changes to a cross-hair when pointing in the workspace of a painting or drawing program. A double-headed arrow appears when the pointer is over a window border, indicating the directions in which you can move the border. After choosing a command, you may see the hourglass, which tells you that Windows is working on a task and temporarily unavailable.

You can click just about anywhere on the desktop with the mouse. What happens when you click depends upon the location of the mouse pointer. In most cases, you click once to activate a Windows command or option, but in some locations you double-click the mouse, as you'll see in the following exercises.

Opening Menus and Choosing Options

The second line of a window, directly below the title bar, is the *menu bar*. It includes the names of one or more *pull-down menus*. To open a pull-down menu, click its name in the menu bar. The pull-down menu then opens to reveal a list of options that you can select by clicking the option with the mouse. You can also click a pull-down menu's title, then hold down the mouse button and drag through the menu options, releasing the mouse button when the option you want is highlighted.

In the following exercise, you click a *toggle option*, which is an option that can be set either on or off (enabled or disabled). When the option is on, a check mark appears in front of the option. Clicking an unchecked option turns it on, and clicking it again turns it off.

1. Point to Options on the Program Manager menu bar, and click the mouse. The Options pull-down menu opens, and stays open when you release the mouse button.

2. On the Options menu, click the last option, Save Settings on Exit.

Clicking a menu option immediately executes it and closes the menu, so in this case, it's hard to see if the option was really turned on.

3. To confirm that the option was enabled, point again to Options on the menu bar, and click the mouse. The Options menu should now appear, with a check mark in front of the Save Settings on Exit option, as shown here:

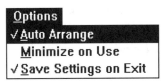

If the Save Settings option was already enabled, you may have just turned it off. Repeat Step 2 to turn it back on.

Caution

4. Now try a different technique to disable the Save Settings option. Point to Options on the menu bar; then click and hold down the mouse button. The menu opens.

5. While holding down the mouse button, drag through the menu until the Save Settings on Exit option is highlighted, and then release the mouse button. Releasing the button disables the option.

6. You can now open the menu again to make sure the check mark is gone. Click Options, note the absence of the check mark beside Save Settings, and click Options again to close the menu.

Scanning Menus

You can use the mouse to scan menus when you're looking for a particular command or trying to remember which command is used to perform a task. Try this:

1. Click File on the Program Manager menu bar, and hold down the mouse button. The File menu opens.

2. Drag the mouse to the right. As you drag, each pull-down menu opens.

3. Release the mouse when the menu you want is open.

If you change your mind and don't want to select a menu option, press the (ESC) *key.*

Note

Using the Minimize, Maximize, and Restore Buttons

Windows come in three sizes:

- A *minimized* window is an icon resting on the desktop.

- A *maximized* window takes up the entire screen. No other windows are visible until the maximized window is minimized or *restored*, which resizes it to its *customized* size (defined next).

- A *customized* window is one you have resized by clicking and dragging its borders and corners to make it any size you want.

Click the Maximize button, as shown here, to maximize a window:

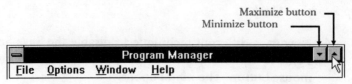

When a window is maximized, its Maximize button converts to the Restore button, as shown here:

Click the Restore button to return the window to its regular or customized size. To minimize a window and reduce it to an icon, click the Minimize button positioned to the left of the Maximize or Restore button.

A typical procedure is to arrange windows in a *cascade* or *tile* formation on the desktop so you can see all your windows, as shown in Figure 3-2. You maximize the window you want to work with; then, when you're finished, you click the window's Restore button, and the cascade arrangement will reappear. You can choose Cascade or Tile from the Window menu to rearrange windows in this way.

Figure 3-2.   *With the Task List, multiple windows can be placed in cascading (left) or tiled (right) arrangements*

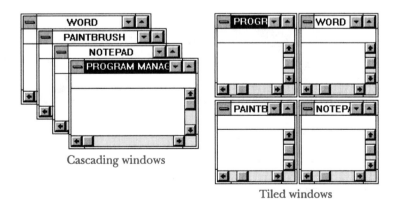

A Word About Maximized Group Windows   Recall that group windows are
subordinate to the Program Manager window. When you maximize a group
window, its name displays in the title bar of the Main window, and its Restore
button appears just below the buttons of the Program Manager window. For
example, when the Main group window is maximized in the Program Manager, it looks like Figure 3-3.

When a group window is maximized in Program Manager, you can't see
other group windows or icons. Remember to click the Restore button to
return the window to its original size.

Activating a Window

Only one group window at a time may be active in the Program Manager,
and only one application window may be active on the desktop. To activate
a window, click the window once, or, if it is minimized to an icon, double-click
the icon.

When a window is not visible because it is overlapped (hidden) by another
window, you can move the overlapping window aside or minimize it to an

Figure 3-3.   *When a group is maximized, it takes up the entire Program
Manager window*

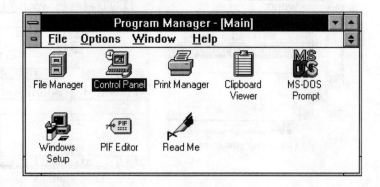

icon. Another method is to pick the window you can't see from a list, as described here:

- To make a hidden group window active in Program Manager, choose its name from the Window menu.

- To make a hidden application window active on the desktop, double-click the desktop or press (CTRL)-(ESC) to open the Task List, and pick the window from that list. (The Task List is covered in "Using the Task List," later in this chapter.)

Tip

You can also choose Cascade or Tile from the Window menu in Program Manager, to rearrange the windows so they are easier to see. (See Chapter 4, "Navigating the Windows Environment.")

Starting Applications with the Mouse

With the mouse, starting an application is easy—just double-click the program icon of the application you want to start. In this exercise, you start the Clock application in the Accessories group. Before doing so, you need to open the Accessories group window. Follow these steps:

1. Locate the Accessories group icon at the bottom of the Program Manager window. If you can't find it, choose Accessories from the Window menu.

2. When the Accessories window opens, point to the Clock icon and double-click the mouse. The Clock appears on the desktop.

3. Minimize the clock by clicking its Minimize button. Note that the time is still discernible in the icon.

Keyboard Techniques and Speed Keys

Though Windows is designed primarily for use with a mouse, you can also use the keyboard. Keyboard techniques are presented here because some actions are actually easier to do with the keyboard, once you have learned the keystrokes. The most important key to remember when using keyboard techniques is the (ALT) key. It is used to access the menu bar and the Control menu of a window; you press (ALT) followed by a letter that represents the menu option.

As you work with Windows menus, you'll notice that some options list *speed keys* to the right of the option. If you don't feel like taking your hands off the keyboard to reach for the mouse, you can always press one of these speed keys to select the option.

Opening the Control Menu

The Control menu is important; it contains commands for resizing, moving, and closing the window. Every window—even the Program Manager—has a Control menu. To access the Control menu of a group window, press the (ALT) key followed by the (HYPHEN) key. To access the Control menu of an application window, press the (ALT) key followed by the (SPACEBAR). Try the following exercise to see how this works:

1. In the Program Manager window, press (ALT)-(SPACEBAR) to open its Control menu. Notice that the options on the menu are commands that can also be invoked with the mouse, like Minimize and Maximize.

2. Press the (ESC) key to close the Control menu.

3. Press (ALT)-(HYPHEN) to open the Control menu of the currently active group window. Notice the similarity in options, then press (ESC) to close the menu.

Remember that group windows in Program Manager are document windows with their own Control menus. Notice the subtle difference in the buttons shown here:

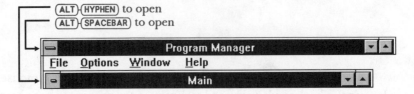

The symbol in the button for the Program Manager Control menu depicts a spacebar as a reminder; the Control menu button in the Main group window represents the (HYPHEN) key.

If you have a mouse, you may never need the Control menu, since most of its commands are easier to execute with the mouse. However, if you don't have the use of your mouse for any reason, you can always revert to keyboard methods for using Windows.

A complete description of keyboard techniques is available by selecting the Keyboard option on the Program Manager Help menu.

Note

Accessing Menus and Menu Options

To access any menu bar, press the (ALT) key, then use the (RIGHT ARROW) or (LEFT ARROW) key to highlight the name of the menu you want to open. When the menu name is highlighted, press (DOWN ARROW) or (ENTER) to open the menu. Once a menu is open, you can use the arrow keys to move through the list of options to highlight the one you want, and then press (ENTER) to display its related dialog box or other screen. (There is an easier way to do all this, as you learn later, but for now, try this next exercise.)

1. Press (ALT) to access the menu bar. The first menu item, File, will be highlighted. Press (ENTER) to open the File menu, shown here:

File	
New...	
Open	Enter
Move...	F7
Copy...	F8
Delete	Del
Properties...	Alt+Enter
Run...	
Exit Windows...	

2. Press the (RIGHT ARROW) key several times to open and examine the other menus.

    As you move from menu to menu, notice that the options in the menu bar, as well as the options on the pull-down menus, each have an underlined character in their name. Instead of using the arrow keys to highlight and select menus and menu options, you can press these underlined characters in combination with the (ALT) key to access the options much more quickly. For example, the combination of keystrokes to open the File menu and choose the Run option is (ALT)-(F) (R). To some users, even the mouse method of accessing menus may seem awkward when compared to the (ALT)-key method.

Let's use this method to work with the Window menu. The names of windows or open documents are listed on the Window menu, preceded by a number. In the following steps you make the Accessories window active by choosing it from the Window menu:

3. Press (ALT)-(W) to open the Window pull-down menu.

4. Type the underlined number preceding the Accessories option to open the Accessories window. (The number representing each window may not always be the same. It changes, depending on the arrangement of windows and the addition of new windows.)

Selecting Other Group Windows

As you've just seen, you can open other group windows by choosing their names from the Window menu. Another way to do this is to press (CTRL)-(TAB) repeatedly until the title bar of the group you want is highlighted. If the group is minimized to an icon, press (CTRL)-(TAB) until the icon name is highlighted, and then press the (ENTER) key to open the group as a window.

In this next exercise, you practice opening, activating, and closing group windows.

1. Press (CTRL)-(TAB) until the Games group icon is highlighted.

2. Press the (ENTER) key. The Games group window opens and becomes the active window.

3. Press (CTRL)-(TAB) until the Main group window is once again active.

4. Press (CTRL)-(TAB) until the Games group is active.

5. Press (ALT)-(HYPHEN) to open the Games group Control menu.

6. Press (C) to choose the Close option.

Note

In the Program Manager, the Close and Minimize commands both minimize a window to an icon. However, when you are working with application windows, these two commands have different results. If you choose Close on the Control menu of an application window, the application is removed from memory, along with any documents in its workspace. You'll be asked to save the documents if you haven't already done so. So if you want to keep the application open and in memory for later use, choose Minimize from the Control menu instead.

Starting Applications with the Keyboard

The main objective of working in the Program Manager is to start applications. To do so, you must first open the group that holds the program icon for the application you want to start. Then highlight the application icon with the arrow keys and press (ENTER).

The following exercise shows you how to open the Windows Control Panel:

1. Activate the Main group by choosing it from the Window menu, or by pressing (CTRL)-(TAB) until the Main window's title bar or icon is highlighted.

2. Press (RIGHT ARROW) until Control Panel is highlighted.

3. Press the (ENTER) key. The Control Panel window overlays the Program Manager window and becomes the active window.

Try pressing (CTRL)-(TAB), and notice that it has no effect in the Control Panel. The (CTRL)-(TAB) key combination is an exclusive feature of the Program Manager window. In the Control Panel, use the arrow keys to highlight the icons.

Returning to the Program Manager

When the Control Panel is open, it becomes part of the desktop, not the Program Manager window. Press (ALT)-(ESC) or (ALT)-(TAB) to switch between desktop windows. Try this:

1. From the Control Panel window, press (ALT)-(ESC) to switch to the Program Manager. The Control Panel window will probably be hidden behind the Program Manager window, depending on your window arrangement.

2. Press (ALT)-(ESC) again to return the Control Panel to the front.

Moving Among Applications on the Desktop

In the previous sections, you learned mouse and keyboard methods for accessing windows. In this section, you learn techniques for working among open applications on the Windows desktop using the mouse and the keyboard.

When more than one window is open on the desktop, you can click the window you want to activate. You can also use keyboard methods to switch among windows, or open the Windows Task List to choose a window from a list. Since you can't always point to a window to make it active (windows may be overlapped by other windows, or the mouse may be inactive, as when you're working in some non-Windows applications), take a look at all of these other techniques:

- Use (ALT)-(TAB) to *preview* windows. Previewing is a quick way to scan through open applications. The title of each application is displayed. Minimized icons open when you release the mouse while the icon is highlighted.

- Use (ALT)-(ESC) to *switch* among application windows. The switching method lets you see the entire contents of each window as you switch. Minimized icons are only highlighted; you must press (ENTER) to open an icon. Though this method is useful, in most cases you'll want to use the faster preview method.

- The *Task List* is opened from the keyboard by pressing (CTRL)-(ESC), or by double-clicking the desktop. The Task List (fully described in "Using the Task List," later in this chapter) provides the same options for the desktop that the Window menu provides for Program Manager. You can use Task List to choose an application, or to arrange windows and icons on the desktop.

The keyboard methods available for moving among applications are summarized here:

Keystroke	Function
(ALT)-(TAB)	Previews windows and icons
(ALT)-(ESC)	Switches between full application windows and icons
(CTRL)-(ESC)	Opens the Task List

Tip

You can reverse the window-switching order by holding down the [SHIFT] *key while pressing* [ALT]-[ESC] *or* [ALT]-[TAB].

Switching Among Applications

3

The following exercise demonstrates how to switch among applications using the mouse and keyboard.

1. In a previous exercise, you made the Clock available on the desktop as an icon. Open it as a window now by pressing [ALT]-[TAB] until the clock name appears and then release the keys.

2. Press [ALT]-[TAB] several times to switch among the windows that are currently open on the desktop. Try going in the other direction by pressing [SHIFT]-[ALT]-[TAB].

In the next steps, you start the DOS Prompt, which temporarily returns you to DOS so you can execute DOS commands. You then switch back to Windows using the [ALT]-[ESC] switching method.

3. Press [ALT]-[TAB] until Program Manager is listed; then release the keys.

4. Press [CTRL]-[TAB] until the Main group is listed, and press [ENTER] if it is an icon.

5. Double-click the DOS Prompt icon, or select it with the arrow keys and press [ENTER].

6. When the DOS prompt appears, press [ALT]-[ESC] to switch back to Windows.

When Windows reappears, the DOS Prompt icon will be part of the desktop since you only switched away from it, rather than closing it. In this way, you can keep a program or task running in DOS while you switch back to Windows.

Using the Task List

The Task List is an integral part of Windows that is always available. You can use it to switch among applications and to reorganize the desktop. The Task List appears when you double-click the desktop or press (CTRL)-(ESC), and is useful when you can't see all the windows on your desktop:

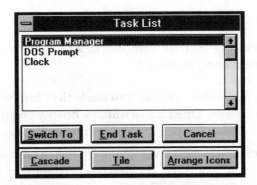

You can also select the Switch To option on the Control menu of any window to open the Task List.

The top portion of the Task List displays the names of currently running applications. To switch to an application, double-click its name with the mouse, or highlight the name using the arrow keys and press (ENTER).

The buttons at the bottom of the Task List window are used to close a window (task) or rearrange the desktop, as described in the following table. Click the button, or press (ALT) along with the underlined letter on the button.

Task List Button	Function
Switch To	Switch to and activate the selected application
End Task	Close the selected application
Cancel	Exit the Task List
Cascade	Rearrange windows in a cascade layout
Tile	Rearrange windows in a tiled layout
Arrange Icons	Arrange the icons on the desktop

Practice using the Task List now by following these steps:

1. Double-click the desktop or press (CTRL)-(ESC) to open the Task List.

2. Double-click Clock in the list box, or press (DOWN ARROW) to highlight Clock and then press (ENTER). Clock becomes the active window.

3. Use Task List to close an application. Repeat Step 1, and choose DOS Prompt from the list box.

4. Click the End Task button or press (ALT)-(E). The following dialog box appears:

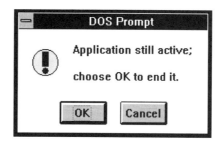

Note

This demonstrates that you can't end a DOS or non-Windows application from Windows without warning. Click the OK button in this case, but keep in mind that you'll normally need to close non-Windows applications using their regular exit routines.

5. Open Task List again by repeating Step 1. Then click the Cascade button to see how Windows rearranges the open windows in a cascade layout.

Resizing and Moving Windows and Icons

You may want to resize and move open windows for several reasons. Perhaps you want to see two windows side by side so you can view the contents of one window while working in another. In Program Manager, you may need to resize group windows and arrange them to improve access to startup icons. In this section, you learn how to minimize, maximize, resize, and move windows on the desktop. Then in Chapter 4, "Navigating the Windows Environment," you see how to reorganize the windows in the Program Manager using the techniques you learn here.

Resizing Windows with the Mouse

Every window has active borders and title bars. You can click and drag the borders with the mouse to resize the window.

Note

You may want to move a window before or after resizing it, by clicking and dragging its title bar. See "Moving a Window," later in this chapter.

The shape of the mouse pointer changes when it is pointed at a window's border or corner. The pointer becomes a double-headed arrow when it is over a window border, and a diagonal double-headed arrow when it is over a corner. The arrows indicate the directions in which you can move the borders or corners. When the mouse pointer converts to one of these symbols, you can click and drag the border or corner, and then release the mouse to resize the window.

In the following exercise, you resize the right border and then the lower-right corner of the Program Manager window. Keep in mind, however, that any border or corner may be resized using the methods described here.

1. Make the Program Manager window active by clicking it with the mouse, or by pressing (ALT)-(TAB) until the title bar is highlighted.

2. Drag the mouse into the right border until you see the double-headed arrow pointer.

3. Click and drag the border to the right. As you drag, a shadow box appears to indicate the new size for the window, as shown in Figure 3-4. Drag the border out about an inch, and then release the mouse to resize the window.

Now resize the window in two directions, by dragging its lower-right corner outward.

4. Move the mouse to the lower-right corner until you see the diagonal double-headed arrow pointer.

5. Click and drag down and to the right. As you drag, the shadow borders appear, as shown in Figure 3-5.

6. Release the mouse to resize the window.

Figure 3-4.   *A shadow border appears when you're resizing a window*

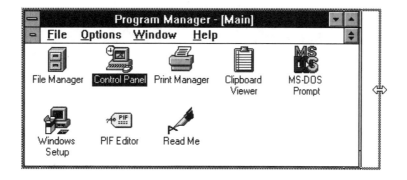

3

Tip

You can click any border or corner to resize a window, but it's most common to drag the lower-right corner because the right and bottom portions of a window's contents are usually hidden.

Using Scroll Bars

Scroll bars appear at the right and bottom of a window when the entire contents of the window's workspace can't be seen—usually after the window has been resized. Scroll bars can only be used with a mouse. In this exercise, you reduce the Program Manager window until scroll bars appear, and then scroll the window vertically and horizontally.

1. Resize the Program Manager window by clicking and dragging its lower-right corner inward. Do this until the horizontal and vertical scroll bars appear, as shown in Figure 3-6. You may need to click and drag inward several times.

Figure 3-5. *Shadow borders appear on two sides when you're dragging the corner of a window*

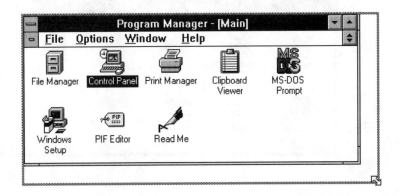

2. Click the down-arrow scroll button on the vertical scroll bar several times. As you do this, the window contents scroll down, and the slider button moves down in the slider bar. Click until the slider button is at the bottom of the bar.

3. Now click the vertical slider button and drag it back up. When you get about halfway up the bar, release the mouse button. Notice how the contents of the window change.

4. Click and drag up again, and watch how the contents of the window change depending upon where you release the slider button. Drag the slider button all the way to the top of the bar and release the mouse.

5. Position the mouse inside the vertical slider bar, and then click and release the mouse button.

Clicking inside the slider bar moves the contents of the window one page at a time. A page is equal to the vertical height or horizontal width of the window itself.

Note

Figure 3-6. *Resizing a window makes the horizontal and vertical scroll bars appear*

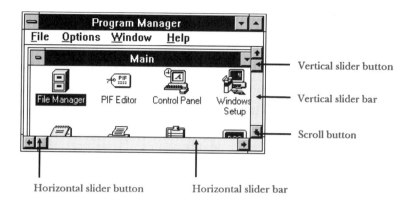

Vertical slider button

Vertical slider bar

Scroll button

Horizontal slider button   Horizontal slider bar

3

If you want, try experimenting with the horizontal scroll bar, clicking on the horizontal scroll buttons, slider button, and slider bar to see how they affect the window.

Removing Scroll Bars

When you want to see the complete contents of a window, resize the window so that the scroll bars disappear. In the previous exercise, you resized the Program Manager until scroll bars appeared. Now reverse these steps to remove the scroll bars:

1. Drag the Program Manager vertical slider button all the way to the bottom, and the horizontal slider button all the way to the right. (Note that this is not a necessary step but will demonstrate an anomaly of the scroll bars.)

2. Click and drag the lower-right corner of the Program Manager window outward several inches.

Notice that the scroll bars don't go away immediately, because you scrolled the window contents to the bottom and to the right. You'll often see this effect when resizing a window to remove its scroll bars. Even though you've made the window large enough to make all its icons visible, they still need to be scrolled into view. Then the scroll bars will disappear.

3. To remove the scroll bars, drag the slider buttons back to the top and far left.

4. If the scroll bars still don't go away, drag the lower-right corner out further.

5. Now drag the borders back in as far as possible to remove white space, but not so far that the scroll bars reappear.

Tightening the window borders in this way resizes the window to its optimum size. The entire window contents can be seen at once, yet the window doesn't take up too much space. Some windows, however, contain so much material that they dominate the desktop if opened in this way. You'll need to resize these windows and arrange them on the desktop in the best way possible.

Moving a Window

Once you resize a window, you can reposition it next to other windows, or just move it out of the way. In this example, you drag the Program Manager window to the upper-left corner of the desktop; then you open the Clock window, resize it, and drag it out of the way to the lower-left corner of the desktop. In the last exercise, you resized the Program Manager window to its optimum size. It should now fit in the upper-right corner, leaving plenty of space on the desktop for other windows.

1. Point to the title bar of the Program Manager; then click and drag until the window is in the upper-left corner.

2. Double-click the Clock icon, which should still be resting on the desktop. (If it's not, open the Accessories group in the Program Manager and double-click the Clock icon.)

3. Resize the Clock window so it is approximately two inches square.

4. Point to the title bar of the Clock; then click and drag the window to the lower-right corner of the desktop.

   Try choosing Analog or Digital from the Clock Settings menu to change the way time is displayed.

3

Closing a Window

There are several different ways to close a window. Keep in mind that closing a window removes the program and its documents from memory. If you want to keep the window open but remove it from the desktop temporarily, minimize the window instead of closing it.

To close a window, double-click the Control button in the upper-left corner of the window. Alternatively, you can press (ALT)-(F4), or you can choose Close from the window's Control menu.

Closing the Program Manager window is the same as exiting Windows. To see how this works, follow these steps:

1. Double-click the Control button on the Program Manager window, and you'll see the following dialog box:

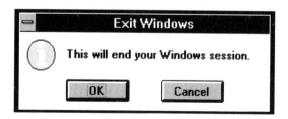

2. If you really wanted to close the Program Manager, you would click the OK button. For now, click the Cancel button to stay in Windows.

When you close applications, you'll see a warning message if the application workspace contains an unsaved document. This warning message gives you a chance to save your work before the application closes.

Dialog Boxes

The *dialog boxes* that appear when you invoke Windows commands display information and additional parameters for commands or options. Dialog boxes usually appear after you select an option that is followed by an ellipsis (...), or as part of a command routine. In this section, you work with the Run command in the Program Manager, which presents the two dialog boxes shown in Figure 3-7. The Run dialog box at the top of the figure appears when you select Run on the Program Manager File menu. The Browse dialog box then appears when you click the Browse button in the Run dialog box.

Many Windows commands use dialog boxes. As a result, you'll rarely need to look up a command's usage in a manual. The dialog boxes present you with all possible options in an easy-to-use format. Keep in mind that you do not need to change all options in dialog boxes. In most cases, the application supplies default settings that you can use to execute the command. Often it is only necessary to change one or two settings.

Dialog boxes consist of *fields*, and some fields are grouped together in boxes. Field options may be turned on or off by clicking buttons or marking check boxes. You can also select options from scrollable list boxes or pull-down lists. When all options are set, click the OK button or press (ENTER) to accept the changes. You can press (ESC) to cancel the dialog box.

Dialog box options and buttons are easily accessed with the mouse, and you can also use the following keyboard techniques to jump between fields and select items:

- Press (TAB) to jump from one field to the next. A dotted rectangle or highlight will appear in the currently selected area.

- Press (SHIFT)-(TAB) to move backwards through the fields.

- If you press (TAB) at the last field, you are returned to the first field.

- If a field has an underlined letter, you can press (ALT) and then press that letter to jump to that field.

- Press (SPACEBAR) to mark and unmark check boxes.

Figure 3-7. *The Run dialog box and its related Browse dialog box*

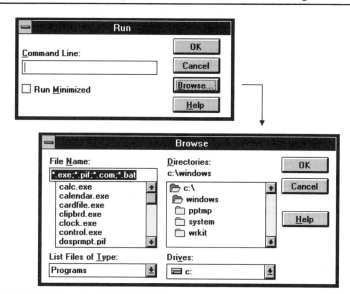

Dialog Box Fields and Buttons

Though every dialog box has a different set of options, the methods used to enter and edit options and settings are the same in any dialog box. Each type of field and button found in a dialog box is described in the following paragraphs.

Command Buttons

Command buttons let you execute or cancel the dialog box, or open another dialog box. For example, some windows contain a Help button that opens a window with help information about the current command. Notice that the Browse button in Figure 3-7 has an ellipsis (...), which means it will present another dialog box if selected.

You click the command buttons to select them. With the keyboard, press (TAB) to move among them; as you tab, a dotted rectangle surrounds the text of the currently selected button. The OK button on the Run box in the following illustration is highlighted:

```
┌─────────────────────────────────────────────────────────┐
│ ─                          Run                            │
├─────────────────────────────────────────────────────────┤
│ Command Line:                              ┌──────────┐   │
│                                            │   OK     │   │
│ ┌───────────────────────────────────┐     └──────────┘   │
│ │                                   │     ┌──────────┐   │
│ └───────────────────────────────────┘     │  Cancel  │   │
│                                            └──────────┘   │
│ ☐ Run Minimized                            ┌──────────┐   │
│                                            │ Browse...│   │
│                                            └──────────┘   │
│                                            ┌──────────┐   │
│                                            │   Help   │   │
│                                            └──────────┘   │
└─────────────────────────────────────────────────────────┘
```

Note

Pressing (ENTER) *is the same as clicking the OK button, so be careful not to press* (ENTER) *until you've set all necessary options and are ready to execute the command.*

Text Boxes

Text boxes let you enter information that a command needs to run. For instance, in the foregoing Run dialog box, you must type the filename of the program to run in the Command Line text box. Sometimes text boxes contain default information. Some text boxes will accept only numbers.

List Boxes

A list box holds the names of one or more items needed by the command. You can scroll through the list by pressing the arrow keys on the keyboard or by clicking arrow buttons in the list box's scroll bar. You can also use the (PGUP) and (PGDN) keys, or type the first letter of the item you are looking for to quickly scroll through the list. As shown in the Browse dialog box in Figure 3-8, selecting a file from the File Name list box causes its name to appear in the File Name text box.

Pull-Down List Boxes

Pull-down list boxes initially display only one item. In Figure 3-8, the List Files of Type box and the Drives box are pull-down list boxes. Clicking the down-arrow button with the mouse opens the pull-down list, as shown in Figure 3-9. You can also press (TAB) to move to a pull-down list box, and then press the (DOWN ARROW) key on the keyboard to scan through the list. Press the (TAB) key when the item you want is highlighted.

Figure 3-8. *The File Name text box with a name selected from the list box*

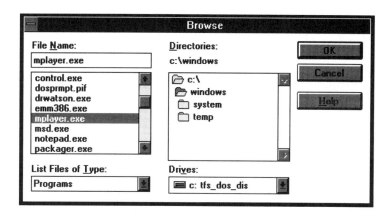

Figure 3-9. *The Drives pull-down list, opened by clicking the down-arrow button in the list box*

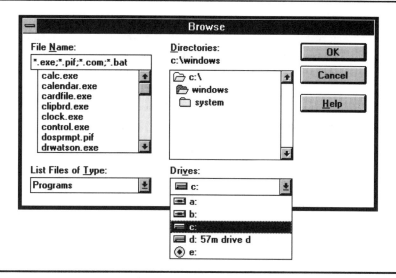

3

Option Buttons

Option buttons (also called radio buttons) are toggles that let you turn an option on or off by clicking the button. When option buttons are grouped together in a box, only one button may be enabled. The next illustration was captured from a Setup dialog box for a laser printer:

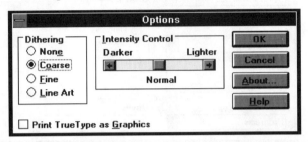

Here only one of the four buttons in the box can be turned on, by clicking the button with the mouse. If one button is already enabled and you click another button in the box, the previously enabled button is turned off. With the keyboard, you can turn on an option button by pressing the (ALT) key and pressing the underlined letter of the button you want to select. Repeat this action and you turn the button off.

Check Boxes

Check boxes work like option buttons; you mark them to turn the option on, and remove the mark to turn the option off. Unlike option buttons, however, you can mark as many check boxes as are necessary to set the options and settings for a command. In the following example, the box is from Microsoft Word for Windows, and is used to set various preferences for a window and the text displayed in it:

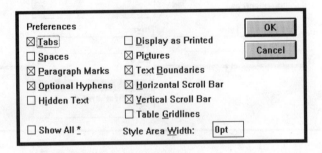

Warning and Message Boxes

Warning boxes are displayed when you attempt to execute a command improperly, or when Windows needs more information related to the command. The following box appears to confirm file deletions:

When a warning or message box appears, click (or select from the keyboard) one of its buttons, depending on the task at hand. If you choose the Cancel button, the entire command is cancelled.

Using Dialog Boxes

Now you'll put together all the information you've learned in this section about dialog boxes. In the following exercise, you open the Run dialog box and then start the File Manager.

1. Make sure the Program Manager window is active by clicking it with the mouse. Or press (CTRL)-(ESC) to choose it from the Task List.

2. Choose Run on the File menu by clicking it with the mouse or pressing (ALT)-(F) (R). The Run dialog box appears (see Figure 3-7).

Now you need to insert the name of the File Manager program in the Command Line text box. If you knew the name, you could type it in the box and click the OK button or press (ENTER). However, in the following steps, you use the Browse option to locate the filename and place it in the Command Line box.

Keep in mind that this is an exercise in using dialog box features and contains more steps than you would actually need to access a file.

Note

3. Click the Browse button in the Run dialog box (or press (ALT)-(B)) to display the Browse dialog box (Figure 3-7).

4. Note the different fields of the dialog box. The Directories field on the right lists the disk drive and directory where your Windows files are located, and the scrollable list box contains the filenames.

5. Click the down-arrow scroll button in the Drives pull-down list box to see a list of alternative disk drives. (You can also press (ALT)-(V) to access the Drives field, and then press the (DOWN ARROW) key on the keyboard to open this pull-down list box.) Choose C or the drive where your Windows files are located.

6. Now press the (TAB) key several times until the File Name list box is highlighted. A dotted rectangle surrounds the first file in the list.

7. Press the (DOWN ARROW) key on the keyboard several times to scroll through the list.

8. Press (W) to jump to the files that start with *W*, and then press (DOWN ARROW) until the WINFILE.EXE is highlighted. This filename now appears in the File Name text box.

9. Click the OK button or press (ENTER) to select the WINFILE.EXE file. The complete path and filename now appears in the Command Line field of the Run dialog box.

10. Click in the Run Minimized check box (or press (ALT)-(M)). This will minimize File Manager when it starts. The Run Minimized option is useful when you want to load an application for later use.

11. Click the OK button on the Run dialog box, or press (ENTER), to start File Manager.

File Manager now appears as an icon at the bottom of the desktop. To open the File Manager as a window, double-click its icon; or hold down (ALT)-(TAB) until its name appears, and then release the keys.

Exiting Windows

That's it for this chapter. If you want to exit Windows and return to DOS, make the Program Manager window active and double-click its Control menu button, or press (ALT)-(SPACEBAR) and select Close from the Control menu.

4

Navigating the Windows Environment

In this chapter, you get a good idea of what Windows can do as you explore the Program Manager, learn more about File Manager, and work with several of the Windows applications and utilities. In the Program Manager section, you see how to rearrange group windows and set some important options. You set the date and time within the Windows environment and change the color scheme of a window. In the File Manager section, you study the structure of the File Manager window and practice working with some files on your disks and hard drive.

Keep in mind that this chapter builds on the techniques you learned in Chapter 3, "Using the Windows Interface," and introduces you to features you'll learn more about later.

Exploring the Program Manager

You've already seen how the Program Manager provides methods for organizing program icons into groups of applications based on the type of work you do. But the main purpose of the Program Manager is to "launch" applications, so this section shows you some interesting techniques for doing just that.

Program Manager Groups

When the Program Manager is first installed, it contains at least four groups: Main, Accessories, StartUp, and Games. Two additional groups, called *Windows Applications* and *Non-Windows Applications*, may have been created to hold icons for applications already installed on your system.

Each group, except StartUp, contains application icons. The StartUp group holds the icons of programs you want to start every time Windows starts. To include a program in the group, copy its icon into the StartUp group, as you learned in Chapter 2, "Starting Windows." The File Manager, Notepad, and Calculator are useful startup utilities you can include in the group. (In addition, you can specify that the programs will run *minimized*, which means they appear as icons on the desktop after Windows finishes loading.)

The Accessories group contains helpful programs you'll want to run daily. In the next section, you see how to rearrange the desktop so that the Accessories group is open and ready when Windows first starts.

Reorganizing the Program Manager

The initial arrangement of groups and icons in the Program Manager, described in the foregoing paragraphs, is useful when you're learning Windows, but as you become more familiar with the program, you may want to rearrange Program Manager to suit your own projects and working style.

Consider, for example, the contents of the Main group. Though its icons represent useful programs, you may find you don't really need to access these programs every day. You can copy the File Manager into the StartUp group so it automatically loads with Windows. The most practical Program Manager arrangement displays a group window of icons to start programs that you use most often, such as those in the Accessories group.

Figures 4-1, 4-2, and 4-3 show three possible arrangements of the groups within Program Manager. In Figure 4-1, the Main and Accessories groups are both open and arranged side by side. Not all icons are visible; rather, the most frequently used icons have been placed so they can be selected without scrolling the window.

The Program Manager in Figure 4-2 places less emphasis on the Main group, which is minimized. Here the Accessories group is open as a window so its applications are easier to select. In this arrangement, the Main group is rarely needed because its most-used application, File Manager, has been added to the StartUp group so that it automatically starts when Windows loads.

Figure 4-3 depicts a custom arrangement in which part of the Main group and most of the Accessories group are visible. The difference between Figure 4-1 and Figure 4-3 may seem trivial, but the methods used to achieve each configuration are quite different, as you'll see.

Figure 4-1. *One method of arranging Program Manager is to place the Main and Accessories groups side by side*

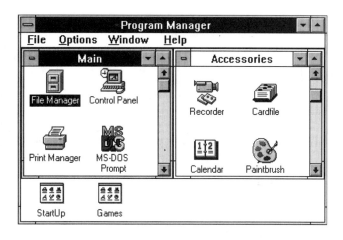

Figure 4-2.   *This Program Manager arrangement places more emphasis on Accessories than the utilities in the Main group*

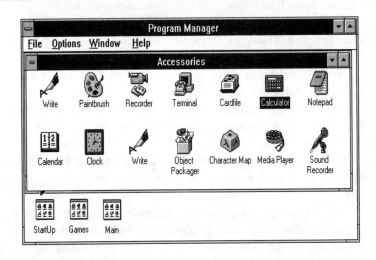

Figure 4-3.   *In a custom window arrangement, you can manually resize the windows*

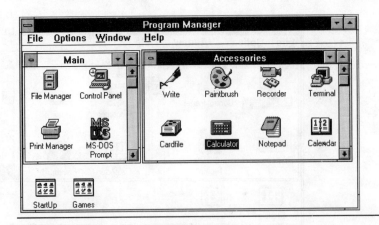

The following exercises show you how to create the arrangement in Figure 4-1 using the Tile command, and then how to create the custom arrangement in Figure 4-3 by manually resizing windows. Throughout this book you'll be using programs in the Main group and Accessories group, so it's a good idea to keep the Main group window open for now. Later, you can create new groups and rearrange windows to accommodate the way you work.

Set Program Manager Options

Before continuing with the exercises, make the following changes on the Program Manager Options menu. Note that if the options have already been checked, do not choose the options when you open the Options menu or they will be toggled off.

1. Choose Save Settings on Exit from the Options menu.
2. Choose Auto Arrange from the Options menu.

The first step ensures that any changes you make to the size of windows and their arrangement are saved for subsequent Windows sessions. The second step causes icons within Program Manager groups to automatically rearrange to fit within a resized group window.

Move and Resize the Program Manager

Now you can begin creating the Program Manager arrangement in Figure 4-1. In this setup, the Program Manager window is moved to the upper-left corner of the desktop and resized so that it takes up about three-quarters of the space. This leaves room for other applications, and yet provides enough room in the Program Manager for rearranging group windows.

1. Point to the title bar of the Program Manager; then click and drag the window to the upper-left corner of the desktop.
2. Point to the lower-right corner of the Program Manager window; then click and drag until the window covers about three-quarters of the desktop.

Tile the Group Windows

Now you can arrange the group windows within the Program Manager, using the Tile command from the Window menu. Follow these steps:

2

2

2

1. Make sure the Main group is open as a window. If it isn't, double-click its group icon to open it.

2. Open the Accessories group by double-clicking its group icon.

3. Choose Tile from the Window menu.

The two open group windows are now side by side, as in Figure 4-1.

The size of tiled windows and the number of visible icons in them depends on the original size of the Program Manager window. For example, when the Program Manager window is maximized and you select Tile, the group windows are tiled to fill all the available space. Try this on your newly arranged desktop by following these steps:

1. Click the Program Manager Maximize button to make the window fill the entire desktop.

2. Choose Tile from the Window menu. The two open windows are resized and fill the Program Manager window.

3. Now click the Restore button on the Program Manager. When the window is restored to its previous size, the tiling arrangement no longer fits the window. This demonstrates that you may need to periodically retile your window arrangements if Program Manager is resized.

4. Choose Tile again, and resize the group windows to fit within the restored Program Manager.

Now that you understand how tiling works, you can adjust and retile the Program Manager window until it is arranged the way you like. You can enlarge the Program Manager window, and then retile to see more icons, or reduce the Program Manager window and retile so the window takes up less space on the desktop. Repeat the steps in the previous exercise until the Program Manager fits optimally on your desktop.

Other Arrangements: Cascade and Custom

The Tile option resizes windows to fit within the boundaries of the Program Manager, making each the same size. You may, however, prefer an arrangement in which all icons within a group are visible. You can do this with the Cascade option on the Window menu, as follows:

1. Choose Cascade from the Window menu. The group windows are resized so you can see more icons, but only icons in one window are visible at the top of the arrangement.

2. Click the title bar of the back window to move it to the front.

3. If you can't see all icons in either of the windows you have observed, resize the Program Manager, and select Cascade again. Repeat this until the group windows are sized so you can see all the icons.

The custom arrangement shown in Figure 4-3 can be created by following these steps:

1. Enlarge the Program Manager window so you have some room in which to work. (Later, you can reduce the Program Manager window to surround the groups.)

2. Click the title bar of the Main group and drag it to the upper-left corner of the Program Manager window.

3. Click and drag the lower-right border of the Main window until it is approximately the size shown in Figure 4-3. You can make it larger or smaller, depending on the number of icons you want displayed.

4. Release the mouse button to resize the window. The icons automatically rearrange to fit its new size.

5. Repeat Steps 2 and 3 until the Main window is sized the way you want.

6. Drag the Accessories window next to the Main group, and then resize its window. If there isn't room to make the Accessories window large enough to suit you, enlarge the Program Manager window.

7. Once the group windows are resized, adjust the Program Manager window border to remove excess white space.

Note

After resizing windows into a custom arrangement, excess space may exist between the icons and the bottom of the group windows. It's easy to move the group icons to reduce this effect; simply click the icons and drag them up. Then you can click and drag Program Manager's bottom border up to eliminate the white space.

Rearrange the Program Icons

If you've created your own custom Program Manager arrangement like that in Figure 4-3, you may want to refine it by arranging the icons so that most are visible without having to scroll the window. In this next exercise, you rearrange icons in the Main group.

1. Click the Maximize button on the Main window so that you can see all its icons.

The icons in the maximized window arrange themselves from left to right in one or more rows, depending on the size of the window. The left to right order is maintained in multiple rows if you shrink the window. The objective of this exercise is to reorder the icons so that the most important icons are still visible at the top of the window even when it is reduced in size.

2. To rearrange the Main group icons, click and drag them over one another. When you release the mouse button after moving an icon, notice how other icons move down through the list or trade places with the one you've moved. Work at rearranging the icons until they appear as shown here:

3. Now click the Restore button on the Main window. Notice that the icon order is maintained in the reduced window.

Organizing the Desktop

As you work with Windows from day to day, you'll probably find that you usually want to open more than one application at a time. Typically, one application is left open while you work in another. You can then use the waiting application later without having to reload it. Having two applications open also allows you to cut and paste information between them, a powerful tool that is described in "Cut and Paste Operations" later in this chapter. But first let's examine some ways of organizing and navigating applications on the Windows desktop.

For this exercise, make sure your Program Manager window is arranged so that it looks similar to Figure 4-3. Activate the Program Manager, open the Accessories group window, and then follow these steps to open several applications:

1. Double-click the Notepad icon, so that the Notepad window appears on the desktop. (If you can't see the icon, scroll the window.)

2. Click the Program Manager window to make it active. If you can't see the window to click it, press (ALT)-(TAB) repeatedly until its menu bar is highlighted; then release the keys.

3. Double-click the Write icon in the Accessories group. The Write window is added to the desktop. By now, the desktop is getting cluttered, but you can still open other applications.

4. Double-click any blank part of the desktop to make the Task List appear, as illustrated next. (If you can't see the desktop, press (CTRL)-(ESC) to bring up the Task List. You'll learn more about the Task List in a later section.)

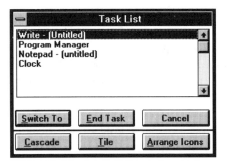

On the Task List you'll see all the currently open applications.

5. Open one more application: double-click the Paintbrush icon.

Window Switching Methods

A Windows session can have as many open applications as will fit in memory. There are three methods for switching among applications. You can try all three methods by following these steps:

1. Press (ALT)-(ESC) several times to switch among the open windows. This switching method displays the entire contents of each window, but is slower than the scrolling method demonstrated in Step 3.

2. Press (SHIFT)-(ALT)-(ESC) several times to reverse the order of the switching.

3. Press (ALT)-(TAB) several times to scroll through a list of names of open windows.

4. Press (SHIFT)-(ALT)-(TAB) several times to reverse the scroll order.

5. Double-click the desktop (or press (CTRL)-(ESC)) to open the Task List. In the List, double-click any application to activate it.

As you can see, there are several ways to activate an application window. You decide which is best based on the number of applications you have open. With many applications open, it's best to use the Task List, because you can double-click the application you want instead of cycling through all the open windows.

Organizing the Desktop with the Task List

The Task List isn't just for opening applications—it is also a helpful tool for reorganizing a cluttered desktop. You've already seen how to select an application from the Task List. Now here are some exercises using the Task List to make task switching easier.

1. Double-click a blank area of the desktop (or press (CTRL)-(ESC)) to display the Task List.

2. Click the Tile button to resize and tile all open windows on the desktop.

Tip

When windows are tiled, you can see some of the contents of each window. This is useful if the same application is open in more than one window and you need to differentiate between the contents of each window. Simply click the Maximize button of the window you want to work in, and then restore the window when you're finished. Try this now:

3. Click the Maximize button on the Notepad window. Notepad opens to a full-screen display. Then click the Notepad Restore button to return it to the tile arrangement.

The number of open windows makes a difference in how windows are tiled. When four windows are open, for example, they are arranged in a checkerboard pattern on the desktop, as you see now. Try this next exercise to see another arrangement:

1. Click the Minimize button in the Program Manager window to reduce it to an icon on the desktop.
2. Open the Task List (double-click the desktop or press (CTRL)-(ESC)).
3. Click the Tile option. The three open windows are arranged side by side.
4. To rearrange the windows in a cascade, reopen the Task List and click on the Cascade button.

Now each window is larger and displays more of its contents horizontally than with the tile method. Click the Maximize button of any window you want to work in, and restore the window when you're finished.

Arranging Desktop Icons

When applications are not in use, there's no need to keep their windows open. It's better to minimize them to icons and thereby reduce desktop clutter; this also makes the applications easier to open if another application is running in a large window. Follow these steps to practice minimizing applications and arranging their icons.

1. Click the Minimize button of each open window.

4

2. Click and drag the icons to new positions anywhere on the desktop.

3. Double-click the desktop to open the Task List (or press (CTRL)-(ESC)).

4. Click the Arrange Icons button to align the icons neatly at the bottom of the Desktop.

Tip

The Arrange Icons button is useful when icons are moved out of place or you've closed some application icons and you want to adjust the position of those remaining on the desktop.

Cut and Paste Operations

The *cut-and-paste* feature in Windows lets you copy or move text and graphics images from one place to another in a document, or from one application window to another. Commands for cutting and pasting are located on the Edit menu of nearly every Windows application.

Cutting and pasting is easy—first highlight the text or image you want to move. Then choose either Cut or Copy. A Cut removes the selected text or graphic from its current location and places it in the Clipboard; a Copy leaves the original text or graphic intact and places a copy of it in the Clipboard. With the text or graphic waiting in the Clipboard, click where you want it inserted, and select the Paste command to complete the operation.

Note

The Clipboard doesn't need to be open for you to take advantage of the cut-and-paste feature. However, you can open it any time by double-clicking its icon to see its contents or save them to disk.

The following exercises demonstrate how the Clipboard works:

1. In an exercise in the foregoing section, you opened Notepad, Write, and Paintbrush in the Program Manager Accessories window. Make sure these applications are still open (double-click their icons if necessary) before you begin this exercise.

2. Activate the Notepad window. Then type the following text, and press the (ENTER) key at the end of the line.

    This is an example of copying and pasting text.

3. Notice that the arrow pointer has changed to an I-beam pointer. Place the I-beam pointer in front of the *T* in the word *This*, and click and drag to the end of the line. This highlights the line.

4. Choose Copy from the Edit menu, or press (CTRL)-(INS). This puts the highlighted line in the Clipboard.

Remember, you don't need to have the Clipboard open to perform cut-and-paste operations, but you can view its contents at any time. In the section "Saving the Clipboard Contents," later in this chapter, you learn how to open the Clipboard.

5. Press the (DOWN ARROW) key to remove the highlight from the text you selected in Step 3 and move the insertion point to the next line.

6. Click the Edit menu again. (Notice that Copy and Cut on the Edit menu are now unavailable because nothing is selected or highlighted in the Notepad workspace.) Select Paste from the Edit menu.

The text you copied to the Clipboard is pasted into the line where you have positioned the insertion point, just below the previous text.

Pasting to Another Application

Let's try pasting the same line into a different window (the text is still in the Clipboard). Follow these steps to paste it in the workspace of the Write application:

1. Click the Write window, or double-click its icon.

2. When the Write window opens, click Edit on its menu bar. Notice that it has the same Cut, Copy, and Paste options as the Notepad Edit menu.

3. Choose Paste from the menu, and the now-familiar line appears in the Write workspace.

Now try copying a graphic image from the Paintbrush window to the Write window. In this exercise, you open a file called WINLOGO in Paintbrush, and use the Cutout tool in that application to mark part of the image so that it can be copied to the Clipboard.

1. Click the Paintbrush window, or double-click its icon.

2. In the Paintbrush window, choose Open from its File menu, or press (ALT)-(F) (O).

3. Double-click the filename WINLOGO in the file list; if you don't see this filename, type **WINLOGO** in the File Name field.

4. When the WINLOGO graphic appears, click the Scissors cutout tool, pictured here:

5. Once you've clicked the cutout tool, use it to surround the relief part of the logo.
   Move the mouse pointer to the Paintbrush workspace (it converts to a cross-hair pointer). Position this pointer in the upper right, and then click and drag to the lower right and release the mouse button. The logo should be surrounded by a dotted line.

6. Choose Copy from the Edit menu. This puts the graphic in the Clipboard and overwrites the line of text you put there earlier.

7. Minimize the Paintbrush window.

Figure 4-4. A Paintbrush image pasted to a Write document window

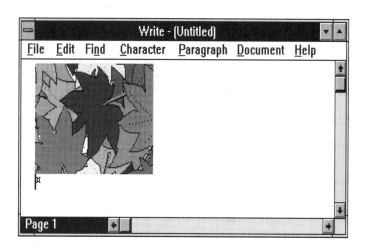

8. Activate the Write window, and press (ENTER) to start a new line. Select Paste from the Edit menu. The image is pasted in the Write document at the position of the cursor, as shown in Figure 4-4.

Saving the Clipboard Contents

You can open the Clipboard at any time to view or save its contents. The image from Paintbrush is still in the Clipboard after the last exercise; follow these steps to save that image to a file:

1. Activate the Program Manager window and double-click the Clipboard icon in the Main group. The Clipboard window opens, as shown here:

2. Choose Save As from the Clipboard File menu.

3. When the Save As dialog box appears, type **LOGO** and press (ENTER).

The Clipboard saves the image in a file named LOGO, with a .CLP filename extension. If you want to insert this image in another document, you can open the Clipboard and use the Open option on the File menu to reload the file LOGO.CLP. Once it's loaded in the Clipboard workspace, you can paste it in any application using the Paste command.

Choosing the Copy or Cut command overwrites the current contents of the Clipboard. If you think you'll need something that's in the Clipboard for another use, you must save it to a file. Chapter 14, "Using the Windows Accessories," describes how to build a catalog of images by pasting them into a Cardfile file.

Remember

Closing Application Windows

Before you go further in this chapter, follow the steps here to close the applications that are open on the desktop. This is especially important if your system is low on memory.

Tip

To close Notepad, Write, and Paintbrush, double-click the Control button in their respective windows. Or, if they are icons on the desktop, click the icon once, and then choose Close from the Control menu. Message boxes will appear and ask you if want to save the contents of Notepad and Write. Unless you want to save something that's there, just click the No button, and the applications will close.

Exploring the Control Panel

In this section you learn important techniques for *customizing* the look and operation of Windows by using utilities in the Control Panel. Double-click the Control Panel icon in the Program Manager Main window now, to display a window similar to this:

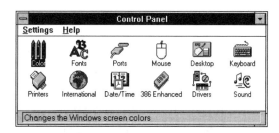

The utilities in the Control Panel are used to control your computer, printers, and various features of Windows. Here in Chapter 4 you examine the Date/Time utility and the Colors utility.

Setting the Date and Time

Because files are tagged with the date and time when they are saved, and because this information can be used to sort and organize files, it is important that your system has the correct settings. To set a new date and time, double-click the Date/Time icon on the Control Panel. This is the Date & Time dialog box:

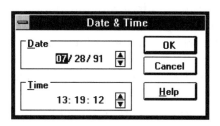

Note

Use the International icon on the Control Panel to change the format of the date and time display. This option is explained in Chapter 6, "Customizing Windows: The Control Panel."

To change the date or time, double-click the item you want to change, and then click the up- or down-arrow button repeatedly until the setting for each element is correct. You can also use the (TAB) key to move to any field and then type in a new setting.

The following exercise shows you how to set the date and time.

1. Double-click the month element in the Date field, or press the (TAB) key until it is highlighted.

2. Click the up- or down-arrow in the Date field to increase or decrease the value for the month element, or simply type in a new value.

3. Tab to the day element and repeat Step 2.

4. Tab to the year element and repeat Step 2.

5. If necessary, change the time field using the same procecure.

6. To save your changes, click the OK button or press (ENTER). To quit without making the changes, click the Cancel button or press (ESC).

Changing the Color Scheme

You can change the color scheme of your Windows environment using the Color utility. Open it now by double-clicking the Color icon in the Control Panel. In the Color dialog box (Figure 4-5), the Color Schemes field at the top of the box lists the current color scheme. When you pick a color scheme, it appears in the sample window in the middle of the dialog box.

There are two ways to change color schemes: you can select one of the predefined color schemes in the Color Schemes field, or you can create your own custom color scheme by clicking the Color Palette button at the bottom of the dialog box. Complete details for creating custom color schemes are covered in Chapter 6.

Follow this exercise to choose one of the predefined color schemes:

Figure 4-5.   *The Color dialog box lets you change the Windows color scheme*

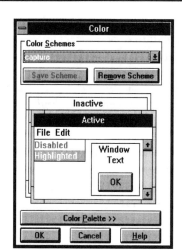

4

1. In the Color dialog box, click the down-arrow button in the Color Schemes field, or better, just press (DOWN ARROW) on the keyboard.

2. Press the up- and down-arrow keys in the list box to scroll through and scan through the sample color schemes.

3. Highlight the color scheme you want, and click the OK button or press (ENTER).

That's how easy it is to change the color scheme. Experiment with different schemes until you find one you like.

Exploring the File Manager

The File Manager helps you organize and manage the programs and files on your hard disk filing system. A *file* is a collection of information, initially created in the RAM of the computer and then saved to a disk storage device. All files have unique names. Hard drive filing systems that use DOS are organized into *directory* structures. Each directory is a separate area where you can store files; for instance, one directory might hold your business files, and another your personal files.

Note

Keep in mind that this section provides only a brief introduction to the File Manager. Chapter 9, "Managing Files, Directories, and Disks with File Manager," contains a complete discussion.

The File Manager window is illustrated in Figure 4-6. Like the Program Manager, File Manager has its own document windows, but they are called *directory windows* because they list the files in a directory. The elements of the File Manager window are described in the next sections.

Menu Bar   The File Manager menu bar contains commands for copying, moving, renaming, and deleting files or directories. It also contains options to change the way files are listed and the way the directory structure is presented.

Figure 4-6.   *The File Manager directory window*

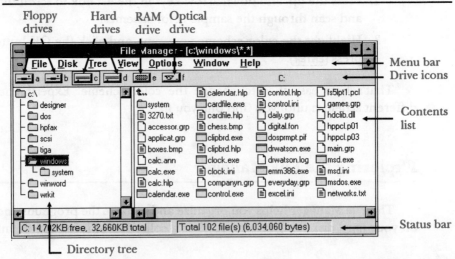

Directory Window   Directory windows provide a view of files in your directories. More than one directory window can be open at once, each presenting a list of files in a different directory. Each directory window includes drive icons, a directory tree, and a contents list (or files list).

Drive Icons   The drive icons represent the disk drives available on your system. Clicking a drive icon displays the directory tree for that drive.

Directory Tree   The directory tree represents the directory structure for the currently selected drive. Click a directory on the tree to display its files in the contents list.

Contents List   The contents list, also called the files list or file listing, displays the files of the directory that is currently selected in the directory tree. Icons are used to represent the various types of files:

4

File Icon	Description
	Executable files are program files and batch files. You can double-click these icons to start programs; thus the File Manager can be used to launch applications in the same way as Program Manager.
	Associated files are created by a Windows application, or have a filename extension recognized by an application. You can double-click the icons of associated documents to automatically load them into the workspace of the application that created them.
	Subdirectories branch from other directories. Double-click a subdirectory icon to access the files in it.
	Parent directories have branching subdirectories. Double-click the parent icon to move back one level in the directory tree.
	The *other file* icon represents all other files.

Using the File Manager

In these exercises, you get a chance to use File Manager and become familiar with what it can do. First, let's take a look at your Windows directory, which is normally on drive C, but may be on another drive in your system.

1. Click the Drive icon where the Windows directory is located.

2. Click the Windows directory icon in the directory tree. The files list then displays the files in the Windows directory.

Change the Order of the Files List

The order of the files included in the files list can be changed using options on the View menu. In this next exercise, you sort the list by file type, which groups files by their filename extension.

1. Click View in the File Manager menu bar.

2. Click Sort By Type, or press (ALT)-(V) (B). Watch as the files are resorted in alphabetical order by their filename extension.

Tip

Listing files by type (filename extension) is a convenient order to use when you need to view or select a group of similar files. For example, scroll through the files list and notice that files with the extension .BMP are grouped together.

Listing File Statistics

Use the View All File Details option to display additional information about files, such as their creation date and size:

1. Select View from the File Manager menu, and then All File Details. (You can press (ALT)-(V) (A) to quickly choose this option.)

2. If you can't see all the file statistics, enlarge the File Manager window, and then enlarge the directory window.

Now you see more than just the filenames and icons. Files are listed in rows with the size, date, and other information.

Listing Only Executable Files

You can specify which files you want to be included in or excluded from the File Manager files list, thus restricting this display to only the files you want to work with. In this exercise, you reduce the file listing to only executable program (.EXE) files. An .EXE file can be double-clicked with the mouse to start a program.

1. Select the View command and choose the By File Type option. The following dialog box appears:

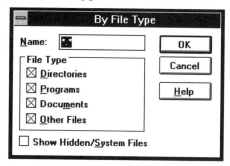

Initially, the Name field includes the file specification *.*, which means all files will be listed. The File Type box offers you another way to specify which files should be listed: Just mark or unmark the check box for the file types you want included or excluded from the list.

2. Unmark the check boxes for Documents and Other Files. Leave only the Directories and Programs check boxes marked.

3. Click the OK button or press (ENTER).

The contents list in File Manager now displays a list of directories and executable program files in the Windows directory. Other files are excluded from the list.

Starting Programs from File Manager

Now that you have the .EXE files listed in File Manager, you can double-click any of them to start those programs. Most of the .EXE files you see in the files list are the same programs that are started when you double-click an icon in the Program Manager. Note CLOCK.EXE (the Clock), CALC.EXE (the Calculator), and CONTROL.EXE (the Control Panel). As mentioned, File Manager just gives you another way to start these programs. Try it now by following these steps:

1. Point to CALC.EXE and double-click. The Calculator opens on the desktop.

2. Click the Calculator Minimize button.

3. Locate NOTEPAD.EXE and double-click its icon. If you already have Notepad loaded, another copy will open in another window. Minimize this window for use in the next exercise.

Loading Associated Files

Associated files are linked, by means of their filename extensions, to the applications that created them. For example, the Notepad editor creates files with the extension .TXT, and the Calendar utility creates files with the extension .CAL. You can double-click an associated file to open it in the workspace of the application used to create it.

Follow these steps to change the files list and open an associated file.

1. Select the View command and choose the By File Type option.

2. When the By File Type dialog box opens, mark only the Documents check box. (After the last exercise, you need to unmark Directories and Programs.)

3. Click the OK button or press (ENTER).

4. When the files list reappears, double-click WINLOGO, which is associated with the Paintbrush application. The file is loaded in the Paintbrush workspace.

Thus File Manager provides a quick way to view and open your various document, graphics, and other files. To do the same in Program Manager, you would need to create an icon for the document in a group, or start the application and then open the document.

Opening a Second Directory Window

You can open a second directory window and view two sets of files side by side for comparison. Try this now:

1. Select the Window command from the File Manager menu bar and choose New Window, or press (ALT)-(W) (N).

2. The new window duplicates and overlaps the first window. To see both windows, choose Cascade from the Window menu.

3. In the directory tree of the new window, click an icon for a directory different from the one selected in the first window. The files for that directory are then listed in the new window, and the title of the window changes.

To open a new window for another disk drive, double-click the icon of the disk in the current window.

Tip

Closing the File Manager

Caution

*When you're ready to close the File Manager, first take a look at the status of the Save Settings on Exit option on the Options menu. If this feature is enabled, any changes you made to directory windows and menu options will be retained for your next File Manager sessions. However, because the changes made in these exercises are not necessary to normal operation of the Windows environment, it's important that you make sure this feature is **not** enabled.*

Save Settings on Exit is a toggle, so if the check box is marked, just select it again to turn it off. You can now double-click the Control button or choose Exit from the File menu to quit File Manager.

5

Using Windows Help

In this chapter, you learn how to use the Windows *help system*. Nearly every window contains the Help option on its menu bar. Use Help to obtain information, assistance, and even tutorials on Windows applications.

Accessing Help

You can access help information in two ways: You can select the Help option on the menu bar of a window to access help for any topic related to the application running in the window. Or, you can highlight a particular command or menu option and press the (F1) key to get help related to that item. For example, if you highlight the Run command on the Program Manager File menu and press (F1), instructions for using Run are displayed, as shown in Figure 5-1. *Help windows* are resizable and movable, and have a menu bar, buttons, and other typical Windows features. They can even be minimized and kept on the desktop for periodic reference.

Figure 5-1.   *A typical Help dialog box*

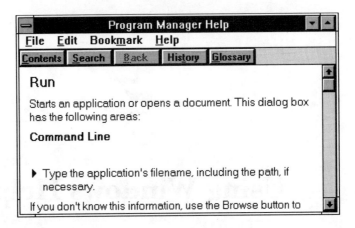

Think of the help system as a reference book with a table of contents, index, and glossary. Most applications have their own "book" of help. The F1 key lets you immediately display a specific part of the book that is related to the task you are working on. To view help information for an entire application from the beginning, click the Help option on the application menu bar or press ALT-H. You'll see a pull-down menu similar to these:

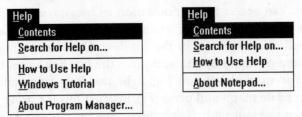

The Help menu on the left is from the Program Manager, and the one on the right is from Notepad. Both menus have options in common, such as Contents and Search for Help on. Search for Help on helps you locate any topic in Help. Some applications have their own tutorials, like the Windows Tutorial option on the Program Manager menu.

How to Get Help

To get help, either open the Help pull-down menu or press the (F1) key to display specific help information related to the task you are working on. A third method is also available in some applications; you can press (SHIFT)-(F1) to change the mouse pointer to a question mark, and then click the area of the screen for which you want help. The exercises in the rest of this chapter illustrate these techniques. Before starting the exercises, make sure the Program Manager is active.

Using the Help Menu

In the Program Manager, choose Help from the menu bar to open the Help menu. Choose the Contents option to open the Help window. The Help window contains a list of topics displayed in green or as underlined letters. Now minimize the Help window by clicking its Minimize button. You will see the following Help icon at the bottom of the desktop:

The Help window is now out of the way, but easily accessible when you need it.

Getting Context-Specific Help

You can get help information related to the command you're using by pressing (F1). In the following exercise, you display help for the Run command on the Program Manager File menu:

1. Activate the Program Manager window, and open the File menu.

2. Press the (DOWN ARROW) key to highlight the Run option (*don't* click the option).

3. Press (F1) to display help for the Run command.

4. Reduce the size of the Help window, and notice that the help text rearranges itself to fit the new window shape.

5. You don't need to read this help now, so close the Help window by double-clicking its Control button.

Some dialog boxes have buttons for accessing help. In this way, you can execute a command and then get help about the command's options. Try this:

1. Choose Run on the File menu.

2. Click the Help button in the dialog box. When the help for the Run command is displayed, notice that the size you gave the Help window in the previous exercise is retained.

3. Close the Help window.

4. Press (ESC) to close the Run dialog box.

Using Help Windows

Help windows look much the same as other windows, except they also have a set of buttons used to navigate the special contents of the window. In the following exercises, you learn how to work with Help windows. Before you start the exercises, you need to open the Program Manager Help window by choosing Contents from the Help menu.

Tip

Keep in mind that you can resize Help windows and position them beside their related application windows. This makes it easy to reference help information when you need it. Alternatively, you can keep Help windows minimized, and maximize them when you need their information.

Scroll the Help Text and Choose a Topic

To scroll through help text, click the down-arrow button on the scroll bar, or press the (PGDN) key. You can click any topic that is highlighted in green or underlined. Follow these steps to practice getting help on various topics:

1. Click the topic called "Organizing Applications and Documents" under the How To heading in the contents list. The following Help window appears:

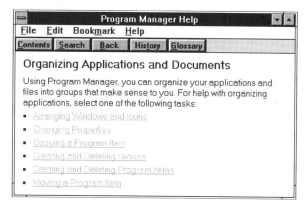

Notice that this topic has branching topics of its own. As you click each topic, you move further into the help text. You use the Back button under the Help window menu bar to move back to your starting place.

2. Click the topic "Creating and Deleting Groups."

Now you see help text that describes how to create and delete groups. Notice the green or underlined words within the text itself. These are *glossary items.* You can click a glossary item to get a quick description of the term.

3. Click the glossary item "title bar" to display the glossary text shown in Figure 5-2.

4. Click the glossary reference to remove it from the screen.

Figure 5-2. *Glossary reference window opened for the selected "title bar" topic*

| □ ▾ | Program Manager Help | ▾ ▲ |

File   Edit   Bookmark   Help

| Contents | Search | Back | History | Glossary |

Creating and Deleting Groups

You can create a group in Program Manager to help organize your
applications and documents.

To create a group

1 From the File menu, choose New.
2 Select the Program Group option, and then choose the OK button.
3 Type a description for the group.   ⌐—— Glossary reference
   This description will appear in the title bar of the group window and

4

title bar

The horizontal bar at the top of a window that contains the title of the   ◄—— Glossary text
window or dialog box. On many windows, the title bar also contains the
Control-menu box and Maximize and Minimize buttons.

This section has shown you how to move into different levels of help text.
The next section shows you how to move back through the help text.

Using Help Buttons

Every Help window has a set of Help buttons, as illustrated here:

These buttons are used to navigate through the help text, or to quickly
relocate to other topics. Some Help windows include the << and >> buttons;
they are used to browse back and forth through help topics. Here is a list of
the buttons and their functions; they are discussed in detail in the paragraphs
that follow:

Help Button	Function
Contents	View Help window contents
Search	Search for specific help topics
Back	Move back one help topic
History	View history
Glossary	Display a list of glossary items
<<	Browse backward
>>	Browse forward

Viewing the History

Every topic you access while using a Help window is recorded automatically in a history file. You can then display the history file and use it to jump back to any previous topic. In the last exercise, you advanced into the Program Manager help text twice by clicking on two topics. To view these steps and return to any one of them, click on the History button or press (ALT)-(T). You'll see a listing of steps similar to this:

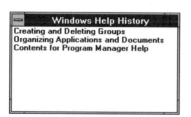

To return to any topic in this history list, double-click the topic with the mouse. The help text for the topic is displayed in the Help window.

The History button provides a convenient way to browse through help text. It lets you advance several steps into a help topic, and then quickly return to the top level and continue with another topic.

The Back Button and Browse Buttons

The Back button is used to go back one step in the help text. You can click this button several times to retrace your steps to any point, and then branch off to another topic.

5

The forward browse button (>>) and the backward browse button (<<) that appear on some Help windows let you step forward or backward through each major topic in the help text. The << button moves backward through the help topics, and the >> moves forward through the help topics. Click the button with the mouse, or press (ALT)-(◄) or (ALT)-(►).

Displaying the Table of Contents

To return to the beginning of the help text and display its list of topics, click the Contents button. Try this now to return to the beginning of the Program Manager help text.

Searching for Topics

You can quickly locate any help topic using the Search button or by choosing Search for Help on from the Help menu. Try the following exercise to locate help for the options on the Program Manager File menu:

1. In the Program Manager Help window, click the Search button. You'll see the Search dialog box (Figure 5-3).

2. In the top text box, where the blinking cursor appears, type **F**. Keywords that start with *F* are displayed in the list box in the top half of the Search dialog box.

3. Double-click the "File menu" keyword, to view a list of topics that have this keyword in their text. The lower list box then displays these topics (see Figure 5-3).

4. Double-click on the "Exit Windows" topic in the lower list box to see that help text.

The Show Topics button and the Go To button can be used instead of the mouse instructions in the foregoing exercise. To use the Show Topics button, first highlight a keyword in the upper list box, and then choose the Show Topics ((ALT)-(S)) button. When the topics appear in the lower list box, you can highlight a topic and choose the Go To ((ALT)-(G)) button to display the help text for that topic.

Figure 5-3. *The Search dialog box for finding help topics*

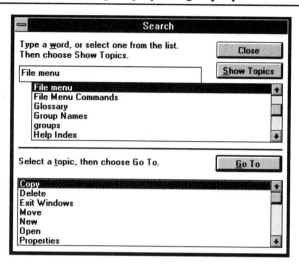

Using the Help Menu Options

Now let's take a look at the options on the Help window menu bar. In the Program Manager Help window, select each option as you read the following text:

- The *File* menu gives you options for opening the help text of another application, or printing the currently displayed help topic.
- The *Edit* menu has options for copying a block of help text to another application, and annotating (adding to) help text.
- The *Bookmark* menu is used to insert a placeholder in help text so you can quickly refer back to a point in that text at any time.
- The *Help* menu provides help about the help system itself.

This section steps you through the menu options. Before beginning, make sure the Program Manager Help window is still open. If it isn't, open it now.

The File Open Option

Most Windows applications have their own help text, which is in a file (with a .HLP extension) stored in the Windows directory of your hard drive. You can look at the help information for any application, even if it's not running, by choosing Open on the File menu of any currently open Help window. This is most useful for teachers or managers who need to create a set of instructions for other users. You can open the help text file of any application, and then use the Copy option on the Help Edit menu to copy specific topics to another document. Do the following exercise to practice opening another help topic:

1. Make sure the Program Manager Help window is still open. If not, choose Contents from the Program Manager Help menu.

2. Choose the Open option on the File menu. You'll see this dialog box:

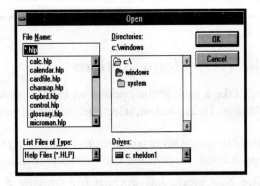

3. Double-click CALC.HLP at the top of the File Name list.

The Help window title bar now displays "Calculator Help," even though the calculator is not running.

Printing a Help Topic

Printing the text of a help topic is one of the most useful things you can do with the Help system. In this next example, you print a list of the standard keystrokes used by the Calculator.

1. Click the topic "Use Standard Calculator Functions" under the Keyboard heading, to display the keyboard methods for accessing the Calculator.

2. Choose Print Topic from the File menu to print the topic.

To print other topics, first display the topic, and then choose the Print Topic option on the Help File menu.

Print the contents of any help topic to create an instant quick-reference that you can post next to your computer or place in a help binder.

Tip

Copying a Help Topic

Teachers, instructors, and managers can open a help file and copy its text to a file in a word processor. Printed or on-line collections of these help topics can be expanded or abbreviated, or otherwise customized, to train students and employees.

Use the Copy option on the Help Edit menu to place the text of any help topic in the Clipboard. You then paste the help text into another application. In the following exercise, you copy the Standard Calculator Functions help information to the Notepad editor and save it for later use.

1. Make sure the Using Standard Calculator Functions topic is still displayed. If not, use the Help window History button and choose it again from the list of Calculator help topics.

2. Select Edit in the menu bar, and choose the Copy option. You'll see this dialog box:

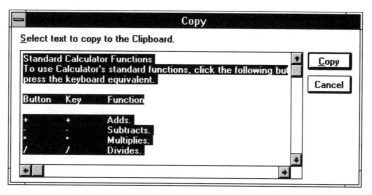

3. Click the Copy button to copy the entire text into the Clipboard.

4. Start Notepad by double-clicking its icon in the Accessories group of the Program Manager.

5. When the Notepad window opens, choose Paste from the Edit menu to place the help text in the workspace.

6. Save the text by choosing Save As from the File menu. When the Save As dialog box appears, type **CALCKEYS** in the File Name text box, and click OK or press (ENTER).

7. Close the Notepad window, and make the Calculator Help text window active again. If you can't see the Help window to click it, press (CTRL)-(ESC) and choose its name from the Task List.

You'll get a chance to use this CALCKEYS file later for other exercises.

 You can highlight any part of the text by clicking and dragging through it with the mouse.

Note   ## The Annotate Option

The Annotate option in the Help Edit menu lets you add *annotations* (notes and comments of your own) to any help topic. When you add an annotation, a paper clip appears at the beginning of the topic's help text. Try adding a comment to the current (Calculator) Help window by following these steps:

1. Choose Annotate from the Edit menu. You'll see this dialog box:

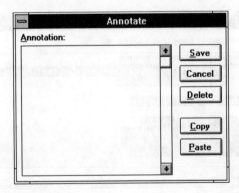

2. In the large text box where the blinking cursor appears, type the following:

   This topic has already been printed.

3. Click the Save button ((ALT)-(S)).

4. Scroll to the top of the Calculator help text until you see the paper clip.

5. Click the paper clip to display the Annotate dialog box, and you'll see your annotation. Press (ESC) to return to the Help window.

You can remove an annotation at any time by clicking the Delete button ((ALT)-(D)) on the Annotation dialog box. The Copy and Paste buttons in that box let you copy existing annotations from one annotation box to another.

Defining Bookmarks

Bookmarks mark a place in a help file to which you want to return later. Bookmark titles are then added to the Bookmark menu. Here's an exercise to define a bookmark:

1. The Standard Calculator Functions help text should still be visible in the Help window. Select Bookmark from the menu bar, and choose the Define option from the menu. You'll see this dialog box:

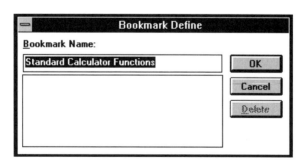

2. In the bookmark name field where the cursor is flashing, type **I was here!** in the top field. Click OK or press (ENTER).

The lower field is used to select and delete an existing bookmark.

Note

3. Open the Bookmark menu. You'll see your new bookmark on the pull-down menu, as shown here:

You can use bookmarks in topics you need to access quickly. Bookmarks are saved from one session to the next. When you don't need a bookmark any longer, open the Bookmark Define dialog box, click the bookmark to delete in the list at the bottom, and click the Delete button ((ALT)-(D)).

6

Customizing Windows:
The Control Panel

To customize your Windows environment, you use the Control Panel utilities, illustrated after the next paragraph. For example, you use the Printers icon to add and configure printers to work with Windows. You can also personalize your Windows screen by changing the color scheme or displaying pictures on the Windows desktop.

To begin working with the Control Panel, double-click its icon in the Program Manager (or select it with the keyboard), and you'll see a Control Panel window similar to this:

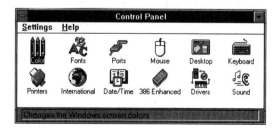

There are three categories of options on the Control Panel:

- **Window and desktop options**   Choose the color of window borders, menu bars, text, and other features with the Color utility. To alter the desktop pattern, cursor blink rate, and window spacing, use the Desktop utility.

- **Hardware settings**   Set the operations of the keyboard, mouse, serial ports, and printers with the Keyboard, Mouse, Ports, and Printers utilities, respectively.

- **Software settings**   Control the internal settings of your system—date and time, language and currency formats, keyboard operation, and screen fonts with the Date/Time, International, Keyboard, and Fonts utilities, respectively. The Network utility lets network users log on and modify various network settings.

The sections in this chapter describe each of the Control Panel utilities in detail, except for MIDI Mapper, which is beyond the scope of this book.

Color

The Color utility lets you change the color of window borders, title bars, menu text, and so on. Choose one of the Windows predefined color schemes, or design your own.

Double-click the Color icon in the Control Panel to display the Color dialog box pictured in Figure 6-1. The highlight should be in the Color Schemes pull-down list box. To scroll through the options in this box, click the down-arrow button with the mouse, or press the (DOWN ARROW) key on the keyboard. As you scroll through the list, the sample window (in the center of the Color dialog box) takes on the currently selected color scheme so you can see what it looks like. Click OK or press (ENTER) to select a new color scheme.

Creating Custom Color Schemes

Windows 3.1 comes with a number of predefined, named color schemes. These are all listed in the Color Schemes box. If you don't like these schemes,

Figure 6-1.   *The Color dialog box*

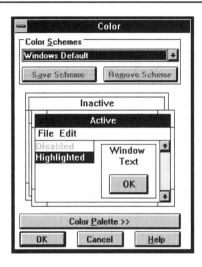

you can create your own. To create a custom color scheme, you pick a window element you want to change (border, title bar, window text, and so on), and then choose a new color for it from the Basic Colors palette. Once you've created a scheme you like, you can save it and make it the current color scheme.

Mouse users can click any part of the Color dialog box to change settings. If you're using the keyboard, press the (TAB) key to move among the fields. Don't press (ENTER) until you're completely finished, because that closes the dialog box.

The following exercise shows you how to create your own custom color scheme:

1. Click the Color Palette >> button in the lower part of the Color dialog box. The Color dialog box expands, as shown in Figure 6-2.

2. Click the down-arrow button on the Screen Element list box until Desktop is highlighted.

Figure 6-2.   *The Color dialog box, fully expanded*

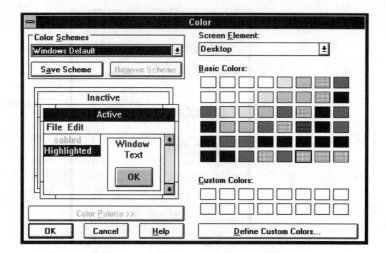

3. In the color boxes of the Basic Colors area, notice that the current color is surrounded by a black border. Click White in the lower-right corner to select white for the desktop color.

4. Choose Menu Bar from the Screen Element list.

5. Click a new color in the Basic Colors area to change the color of the menu bar.

Repeat Steps 4 and 5 to change any screen element you want, watching the sample window on the left as you select each new color. Once you've designed a color scheme, save it by following these steps :

1. Click the Save Scheme command button ((ALT)-(A)) to display the following dialog box:

2. Type a name for your scheme in the text box.

3. Click OK or press (ENTER) to save the scheme.

To edit your color scheme, highlight its name in the Color Schemes box and make changes as outlined in the previous procedure. Or click the Remove Scheme button ((ALT)-(M)) to delete it altogether. To make your new scheme active, display its name in the Color Schemes list box, and click the OK button or press (ENTER).

Creating Custom Colors

You can also create your own colors for use in the color schemes. Open the Color dialog box from the Control Panel; then click the Color Palette >> button to display the expanded Color dialog box (Figure 6-2). Next, click the Define Custom Colors button to open the Custom Color Selector box, shown in Figure 6-3.

The slider bar and text boxes on the Custom Color Selector box are used to adjust the mix of red, green, and blue (RGB Color Model), or the hue, luminosity, and saturation (HLS Color Model) that make up colors. All these concepts are described in the following paragraphs.

- The large color refiner box, or grid, is for selecting a color by using the mouse.

- The luminosity slider bar to the right of the color refiner box is used to change the luminosity of the current color.

- Click the Color|Solid box to pick a dithered or solid version of the current color.

6

Figure 6-3.   *The Custom Color Selector Box*

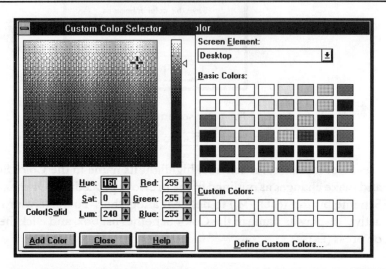

- In the value boxes, select or enter numeric values for colors, rather than using the mouse methods.

Once you've created a color, you click the Add Color button to add the new color to one of the 16 Custom Color boxes.

When you use the Custom Color Selector, you need to understand the following terminology about the custom colors you are creating. *Hue* is the intensity of red, blue, and green that combine to make the color, and corresponds to a *horizontal* movement across the color refiner box. *Saturation* is the purity of a color (or its lack of gray content), and corresponds to a *vertical* movement in the color refiner box. *Luminosity* is the brightness of a color on a scale from black to white.

You can also mix colors by specifying the darkness or brightness of their red, green, and blue elements. When the Red, Green, and Blue fields are set to 0, the color is black. When all three fields are set to 255, the color is white. Any combination in between is a custom color.

Because some monitors are incapable of displaying the full range of colors supported by Windows, a dot pattern is used to approximate the color as closely as possible. This is known as *dithering*. As you work with a color, the Color|Solid box displays the dithered color on the left. The box on the right is the closest solid, or nondithered, color that can be displayed. Once a custom color is created, you can choose between the dithered or solid version of that color by clicking in either side of the Color|Solid box.

This next exercise shows you how to create and add a custom color:

1. Start by dragging the luminosity slider bar pointer about midway on the scale.

2. In the color refiner box, point to the approximate color you want. (You'll see a cross-hair color refiner cursor.)

3. To make adjustments to the color, drag the mouse around in the refiner box or slide the luminosity pointer. Watch the colors in the Color|Solid box until you see a dithered or solid color that you like.

4. Try making some finer adjustments by clicking the up- or down-arrow buttons of the value boxes below the refiner box. Click and hold these buttons to get an idea of how hue, saturation, and luminosity determine the position of the pointers in the refiner box or luminosity bar.

5. Add the new color to a box in the Custom Color field by clicking either the dithered or solid color in the Color|Solid box, and then clicking the Add Color button.

The new custom color will fill the first available color box in the Custom Colors field. To change a custom color, click its color box and follow the above procedure again. Use your custom colors to design custom color schemes.

Fonts

Fonts are sets of characters with a specific typeface that can be altered by changing their size and using different type styles, like italic and boldface. Using varied fonts can change the look and readability of your documents.

In most applications, fonts are changed by opening a fonts dialog box. To understand fonts and how they are translated on your screen and printer, follow these steps to open Windows Write and choose Fonts from the Character menu:

1. Double-click the Accessories group in Program Manager.
2. Double-click the Write icon.
3. Choose the Fonts option from the Character menu, and you'll see the dialog box shown in Figure 6-4.

The Font dialog box includes list boxes for selecting a font, font style, and font size. Scroll through the Font list now by clicking the down-arrow button or pressing (DOWN ARROW) on the keyboard. Watch the Sample box as you do this, and notice that fonts are either printer fonts or TrueType fonts (explained next).

Windows, Your Printer, and Fonts

The fonts available in the character formatting menus of any Windows application depend partly on the currently installed printer. For example, the fonts named Avante Garde, Bookman, and Zapf Dingbats will appear when a PostScript laser printer is installed. If you install a dot-matrix printer, a different set of fonts is available. Special printer definitions are added when you install printers during Windows Setup or with the Printer utility on the Control Panel. These printer definitions tell Windows what it needs to know about your printer and its fonts.

Windows 3.1 includes a new kind of *scalable font* called TrueType. You can reduce or enlarge these fonts to many different sizes. In addition, their appearance on the screen is very close to the printed version. TrueType fonts will print on any graphics-capable printer, so you are not limited to the fonts built into your printer.

It is important to make a distinction between the fonts displayed on the screen and those printed by the printer. Windows uses *screen fonts* to display

Figure 6-4. *The Font dialog box in Windows Write is used to change the formatting of selected characters*

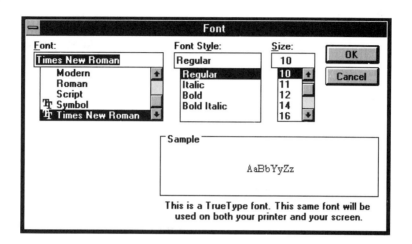

characters as near as possible to how they will look when printed. Sometimes the match isn't perfect, but it's close enough for you to get a good idea of what you'll get on paper. Character size and spacing is sometimes off, but the location of line breaks and the spacing of lines will be accurate enough to give you an idea of the page layout. The advantage of TrueType fonts is that they look good on the screen and in your printed documents.

To better understand fonts, consider the following methods your printer uses to print text.

Built-in Printer Fonts A font that your printer already knows how to print is called a *built-in* font. To work with this font, the printer does not need additional information from the computer, except a direction for which style and size to print. When using built-in printer fonts, you are limited to the range of fonts, styles, and sizes available in the printer. In some printers, the available fonts can be expanded by adding font *cartridges*, or by sending font descriptions stored in the computer to the printer's memory.

6

Computer Fonts   Instead of using a predefined font built into the printer, you can generate fonts in the computer and send them to the printer as graphic information. Windows puts the printer in *graphics mode* and makes it print any font, style, or size you request. The TrueType fonts supplied with Windows 3.1 are scalable in the range of 4 points to 127 points and can be printed on any graphics-capable printer supported by Windows.

Note

Printer fonts have corresponding screen fonts. The screen fonts mimic the way the font appears when printed. In some cases, you can acquire a screen font that provides an even better match to your printer's fonts, by contacting the manufacturer of the printer or by buying third-party font packages.

Viewing, Installing, and Removing Fonts

The Fonts utility on the Control Panel is used to install new fonts, or to install screen fonts for the fonts built into your printer. You can also use the Fonts utility to optimize system memory by removing fonts you don't use. In this section you see how to remove a font from memory and then reinstall it, using the Fonts utility.

Note

Keep in mind that most third-party fonts come with their own installation programs. Before using the Fonts utility, refer to the installation manual for any third-party fonts you have purchased.

Start the Fonts utility by double-clicking its icon in the Control Panel. You'll see the Fonts dialog box pictured in Figure 6-5.

To view currently installed fonts, scroll through the Installed Fonts list box. This displays a sample of each font in the lower box, as you scroll in the Installed Fonts box. As you scroll through the list, you'll see TrueType fonts and other fonts. For example, the Courier 10,12,15 font in the Installed Fonts list in Figure 6-5 is a screen font for VGA screens. It may be used to display a built-in printer font on screen.

Figure 6-5.   *The Fonts utility lets you view, add, and remove screen and printer fonts*

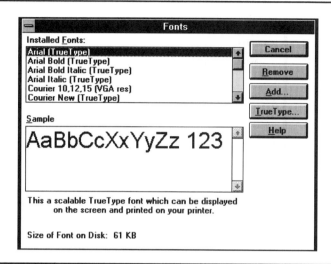

Adding Fonts

Fonts are available from a wide variety of sources. You can buy them off the shelf, or you can download them from bulletin board systems (BBSs) or the Windows forums on CompuServe. To make new fonts available to Windows applications, you need to install them using the Fonts utility. In the following example, fonts downloaded from a CompuServe Windows forum are stored in the directory TRUETYPE on drive C.

1. Choose the Fonts icon from the Control Panel. The Fonts dialog box appears, as shown in Figure 6-5.

2. Click the Add button on the Fonts dialog box.

3. Choose the drive and directory where the fonts are located in the Drives and Directories list boxes. The available fonts will be listed, as shown here:

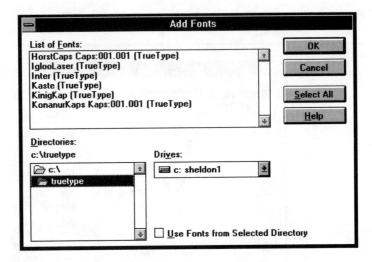

4. Click the fonts you want to add, or click the Select All button to add them all.

5. Click the option Use Fonts from Selected Directory if the fonts are already stored on your hard drive, otherwise Windows will make a duplicate copy of the font files in the \WINDOWS\SYSTEM directory. Leave this option blank if you are copying the files from a floppy disk or from another source such as a network server. Windows will then copy the files for you.

6. Click OK to install the new fonts.

Using TrueType Fonts

By default, Windows displays TrueType fonts in the Fonts dialog boxes of your applications. In some cases, you may prefer to use only your printer's fonts. In other cases, you may prefer to use TrueType fonts exclusively. To change the type of fonts that Windows displays, click the TrueType button on the Fonts dialog box to display the TrueType dialog box, as shown here:

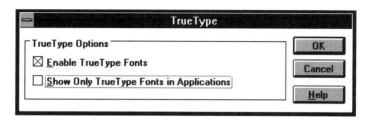

Mark the Enable TrueType Fonts check box to use TrueType fonts, or clear the box to use your printer's fonts only. Mark the Show Only TrueType Fonts in Applications check box to use TrueType fonts exclusively, or clear it to see all installed fonts. Note that checking this option frees memory for other applications.

Removing Fonts

There are two options available for removing fonts. You can remove a font to free RAM for other applications, but keep it available on disk if you need it in the future. Or you can permanently remove a font from your system by removing the disk file of the font. This not only frees memory, but makes disk space available as well.

To remove a font, follow these steps:

1. Choose the Fonts option in the Control Panel.

2. Highlight the font you want to remove in the Installed Fonts list box.

3. Click the Remove button. The dialog box shown here appears:

4. To remove the font from disk as well as from RAM, mark the Delete Font File From Disk option.

5. Click Yes to remove the font.

Freeing RAM by Removing Fonts

As mentioned earlier in this chapter, there are two methods of freeing system memory by removing fonts.

To free the greatest amount of RAM, click TrueType on the Fonts dialog box to display the TrueType dialog box. Then mark the Show Only TrueType fonts in Applications option on the TrueType dialog box. Alternatively, clear the Enable TrueType Fonts option to remove all TrueType fonts from memory. Note that doing so does not remove the fonts from disk. You can reenable them at any time.

The second method of freeing RAM is to remove individual fonts using the Remove button on the Fonts dialog box. In this way, you can selectively remove only the fonts you don't use, rather than all the TrueType fonts or all the non-TrueType fonts as described in the previous paragraph.

Ports

The Ports utility in the Control Panel is used to configure the serial ports on the back of your computer. Most computers have only one or two serial ports, but the Ports utility has options for configuring up to four. Each serial port is referred to as COM1, COM2, and so on. Serial ports are used to connect modems and serial printers to your computer.

If a modem is attached to one of your serial ports, use the modem's communications software to configure the port, rather than the Windows Ports utility.

Note

Double-click the Control Panel Ports icon to display the following dialog box:

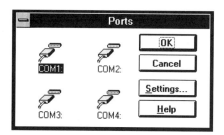

Here you can view and change the configuration for any port, by highlighting the icon for the port and then clicking the Settings button ((ALT)-(S)). If you're not actually setting up a COM port, but just learning about Windows, you can still follow along with this discussion to learn more about communications settings.

For this example, highlight the icon for COM1. Click the Settings button or press (ALT)-(S) to open the Settings dialog box for the COM1 port, as shown here:

Following are descriptions of the settings in this box. To change a setting, click the down-arrow button to display a list of options and then click a new option.

In each case, the setting should match the requirement for the device that is connected to that port.

Note

Baud Rate   The *baud rate* is the speed at which information is transmitted through the port. Click the down-arrow button in the Baud Rate field to see the choices in the list box.

Data Bits   The *data bits* setting is the length, in bits, of each character sent. The bit size is either 7 or 8. Match this to the setting of the device you are connecting.

Parity   *Parity* is an error-checking parameter used by some devices. If the printer or remote device connected to the port uses parity, determine the type, and select the appropriate setting in the Parity list box.

Stop Bits   *Stop bits* are used to indicate the beginning and ending of each transmitted character.

Flow Control   *Flow control* provides a way for the receiving device to tell the sending device to temporarily stop sending data because it has more than it can handle at the moment. After the current data is printed or processed, more can be sent. The Xon/Xoff setting is software-level handshaking and is most commonly used. The Hardware setting designates hardware-level hand-shaking, which takes place between pinouts on the serial connectors. Hand-shaking is usually not required when the baud rate is lower than the printer speed, in which case you can designate None.

To duplicate the settings of one port to another, use the mouse to drag the port icon with the existing settings to another port icon.

Tip

Mouse

To change the operating characteristics of your mouse or other tracking device, select the Mouse icon on the Control Panel. You'll see the following dialog box:

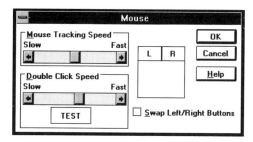

Set Mouse Tracking Speed

When the dialog box first opens, the slider button in the Mouse Tracking Speed box is flashing. Changing the position of this button allows you to change the speed at which the mouse pointer moves across the screen in relation to the movement of the mouse.

Try sliding the Mouse Tracking Speed button all the way to the left, and then drag the mouse pointer on the desktop to try the new speed. Then slide the button all the way to the right, and drag the mouse pointer again to try the new tracking speed. Then set the slider button in the position you prefer, and go on to the next section.

Beginning users, or those of you who are creating precise drawings, may want to set the mouse for slower tracking. As you become more familiar with your mouse, you can increase the tracking speed as desired.

Tip

Setting the Double Click Speed

The Double Click Speed setting tells Windows when to interpret two mouse clicks as a double-click, by defining the length of time between the two clicks. Here's an exercise to practice using the slider bar for this setting:

1. Click the slider button in the Double Click Speed box, and slide it to the left.

2. Try double-clicking with the mouse in the TEST box below the slider bar. When your double-click speed matches the new setting, the TEST box changes colors.

3. Slide the button to the right, and test the double-click speed again in the TEST box.

4. Set the slider button to the position you prefer.

Swapping the Mouse Buttons

If you are left-handed, you can swap the functions performed by the left and right mouse buttons. Just click in the Swap Left/Right Buttons check box (this is a toggle setting). When the box is checked, the right button becomes the button used for the majority of tasks, such as selecting items and executing commands.

Mouse Trails

Click the Mouse Trails option to leave a trail of mouse pointers as you drag the mouse. This option takes effect immediately. It is most beneficial for liquid crystal displays (LCDs) like those on notebook computers, where screen response is slow.

After making changes to the Mouse dialog box, click the OK button or press (ENTER) to return to the Control Panel.

Desktop

The Desktop utility lets you change certain features of the desktop: the desktop color and pattern, the cursor blink rate, and the grid that windows "snap" to when they're resized. Double-click the Control Panel Desktop icon now to display the dialog box shown in Figure 6-6. The options in this dialog box are described in the following paragraphs.

Figure 6-6. *The Desktop dialog box and its many features*

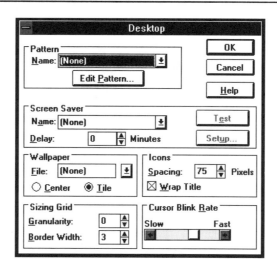

Desktop Pattern

The first time you start Windows, there is no desktop pattern—only the color of the desktop you selected in the Color dialog box (discussed earlier in this chapter). Using the Pattern features in the Desktop dialog box, you can change the appearance of the desktop to a pattern, providing a background that helps differentiate windows and icons on the desktop, or just because you want to see something new. You can install a predefined pattern, like Critters, Quilt, Waffle, or Weave, or create patterns of your own.

Installing a Pattern

Follow these steps to install a pattern on the desktop:

1. Click the Edit Pattern command button ((ALT)-(P)). You'll see the Desktop - Edit Pattern dialog box shown here:

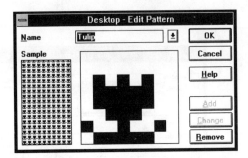

2. Press (DOWN ARROW) on the keyboard to open the Name pull-down list box. Continue to press the (DOWN ARROW) key repeatedly to display each name and pattern.

3. Highlight the Tulip pattern; then click the OK button or press (ENTER).

4. Although the Pattern Name list box now displays the name of the Tulip pattern, to make it appear on the desktop you have to click the OK button in the Desktop dialog box (or press (ENTER)). Do this now to see how the pattern appears on the desktop.

Changing the Pattern Colors

You can change the color of the desktop pattern, as well as its background, to make items on the desktop easier to see and read. These changes are done in the Color utility, as discussed earlier in this chapter. Let's change the colors of the pattern you have added to your desktop.

1. Return to the Control Panel, and double-click the Color icon.

2. Click the Color Palette >> button to open the dialog box.

3. In the sample window, click Window Text, or select it in the Screen Element list box.

4. Select any color box from the Basic Colors area. This will be the color for the tulips in the desktop pattern.

5. Click the desktop in the sample window, or choose Desktop in the Screen Element list box.

6. Choose a color that you want as the underlying background color for the tulips.

7. Click the OK button or press (ENTER), and look at the results on your screen.

Repeat these steps to try other colors in your patterns.

Editing a Pattern

You can also create your own Desktop patterns, as described in this next exercise.

1. Open the Desktop dialog box.
2. Click Edit Pattern ((ALT)-(P)). The Desktop - Edit Pattern dialog box appears, with the current pattern and its color visible in the Sample box.
3. Click the elements or *bits* in the editing area to turn them on or off. Experiment by clicking at various locations and watch as the pattern changes in the Sample box.
4. When you've created a pattern you like, save it by typing a new name in the Name field and clicking the Add button ((ALT)-(A)).
5. Click the OK button or press (ENTER).

The new pattern name now appears in the Pattern Name list box. To place this new pattern on the desktop, click OK or press (ENTER).

In the Desktop - Edit Pattern dialog box, the Add, Change, and Remove buttons are used to edit, save, or delete existing patterns. After editing a pattern, you can click Change and save it under that pattern name. However, it's best to save patterns under new names so you won't lose the original ones. To do so, begin typing a new name in the Name box; the Add button can then be used to save the pattern under a new name. To remove a pattern you have created, highlight its name in the Name box and press the Remove button.

Using a Screen Saver

The Screen Saver feature blanks the computer monitor screen or displays a moving object if you don't press a key or move the mouse for a set period of time. This prevents an image from burning itself onto your screen when left on too long. Use the Screen Saver options in the Desktop dialog box to designate the type of screen saver you want and the interval of inactivity that must pass before the saver takes over the screen.

Here is an exercise to install a screen saver:

1. Open the Desktop dialog box, and click the Screen Saver Name field. A list of available screen savers appears, as shown here:

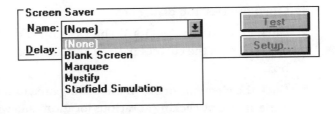

2. Click Starfield Simulation.

3. In the Delay text box, type the number of minutes of inactivity you want to allow before the screen saver comes on. For this example, type **1**.

4. Click the Test button to see a sample of the screen saver.

5. Move the mouse or press any key on the keyboard to return to normal screen mode.

If you want, select any of the other screen savers and click the Test button to see how they look. The Marquee screen saver is described in "Creating a Marquee" later in this chapter.

Customizing a Screen Saver

You can change the features of a screen saver by selecting it and then clicking the Setup button. Follow these steps to change the look of the Starfield Simulation screen saver:

1. Make sure the Starfield Simulation screen saver is selected in the Name list box; then click the Setup button. You'll see this dialog box:

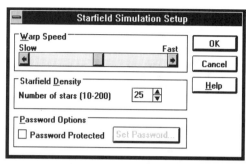

2. To change the speed of the moving starfield, click the slider button in the Warp Speed field and drag it left or right toward Slow or Fast.

3. To change the starfield density (number of stars), click on the up- or down-arrow buttons in the Starfield Density text box.

4. Click the OK button or press (ENTER) to execute the changes, and click the Test button to see the changes.

You can also change the settings of the Mystify and Marquee screen savers. When you open their Setup dialog box, click the Help button to view instructions for setting options.

Setting a Password

Setting a password for a screen saver prevents others from accessing your system when you're not around; this is especially useful when you have an application running, or if the desktop is set up in a way you don't want disturbed.

Before you decide to use a password, keep in mind that typing a password to recover your screen every time it blanks may be a hassle. Only use a password when necessary, like when you're leaving your desk for a while. If you do set a password, don't forget it.

Caution

To change the password for the Mystify screen saver, follow these steps:

1. Choose Mystify in the Screen Saver Name field, and click the Setup button.

6

2. Click the Password Protected check box to make the Set Password button available.

3. Click the Set Password button. The Change Password dialog box appears, as shown here:

4. Type a password in the New Password box, and type it again in the Retype New Password box. *Memorize the password*, and then click OK or press (ENTER).

5. When the Mystify Setup dialog box returns, click OK or press (ENTER) to return to the Desktop dialog box.

6. Change the Delay value to one minute (if it isn't already set), and click OK or press (ENTER).

7. Don't touch the keyboard or mouse for one minute. When the screen saver takes over, press any key. The password dialog box appears.

8. Type the password you entered in Step 4 to return to Windows.

If you forget the password for a screen saver, you'll need to restart your system to get back into Windows. You should then turn the screen saver off.

Note

Creating a Marquee

The Marquee screen saver is unique—it lets you define your own message to display on your screen during periods of inactivity. For example, if your system is busy sorting a large list of addresses and you don't want this process interrupted, a marquee message of "Don't Touch!" is appropriate. You might also create a marquee to inform coworkers that you've gone to lunch, or create a marquee that gives an instructional message like "Press any key to see a demo."

To create a marquee message, follow these steps:

1. Select Marquee from the Screen Saver Name list box; then click the Setup button. You'll see the Marquee Setup dialog box, as shown here, with text scrolling in the Text example field:

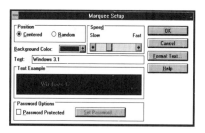

2. Type the marquee text in the Text field.

3. Click the Format Text button; then pick a font, style, size, and color for the text. Click OK.

4. In the Position box, choose where you want the text to scroll—across the center, or randomly on the screen.

5. In the Speed box, select a scrolling speed for the marquee.

6. Choose a color in the Background Color box.

7. If you want a password, fill out the Password Options box as described in the last exercise.

8. Click OK or press (ENTER) to return to the Desktop dialog box.

9. In the Screen Saver Delay box, enter a delay value if desired.

10. Click the Test button to test the marquee, and then press any key to return to the Desktop dialog box.

11. If you are happy with the marquee, click OK or press (ENTER) to close the Desktop dialog box and execute the changes.

6

Putting Up Wallpaper

The Wallpaper option lets you display a Paintbrush bitmap file on the desktop, as a single display or in a tiled pattern. Thus you can display a picture or a list of birthdays and important phone numbers as the desktop background. You can draw bitmapped images in Windows Paintbrush, or you can use images provided in the Windows directory. Try placing one of them on the desktop using this exercise:

1. From the Control Panel, open the Desktop dialog box.
2. In the Wallpaper area, click the down-arrow button beside the File list box.
3. Select WINLOGO.BMP in the file list. (The .BMP signifies a bitmap image file.)
4. Click the Center button; this tells Windows to center the picture on the desktop.
5. Click the OK button or press (ENTER).

The Desktop dialog box closes, and the Windows logo covers the desktop, overlaying any desktop patterns you may have selected previously.

Try other images, following the same steps. Note that most images are much smaller and are designed for tiling. Select LEAVES.BMP, and click the Tile button in the Wallpaper box. When you click OK or press (ENTER), the image is tiled (repeated) in a consistent pattern. Your desktop looks like your front yard in Fall.

Tip

Feel free to experiment with the other image files in the Wallpaper list box, but keep one thing in mind if you are short on memory: wallpaper images may require as much as 164K of RAM, so you may want to remove wallpaper from your desktop when you are running large applications.

Creating Your Own Wallpaper   You can create your own wallpaper images, using Windows Paintbrush. One practical example is to create a wallpaper image using scanned pictures of your kids or your friends; then type in their birthdays and other information under each picture. You might also create a list of phone numbers or other important information. Creating bitmapped images with Paintbrush is covered in Chapter 12.

Changing Icon Spacing

The options for Icons in the Desktop dialog box let you change the default spacing between icons, and set the Wrap Title feature on or off. Figure 6-7 shows how the settings in the Icons box affect the icons on the desktop of a VGA display. In the first line of icons, the Spacing value is 75 pixels, and the Wrap Title option is off. Notice that icon titles overlap. In the middle row, spacing has been increased to 100 pixels, and the titles no longer overlap. In the last row, spacing is again at 75 pixels, but Wrap Title is on—this is the best layout when you have a lot of icons on the desktop.

In this exercise, you'll increase the spacing between icons.

1. In the Control Panel, click the Desktop icon.

2. In the Icons area of the Desktop dialog box, click the up-arrow button in the Spacing text box until the spacing value is 100.

3. Mark the Wrap Title check box, if it is not already marked.

4. Click the OK button or press (ENTER).

6

Figure 6-7.   *Change the spacing between icons and the setting of the Wrap Title feature to make icons easier to see on the desktop*

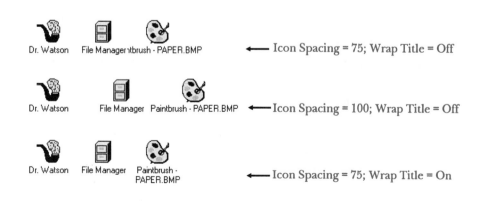

Dr. Watson   File Manager Paintbrush - PAPER.BMP   ⟵ Icon Spacing = 75; Wrap Title = Off

Dr. Watson   File Manager Paintbrush - PAPER.BMP ⟵ Icon Spacing = 100; Wrap Title = Off

Dr. Watson   File Manager   Paintbrush - PAPER.BMP   ⟵ Icon Spacing = 75; Wrap Title = On

5. The changes in icon spacing will not take effect until you rearrange the icons. To do this, open the Task List by double-clicking the desktop or pressing (CTRL)-(ESC).

6. When the Task List appears, click the Arrange Icons button. Then you can observe the changes you've made.

Adjusting the Sizing Grid

The Sizing Grid box in the Desktop dialog box controls the *granularity* of the desktop. Granularity is like an invisible grid pattern on the desktop that windows "snap" to when being moved or resized. The purpose of the grid is to help you align windows and give your Desktop a neat appearance. The granularity value is initially set to zero, but you can set it from 1 to 49, with each increment representing 8 pixels. (To get an idea of pixel size, note that the default border width is 3 pixels.) Just setting the grid to 1 makes it easier to align windows when moving or sizing them.

There is also an option in this box to change the border width of desktop windows. If you are having trouble differentiating windows on the desktop, you can increase their border width to make them easier to see or grab when resizing.

To set the Granularity and Border Width values, follow these steps:

1. From the Control Panel, open the Desktop dialog box.

2. In the Sizing Grid box, click the up-arrow button in the Granularity text box until the value is 5. This sets a grid 40 pixels wide.

3. Click the up-arrow button in the Border Width text box until the value is 5 pixels.

4. Click the OK button or press (ENTER).

At the desktop, notice that the window border is now wider. Now try sizing the Program Manager window with the mouse or keyboard. Notice that the window border snaps to the new grid pattern. In most cases, a grid pattern of this large size is only useful if you have a large monitor and are working in a higher resolution, such as 1024 by 768 pixels.

Setting the Cursor Blink Rate

Use the Cursor Blink Rate option to change the rate at which the cursor blinks. You can set the blink rate so that you can more easily find the cursor when editing documents in Windows Write, Notepad, or other Windows applications. Here's how to change the blink rate:

1. Open the Desktop dialog box in the Control Panel.

2. Click and drag the button in the Cursor Blink Rate slider bar. As you do, watch the blinking cursor on the right until it is blinking at the rate you want.

3. Click the OK button or press (ENTER) to set the new blink rate.

Printers

The Printers icon is used to install and configure printers. You can also use it to select a different port for a printer, or to install new fonts. For a complete discussion of the Printers utility, refer to Chapter 10, "Printing with Windows."

6

International

Use the International icon to set country-specific formats for such elements as date, time, currency, numbers, and keyboard settings used in Windows. The default settings are for the United States, so you won't need to make any changes to these settings unless you are using Windows in another country or under other special conditions. The International dialog box is shown in Figure 6-8.

If you need to use different international settings, select your country from the Country list box. This updates all the other settings in the International dialog box. However, if you need to specifically customize the date, time, and currency formats, click the appropriate field in the dialog box and

Figure 6-8.   *The International dialog box*

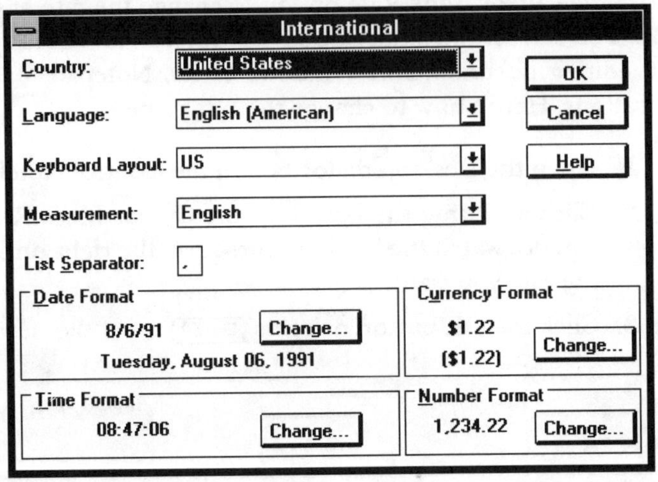

enter changes as necessary. To see how selecting a different country affects the other settings in the dialog box, try the following exercise:

1. Open the International utility by double-clicking its icon in the Control Panel.

2. The highlight is in the Country pull-down list box. Press the (ALT) key, and then the (DOWN ARROW) key on the keyboard. As you scroll through the list, notice the changes in the other fields and in the formats at the bottom of the dialog box.

3. To select a new country, highlight its name in the Country list box, and click OK or press (ENTER). To cancel the dialog box without changing the country, click the Cancel button or press the (ESC) key.

If your country is not listed in the Country list box, you can pick a country that has the most appropriate settings, and then make additional changes in the other fields of the dialog box to match the formats used in your country.

Keyboard

To adjust the operations of your keyboard, use the Keyboard icon on the Control Panel. You can adjust the delay, which is how long a key must be held down before it starts repeating, and the repeat rate, which is how fast the key repeats as you hold it down. To change the delay and repeat rate, follow these steps:

1. Select the Keyboard icon on the Control Panel, and you'll see this dialog box:

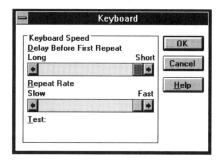

2. To adjust the delay interval, click the button in the Delay slider bar and slide it left or right.

3. To adjust the repeat rate, click the button in the Repeat Rate slider bar and slide it left or right.

4. Test the new settings by placing the cursor in the Test box and holding down a key.

5. Adjust the slider buttons until the settings are as you want them; then click OK or press (ENTER) to save the changes.

Date/Time

To set a new date and time, select the Date/Time icon on the Control Panel. (If you worked through Chapter 4, you've already had the opportunity to change the date and time.) If you have a mouse, double-click on the portion of the date or time that you want to change; then type a new value or click the up- or down-arrow keys on the dialog box. Click the OK button or press (ENTER) to save the changes.

Installing Drivers

The Drivers utility is used to install new drivers as they become available. Many of the drivers are associated with Windows's new multimedia capabilities. Double-click the Drivers utility to display the following dialog box:

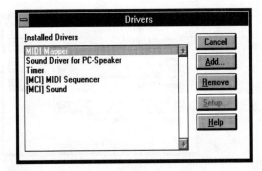

Note the following regarding the Drivers utility:

- Use Drivers to install preexisting drivers for sound cards, such as those listed in the previous illustration.

- Use Drivers to install the driver file supplied with a new hardware device you've attached to your system.

- Device drivers for a mouse, keyboard, display, and network, as well as international key code support, are installed with the Setup utility.

- Device drivers for printers are installed with the Printer utility.

- You must remove an existing driver before installing a new version over it.

 If you have a CD-ROM drive, install the [MCI] CD Audio driver so you can play CD audio disks in the drive.

Tip

Adding a New Driver

Microsoft supplies some drivers for sound and MIDI (Musical Instrument Digital Interface) devices on the Windows disks. Other devices must be copied from disks supplied by manufacturers, or from the Microsoft Driver Library (MDL). The MDL is available via modem on the Microsoft electronic downloading service at (206) 637-9007, or you can call Microsoft Customer Support at (800) 426-9400.

To install a new driver, follow these steps:

1. Open the Drivers dialog box.

2. If you are installing an updated version of a driver, highlight the existing driver and click the Remove button.

3. Click the Add button to display the following dialog box:

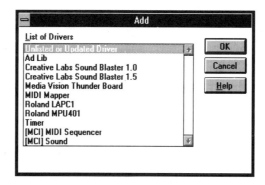

4. A list of available drivers on the Windows disk set is listed. Choose the driver to install and click the OK button.

To install a driver from a floppy disk, use the Unlisted or Updated Driver option. In the remaining part of this example, the SPEAKER.DRV file (available from Microsoft) is added to allow .WAV sound files to be played on the computer's speaker.

5. Click the Unlisted or Updated Driver option in the Add dialog box, then click the OK button. The Install Driver dialog box appears, asking for the letter of the drive containing the driver disk.

6. Place the floppy disk in the appropriate drive and click OK. In a moment, the following dialog box appears, which lists the speaker driver (or any other driver you may be installing):

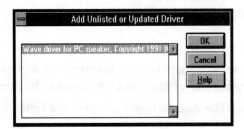

7. Choose the driver if it is not highlighted and click OK to install it.

Driver Settings

When a driver is installed, you may need to adjust some of its settings, such as the interrupts or I/O ports. Refer to the device's manual for details on how the settings should be made for your device. When installing the speaker driver, adjustments are made to its pitch and volume in a dialog box that appears after the driver copies to your system. You can change the setup for most drivers by highlighting the driver entry on the Drivers dialog box and clicking the Setup button.

Once a driver is installed, you must restart Windows to enable it.

Note

Sound

Use the Sound utility in the Control Panel to assign various .WAV file sounds to system events. Sounds play through a sound board such as the Soundblaster, or through your system's speaker if you have the SPEAKER.DRV file installed, as discussed in "Installing Drivers," earlier in this chapter. The following dialog box appears when you double-click the Sound icon:

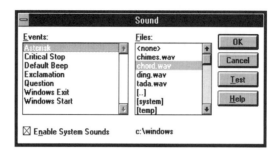

A list of events appears on the left and a list of sounds appears on the right. Do the following to assign a sound:

1. Click any event.
2. Click a sound to assign to it.
3. Click the Test button to hear the sound.
4. If you don't like the sound, try another. When all the sounds are the way you want, click the OK button.

Network

The icon for Network appears in the Control Panel if you are connected to a network system. Network users can print on network printers and save files to network servers. In addition, the File Manager can manipulate files stored on the server. For additional information on using Windows with networks, see your network supervisor.

386 Enhanced Mode

Windows can run in 386 enhanced mode on 80386 or 80486 systems. When Windows starts in this mode, a 386 Enhanced icon appears in the Control Panel. Clicking the icon displays this dialog box:

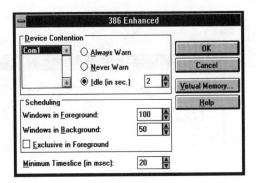

The Virtual Memory button is used to install or change the settings of the swap file used to swap memory from RAM to disk. The dialog box is used to set the following options for multitasking non-Windows applications:

- *Device Contention*   These options set alarms that warn you when applications simultaneously access devices like printers and modems. The warnings are designed to keep you aware of how applications are working in the background, so you can adjust other settings.

- *Scheduling Options*   The Scheduling options are used to specify the percentage of processor time used by applications in the foreground and background.

Because of the technical nature of these settings, they are explained in Appendix B. If you need to multitask non-Windows applications, refer to this Appendix for more information.

7

Working with Files

Windows works together with the DOS operating system to manage, among other things, the files on your computer's hard drives. As you work with files in Windows, you must still follow the rules and regulations for DOS-level files, but Windows makes it easier to organize and use your files. This section provides an overview of how the Windows and DOS file systems work together, plus some exercises to familiarize you with methods for listing, saving, and retrieving files in Windows.

DOS and Windows File Types

Files are collections of information, initially created in the memory of the computer, and then saved to a disk storage device. On DOS-based systems, a *directory* is used to organize the hundreds of files that may be stored on the hard drives and floppy disks. Directories give you a way to separate and organize your files into distinct groups, in the same way a filing cabinet uses drawers, hanging folders, and file folders to separate groups of files.

Keep the following guidelines in mind as you work with files in Windows:

- Files on the same disk or in the same directory must have unique names.

- Filenames consist of an eight-character name and a three-character extension, separated by a period. Similar types of files often have the same extension.

- Files are portable. They can be copied to other disks or directories.

- Files vary in size during their lives. When no longer needed, they can be deleted to make room for other files.

- The location of a file is important. You may need to specify its drive letter and directory name when accessing the file. This information is called the *search path* (or just *path*) to the file.

Files are differentiated according to the information they contain, and their names reflect this information. Several types of files are discussed next.

Program Files   *Program files* contain computer-readable code written by programmers. When you open and look at the contents of a program file, all you see is a string of code that looks like scrambled text. The names assigned to program files have *filename extensions* such as .COM and .EXE. These files are often called *executable* files, meaning that you can execute the program by typing its filename at the DOS prompt. Double-clicking a program icon in Program Manager executes a .COM or .EXE file.

Support Files   Some programs use auxiliary *support files* that also contain program code, but are not executable independently. Support files have filename extensions such as .OVL (overlay), .SYS (system), .DRV (driver), and .DLL (dynamic link library). You'll often see these files in the same directory as your program files.

Text Files   *Text files* contain readable, alphanumeric characters that follow the American Standard Code for Information Interchange (ASCII) format. These files are often called ASCII files and can be opened by a wide range of programs on many types of computers, not just those with DOS systems. Text files are easily transferred to other systems over a telephone line, using a modem.

Formatted Text Files   *Formatted Text Files* contain text and special codes that define how the text is formatted. They must be converted before you can open them in an application besides the one used to create them.

Graphics Files   *Graphics files* contain graphics information in several possible formats. The most common is the *bitmap* image format, which saves the actual dot-by-dot representation of the screen image. Other types of graphics files contain the actual series of commands used to create the image; when this type of file is opened, the commands are replayed to create the image.

Data Files   *Data files* contain information such as that created by a database or spreadsheet program. These files are readable only by the creating application, or by an application that can translate the information in the files to its own format. Data file information is separated in various ways to form the *fields* of a database or the *cells* of a spreadsheet. Common formats are comma-delimited files for databases, and SYLK (Symbolic Link) or DIF (Data Interchange Format) for spreadsheet data. Note that some data files may not contain special formats and are really simple text files.

Note

This book divides files into two broad categories: program files and document files. Applications like Windows Write and Notepad are stored on disk as program files. The files you create with these applications are document files, and may contain text, graphics, and other types of data. Document files are loaded into the workspace or document windows of Windows applications.

7

File-Naming Conventions

It is important to understand the conventions used to name and open files. Files within the same directory cannot have the same name, but you can use names that have characters in common as part of a strategy to keep your files organized. Windows gives you a warning message if you try to create a file with a name that's already in use.

The basic filename consists of an eight-character *name*, followed by a period and then an optional three-character *extension*. The filename may be fewer than eight characters, but any characters beyond the maximum eight are truncated. Here is a typical filename:

YOURFILE.TXT

Another important aspect of a filename is its location, or path. When referring to files not in the current directory, you need to include the drive and directory along with the actual filename. For example, if the YOURFILE file referenced previously were in the WINWORD directory on drive D, its complete path would be

D:\WINWORD\YOURFILE.TXT

Notice that backslashes are used to separate the directory and filename information, and a colon always follows the drive letter. If you need more information on file-naming conventions, refer to your DOS manual.

File-Naming Strategies

To keep your files organized and to help you remember the contents of files, it is useful to develop a strategy for naming your files. You may want to use the filename and its extension to describe a file's contents, the program that created it, and possibly the type of data in the file (text, graphics, or numbers).

Filename Extensions

Many programs automatically add a filename extension when you save a file. Table 7-1 lists the extensions attached to filenames by the Windows accessory programs. These extensions are used whenever you save a file, unless you specifically type a different extension after the filename. Notice that Paintbrush is capable of creating three different types of files, each with its own extension. You use filename extensions to list and work with specific files. For example, you could list all files with the extension .WRI to see the documents you've created in Windows Write.

Table 7-2 lists other extensions you may want to use when creating files with the Windows accessories or any other program. (These extensions are commonly used in the computer industry.) As with the accessories listed in Table 7-1, other Windows applications frequently add their own filename extensions to files you save. For example, Microsoft Excel spreadsheet files

Table 7-1.   *Filename Extensions Used by the Windows Accessories*

Program	Extension	Meaning
Paintbrush	.BMP	New Paintbrush bitmap image
Paintbrush	.MSP	Old Paintbrush bitmap image
Paintbrush	.PCX	PC Paintbrush bitmap image
Calendar	.CAL	Calendar file
Clipboard	.CLP	Saved Clipboard image
Cardfile	.CRD	Index card file
Program Manager	.GRP	Group information file
PIF Editor	.PIF	Program Information File
Recorder	.REC	Set of Recorder macros
Notepad	.TXT	Notepad text file
Write	.WRI	Windows Write text file

usually have the extension .XLS; Lotus 1-2-3 worksheet files may have the extension .WKS or .WK1.

Associating Files and Programs   Filename extensions can help you locate the files created by a particular program. In fact, the extension can be used to *associate* a document with its creating program. Then you can double-click that associated file to simultaneously start up the application and load the document into its workspace. If you save files with extensions other than those associated with the program, you'll need to create a new association. You learn more about associations in Chapter 9, "Managing Files, Directories, and Disks with File Manager."

Filenames

The filename itself can be used to describe and categorize the contents of files. Try to create filenames that make sense to you and others. Names like NOTE.TXT and FILE.DOC are meaningless if you create dozens of notes and files because you'll soon lose track of their contents. A name like JANREPRT.TXT

Table 7-2.   *Common Filename Extensions*

Extension	Usage
.BAK	The backup version of an edited file (some programs create these automatically)
.BAT	Reserved for DOS batch files
.DAT	Commonly used for data files
.DTA	Another extension commonly used for data files
.DOC	Commonly used for document files
.HLP	Commonly reserved for help files
.MNU	Commonly used for menu files
.MSG	A message file
.TMP	Commonly used for temporary files

is a little better at describing the contents of a report file for January, but if you have several report files for January, you'll need to be even more specific.

Take a look at the following strategy for naming monthly report files created with the Excel program. This technique can be imitated in your own filing system or that used throughout your business or organization.

```
RA92130.XLS
RB92130.XLS
RC92130.XLS
RA92228.XLS
RB92228.XLS
RC92228.XLS
```

At first these filenames may seem cryptic, but consider the strategy: The R designates the files as reports (files containing budgets might be indicated by B). The second letter indicates the type of report; here three separate reports are created at the end of each month (A, B, and C). Next comes the report date, followed by the .XLS extension added by Excel.

In the foregoing strategy for naming files, putting the year first, then the month, then the day, for the report date makes it easier to list the files later.

Note

Using Wildcard Parameters to List Files

Wildcard characters can be used as substitutes for any letter or group of letters when specifying filenames. The question mark (?) is used to represent a single character, and the asterisk (*) to represent two or more characters. Wildcards are typically used to list files at the DOS level, but you can also use wildcard characters when working with Windows dialog boxes and the File Manager.

Using the previous list of monthly report files as an example, you can see how wildcard parameters are used to indicate specific files. If you specify RA*.*, the following files are listed:

RA92130.XLS
RA92228.XLS

The specification R???1*.* lists these files:

RA92130.XLS
RB92130.XLS
RC92130.XLS

And the specification RA??1*.* lists only this file:

RA92130.XLS

Notice how the ? serves as a placemarker; that is, any character may occupy its position. The *, on the other hand, is used to represent any group of characters in the filename, and the extension.

This next exercise will help you learn how to use wildcards. Start File Manager now by double-clicking its icon in the Main group of the Program Manager. When the File Manager window appears, follow these steps to view the files in the WINDOWS directory:

1. Click the C drive icon (or the drive where your Windows directory is located) to list the directories on that drive. You can also press (CTRL) and the drive letter to accomplish the same thing.

2. Point to the Windows directory icon and click. The window on the right now lists the files in the Windows directory.

3. Now let's use wildcard characters to list files that have the .TXT extension. Choose By File Type from the View menu.

4. The By File Type dialog box appears. Notice that the Name field includes the *.* wildcard specification. If you execute the command with this specification in the Name field, you'll list all files. To list only files with the extension .TXT, type ***.TXT** in the Name field.

5. Click the OK button or press (ENTER).

A list of the files that have the extension .TXT is displayed. Notice that the title bar of the window includes the file specification *.TXT to indicate which files are being listed.

Use the foregoing procedure again, to list other groups of files. For example, type ***.EXE** in the Name box (Step 4) to list the Windows executable program files. Next, try entering **PROG*.*** to see files related to the Program Manager. Finally, put the ***.*** designation back in the Name box and display the complete list of files in the directory window.

Directory Concepts

Directories provide a way to separate files on hard drives in much the same way you would organize files in a filing cabinet. The following illustration shows a *directory tree* from the File Manager:

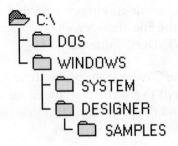

The top folder icon is the *root* directory. All disks and drives have a root directory, and all other directories on that disk or drive branch from that root. In the illustration you can see that the DOS directory and the WINDOWS directory branch from the root directory; they are *subdirectories* of the root. The WINDOWS directory has two subdirectories of its own, SYSTEM and DESIGNER, and DESIGNER has a subdirectory called SAMPLES.

Note

*The terms directory and subdirectory are often used interchangeably. You could say that the SYSTEM **directory** is a **subdirectory** of the WINDOWS directory.*

As mentioned earlier in this chapter, in "File-Naming Conventions," you may need to specify the full path of a file when referring to a file outside of your current directory. For example, a file called HOUSE.DRW in the SAMPLES subdirectory of the previously illustrated directory tree has the path shown here, assuming it is stored on drive C:

C:\WINDOWS\DESIGNER\SAMPLES\HOUSE.DRW

In most cases, you won't need to type out such long paths when working with files. The Windows File Manager lets you open two windows side by side to make copies of files between directories or do other work within directories. In other Windows applications, a dialog box helps you pick the drives and directories where files are located, as described later in this chapter.

Organizing with Directories

You can use directories to organize your files on disk. For instance, always maintain a separate directory for each program. This directory is usually set up by an application when you run its installation utility. In addition, it's a good idea to store the data files for an application in their own subdirectory. This prevents the data files from mixing with the program files, and makes it easy for you to find and list the data files for a particular program.

Backing Up Data Files   If you use subdirectories to separate different types of data files, this will make your backup procedures easy to perform, because you can easily back up an entire directory and its subdirectories at once.

Consider the following illustration, where several subdirectories for data files branch from the DATA directory:

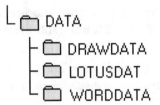

With this arrangement you'll only need to back up the DATA directory, assuming you specify to the backup program that all branching subdirectories should also be backed up. Typically, directories containing data files are the ones that have new or changing files needing backup on a regular basis. Program directories can be included in your occasional "full-system" backup; because their contents rarely change, you won't need to back them up every day.

Using File Menu Options

In this section you explore the Windows commands and dialog boxes for opening, saving, browsing, and searching for files. What you've learned about files and directories so far in this chapter will help you access the common features of these commands. Their features are the same throughout a wide range of Windows applications, so you only need to learn them once.

For the exercises in this section, open Notepad by double-clicking its icon in the Accessories group of the Program Manager. When the Notepad window appears, click the File menu option. The first four options of the File command are used to open and save files in many Windows applications. What you learn about them in Notepad applies to other applications, as well.

The File New Option

Use the File New option to clear the screen of any existing work and begin a new file. If the existing work has not yet been saved, Windows will ask if you want to save it before clearing the screen.

Some applications, such as Word for Windows, let you open several documents at once. In this case, the workspace is not cleared when you select New. Instead, another document window is opened for the new file. You can thus edit two documents at once, compare their contents, cut and paste text or graphics between them, and so forth. Keep in mind that each new document window requires additional memory, so you may be limited in the number of new windows you can open.

The File Open Option

The File Open option lets you open an existing file. Select Open on the Notepad File menu now, to display the Open dialog box shown in Figure 7-1.

This dialog box has four areas where you can make selections or type text. If the file you want to open is in the current drive and directory, just type its name in the File Name text box and press (ENTER). To open a file on a different drive or in a different directory, first select a drive in the Drives list box and/or select a directory in the Directories list box. Changing the drive or directory causes a new list of files to appear under the File Name text field. You can then double-click one of the files to open it.

To narrow down the list of files, if you know part of the filename of the file you want to open, type a wildcard file specification in the File Name text field. This is discussed in greater detail in "Change the File Listing," later in this chapter.

Note

The following steps outline a typical procedure for opening a file:

1. Choose Open from the Applications File menu.
2. Choose a drive in the Drives pull-down list box.
3. Choose a directory in the Directories list box.
4. Double-click the file you wish to open in the File Name list box.

Figure 7-1.   *The File Open dialog box*

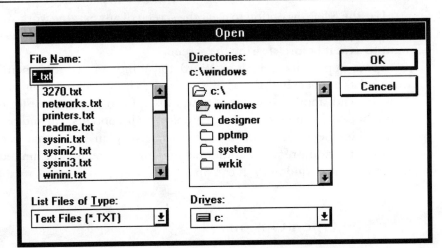

The following exercises help you become familiar with the File Open dialog box and techniques you can use to search for and list files.

Pick a Drive

When you first see the Open dialog box, the highlight is in the File Name text box. If the drive and directory listed in the dialog box are correct for your needs, you can simply type the name of the file you want, or select it from the File Name list box and click the OK button. In this exercise, you pick the drive where your WINDOWS files are located. Even if WINDOWS is already your current directory, work through this exercise for practice.

1. Click the down-arrow button in the Drives list box. You'll see a list similar to this one:

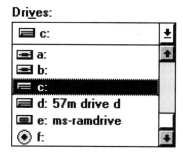

Drives:

- c:
- a:
- b:
- c:
- d: 57m drive d
- e: ms-ramdrive
- f:

2. Your current drive is highlighted. Scan through the list with the arrow buttons or keys, and highlight the drive that contains your WINDOWS directory and files. If you're not sure, select the most likely drive.

3. Press (ENTER) to select the drive. Notice that the contents of the other fields in the dialog box change to reflect the contents of the new drive.

Note

You can follow this same procedure to list the files on a floppy disk or any other drive in your system. Notice from the icons in the previous illustration that drive E is a RAM drive, and drive F is a CD-ROM optical disk.

Pick a Directory

Before opening or saving a file, you always need to make sure you are in the correct directory on a drive. Though files in the same directory have unique names, two files in different directories may have the same name—they are distinct only because they are separated by the directory specification. Be careful to open the file you want in the directory you want.

Just above the Directories list box you'll see the name of the current directory. To select a new directory with the mouse, double-click the directory's icon or name in the list box. If you can't see the directory you want, click the down-arrow button until the directory moves into view, and then double-click its icon or name. Try this:

7

1. Select the Directories list box by pressing (ALT)-(D).

2. Press the (UP ARROW) key on the keyboard until the root directory is highlighted, as shown here:

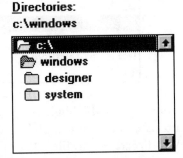

Note that the current drive is C in this illustration; your drive may be different if you chose another drive in the last exercise.

3. Press (ENTER). This changes the listing so it shows the subdirectories that branch from the root directory. The Directories list box will now look like this:

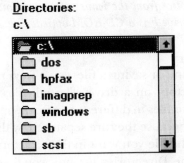

Notice that the current directory is listed at the top as c:\, and its icon is an open folder.

4. Select the WINDOWS directory. (If you can't find the WINDOWS directory, you need to switch to the drive where that directory is stored.)

Once you've selected the WINDOWS directory, a list of its subdirectories appears under its folder icon, and a list of files in the directory appears in the

File Name list box. You can open subdirectories by highlighting them and pressing (ENTER), or you can go back and open any other directory using the same technique.

Change the File Listing

Now you're ready to work with the File Name text box and list box. The previous exercises showed you how to use the Drives and Directories list boxes to make the WINDOWS directory the current one. These next exercises assume you are still in the WINDOWS directory.

When you first bring up the Open dialog box, the highlight is in the File Name text box. This makes it easier to type the name of the file you want and then click OK or press (ENTER). But if you're not sure of the file's name, you can type a new wildcard file specification in the File Name text box, and thus list files that might match it.

Note that *.txt currently appears in the File Name text box because you're using Notepad, which creates files with the .TXT extension. This file specification automatically appears whenever you start Notepad. In other applications, different file specifications are used. For example, Windows Write creates files with the .WRI extension. When you first open Write's Open dialog box, the File Name text box contains *.wri, and files with this extension are listed in the File Name list box.

To change the File Name listing:

1. Make sure the highlight is still in the File Name text box. If it isn't, double-click the box.

2. Type ***.INI** in the text box and press (ENTER). A listing of .INI files appears, similar to this one:

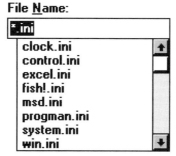

3. Press (TAB) to access the file listing. Note that the first file is surrounded by a dotted line.

4. Press the (DOWN ARROW) key on the keyboard until the file WIN.INI is highlighted. As you scroll, notice that each filename is placed in the File Name text box.

5. Click OK or press (ENTER) to open the WIN.INI file.

The WIN.INI file, and other .INI files, contain Windows startup parameters that advanced users often edit using Notepad.

Note

6. You don't need to have this file open now, so choose New from the Notepad File menu. This clears the workspace.

There are several other techniques for listing files. For instance, you can change the parameter in the List Files of Type text box, or you can specify other wildcard parameters for File Name. Try the following:

1. Choose Open from the File menu. In the Open dialog box, notice that the previous file specification is in the File Name text box.

2. Type **PROG*.*** and press (ENTER). You see the following listing:

File **N**ame:

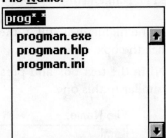

```
prog*.*
    progman.exe
    progman.hlp
    progman.ini
```

3. Try another wildcard specification, using the ? parameter, too. Type **???INI.*** and press (ENTER). You'll see a list like this:

File **N**ame:

4. Choose a file specification from the List Files of Type box. Click the down-arrow button in the field, and the following appears:

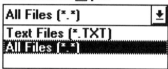

List Files of **T**ype:

5. Highlight the All Files [*.*] option in the list. Press (ENTER), and you'll see the complete list of files in the WINDOWS directory.

In some applications, there may be more options in the List Files of Type box. For example, in the List Files of Type box for Paintbrush, shown next, you can choose from three different types of graphics files that Paintbrush can open:

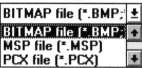

List Files of **T**ype:

On the other hand, in Notepad, you won't be able to load all the files you see listed with the *.* file specification. Because Notepad is a simple text editor, you can only open text files, such as those with the extensions .TXT, .INI, and in some cases .DOC and .DAT. For now, just click the Cancel button or press (ESC) to end this exercise.

The File Save Option

The File Save option is used to save a file using the name that appears in the title bar. This assumes you previously saved the file and assigned a name to it using the Save As option. If you choose Save, and the file has not yet been named, the File Save As dialog box appears.

Note

Keep in mind that the Save option saves changes without asking for verification. In most cases, this will be fine, but there may be times when you want to load a file, edit it, and then save it under a different name. You should then use the Save As option to rename the file before saving it.

Some applications have a Read Only check box that can be marked to force you to save the file under a different name, thus preserving the original. Alternatively, you can mark files as read-only using the Properties command in the File Manager to prevent them from being altered. Files that are used in this way are often referred to as *template* files.

The File Save As Option

The Save As option on the File menu is used to save a file for the first time and specify its filename. It also lets you save an existing file under a new name. The File Save As dialog box has the same features as the File Open dialog box. You type the new name for the file in the File Name text box, and specify the drive or directory where you want to store the file in the Drives and Directories boxes.

The following exercise will familiarize you with the Save As box:

1. Open Notepad if it is not already open.

2. Type your name at the flashing cursor in Notepad's workspace.

3. Choose the Save As option in the File menu, or press (ALT)-(F) (A).

4. When the Save As dialog box opens, notice its similarities to the File Open dialog box. This is the common Windows dialog box format that you'll see in many other applications.

5. Type **NAME.TXT** in the File Name text box, and click OK or press (ENTER).

6. Choose New from the File menu to remove the NAME.TXT file from the screen.

7. Type some other text, such as the make of your car, and select the Save As option again.

8. Type **NAME.TXT**, and click OK or press (ENTER). In a moment, the following dialog box appears:

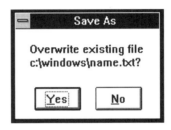

Because NAME.TXT already exists, Windows warns you that you're about to overwrite an existing file.

9. Click the No button, or press (ALT)-(N).

7

When you select No in answer to the "Overwrite...?" prompt, the Save As dialog box remains active, so you can try a different filename. Notice that the File Name list box contains grayed-out filenames. You can scan this list to see what filenames are already in use, and avoid any conflicts. In addition, this list is helpful when you're saving files that follow a naming strategy. You can display the file list to remind you of the naming scheme, or to see what names have been used so far. Or you might need to choose an option in the Save File As Type field to see a different list of files.

You're now at the end of this tutorial. You can click the Cancel button or press the (ESC) key to close the Save As dialog box, and then close Notepad or reduce it to an icon for future use.

8

Organizing Applications

In this chapter, you learn how to organize the applications, utilities, accessories, and other program items in the Program Manager. You create new startup icons and group windows, and rearrange startup icons into new groups that best fit the way you work.

Creating a New Group

To have easy access to the applications and documents in your system, it's a good idea to arrange them according to your work habits. Windows lets you move a program icon into another existing group, or create new groups as you need them. For example, you can organize all of the applications and

tools that you use for writing into a window called "Writing Tools," and all
the applications and tools that you use to create pictures and art into a window
called "Drawing Tools."

Figure 8-1 illustrates two groups that contain *document startup icons*. When
you set up document icons (described in "Creating a Document Icon," later
in this chapter), double-clicking an icon starts the program represented by
the icon itself, and loads a document represented by the name under the icon.
Creating group windows such as these improves your access to the files you
work with regularly. Note that the DAILY group has startup icons for business
and personal appointment calendars, a Notepad TIMELOG, and a Notepad
DAILY file. The COMPANY NEWSLETTER group includes startup icons for
many different files and programs that you might use when creating a
newsletter.

The initial organization of the icons in the Program Manager window may
very well be helpful as you're learning to use Windows, but eventually you'll
find it beneficial to reorganize these icons to fit your personal taste and the
way you work. The following exercise demonstrates how to create a new group
window and add program items to it.

Figure 8-1.   *Groups help organize the way you work*

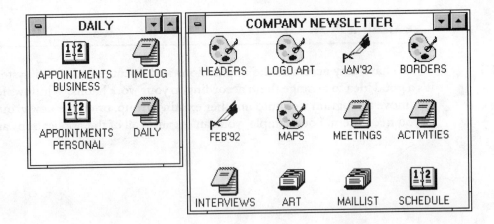

Creating a New Group Window

This exercise shows you how to create a new group window using the New command on the Program Manager File menu. The group will be named Everyday Tools.

1. Choose New from the Program Manager File menu. This opens the New Program Object dialog box, shown here:

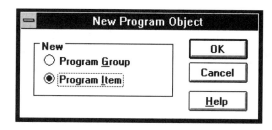

2. Click Program Group (if it is not already selected) to indicate that you want to create a group, not an icon for a group.

3. Click the OK button or press (ENTER) to display the Program Group Properties dialog box:

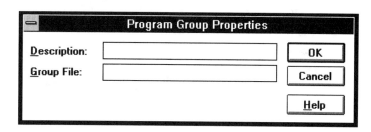

4. Start with the blinking cursor in the Description text box, and type **Everyday Tools**.

Leave the Group File box blank; Windows supplies this using the first eight characters from the Description box. The group file will hold information about the group, such as its name and the icons it contains.

Note

5. Click the OK button or press (ENTER).

When the dialog box closes, the Everyday Tools group appears in the Program Manager as an empty group window. Now you're ready to add icons to the new group.

Copying Program Items to a New Group

Now that the group window exists, you can add application and document icons to it. In this next exercise, you copy existing application icons from the Main and Accessories windows to the Everyday Tools window.

Start by considering which Windows applications and accessories you'll want to include in the Everyday Tools window. For this example, let's copy the File Manager, Control Panel, Print Manager, Write, Paint, Calendar, and DOS Prompt icons to the new window. Later you can add other icons to the group to fit your needs.

The easiest way to copy icons from one window to another is by dragging them with the mouse. However, if you prefer to type the destination group name, you can use the Copy command on the Program Manager File menu. To copy an icon from the Main group to the new Everyday Tools group, follow these steps:

1. Open the Main group window. Make sure you can still see at least a part of the Everyday Tools window, so you can click it later to select it. (You could resize both windows and place them side by side, but it is not necessary for this operation.)

2. Press the (CTRL) key, and then point to the File Manager icon in the Main group. Click and drag the icon to the Everyday Tools group while holding down the (CTRL) key. A copy of the icon now appears in the new group.

If you fail to hold down the (CTRL) key while dragging, the icon will be moved, not copied. Moving an icon removes it from the source group and places it in the destination group.

Caution

3. Repeat Step 2 and copy the Control Panel icon to the Everyday Tools group.

Now try the keyboard method, by copying the Print Manager from the Main group to the Everyday Tools group, as follows:

1. Make the Main group active by pressing (ALT)-(W) and choosing it from the Window menu.

2. Use the arrow keys to highlight the Print Manager icon.

3. Press (ALT)-(F) (C) to choose Copy from the Program Manager File menu. Note that the resulting dialog box describes the operation you are performing, as shown here:

4. Press the (DOWN ARROW) key until the Everyday Tools group name appears in the To Group box, and then press (ENTER).

On your own, copy the DOS Prompt icon in the Main group window to the Everyday Tools group, using either the mouse or the keyboard method described previously. The DOS Prompt is good to have handy if you access DOS on a regular basis. Next, copy the Write, Paint, and Calendar icons from the Accessories group to the Everyday Tools group. First open the Accessories group, and then use the mouse or keyboard method to copy the icons.

8

Resizing and Arranging the New Window

Once you've finished copying the icons listed in the previous paragraph, close the Main and Accessories windows; then follow these steps to resize and move the Everyday Tools window:

1. Click the Program Manager Options menu; if the Auto Arrange feature is not checked in the dialog box, turn it on.

2. Resize the Everyday Tools group window to fit around its icons. Point to a border or corner of the window, then click and drag. The icons will rearrange as you change the window's size.

3. Move the resized window to the upper-left corner of the Program Manager.

The Everyday Tools window should now look like Figure 8-2.

Saving Arrangements

Once you've arranged Program Manager, you need to make sure the new arrangement is available the next time you start Windows. To always save any changes, choose Save Settings on Exit in the Options menu. To immediately update the changes, hold down the (SHIFT) key and choose Exit from the File menu. You won't exit Windows, but the changes will be saved.

Figure 8-2.   *The resized, rearranged Everyday Tools group*

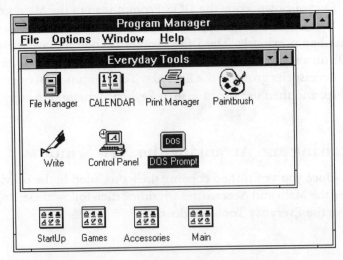

Creating New Program Item Icons

In this section, you create icons for program items, using the New command on the Program Manager File menu. In addition, you learn about using the Setup utility to automatically search your hard drives for applications and create startup icons for them.

The New Option

The New option on the Program Manager File menu is used to create new program item icons, as well as new groups. In this example, you create a new program startup icon in the Main group window for a program called SYSEDIT. This program resides in the \WINDOWS\SYSTEM directory and is used to edit your system startup files and the Windows startup files.

Follow these steps to add the new startup icon:

1. The Main group window was minimized in the last exercise, so activate it now by double-clicking its icon.

Note

To add a program item to a group, you must first make the group active.

2. Choose New from the File menu to open the New Program Object dialog box.

3. This time you are creating a new program item icon, so click the Program Item button; then click OK (or press (ENTER)). You'll next see the following Program Item Properties box (which is described in the next section):

8

Program Item Properties
Description:		OK
Command Line:		Cancel
Working Directory:		
Shortcut Key:	None	Browse...
	☐ Run Minimized	Change Icon...
		Help

Working with the Program Item Properties Box

The text boxes of the Program Item Properties box allow you to describe to Windows all it needs to know about a new program item. In most cases, you don't need to fill out all the options, but you'll find examples of all of them as you work through this section. The next paragraphs are descriptions of each box and button in the dialog box.

Description   In the Description box, type the name you want to appear under the icon or in the title bar of the window that runs the program.

Command Line   In the Command Line box, type the name of the executable (.EXE or .COM) file used to start the program, with a drive letter and path if necessary. Optionally, you can include the name of an associated file to load with the application when it starts, thus creating a document icon. Recall that a document icon starts the application and loads the associated file into the application's workspace. If you don't know the name of the file, you can click the Browse button in this dialog box (explained shortly) to activate a search.

Working Directory   In the Working Directory box, type the name of the directory where you want the application to open and save files. The program itself doesn't have to be in this directory, but it will access files in this directory while it runs.

Shortcut Key   In the Shortcut Key box, specify a keystroke used to start the application. For example, you could assign the keystroke (CTRL)-(ALT)-(W) to an icon for a word processing program. Note that keystrokes must include either (CTRL)-(ALT) or (CTRL)-(SHIFT)-(ALT). In the Shortcut Key text box, if you type a single character such as (W), (CTRL)-(ALT) will automatically be added, making the shortcut key (CTRL)-(ALT)-(W). Press (SHIFT) and a letter to create a (CTRL)-(SHIFT)-(ALT) keystroke.

Run Minimized   Check the Run Minimized box if you want the application to reduce to an icon on the desktop whenever the program starts. This is useful if you have set up the application to start when you turn your system on, but you don't always use it right away.

Browse   If you don't know the name of the executable file to enter in the Command Line field, press the Browse button to open a dialog box so you can search for the file.

Change Icon   Use the Change Icon button to select an icon to use for the program.

Now let's complete the creation of the SYSEDIT startup icon, by indicating the Description and Command Line properties of the program item, as follows:

1. The blinking cursor should be in the Description field. If it isn't, click the text box or press (ALT)-(D).

2. For Description, type **SYSEDIT**. This is the name that will appear under the icon.

3. Press (TAB) to jump to the Command Line text box. Here you need to specify the command that starts the SYSEDIT program. If you know the drive, directory, and filename where the program is stored, you can type them in the Command Line field. Or you can browse the files on your hard disk to locate the .EXE or .COM file, as discussed next.

Browsing for the Filename

Note

As you work through this exercise and some of the others that follow, you'll notice that Windows programs and accessories open and save files in the Windows directory–this happens unless you indicate otherwise. As you know, this book assumes your Windows directory is C:\WINDOWS. However, if you've installed Windows on another drive, or are accessing it from a network drive, you'll always need to specify the appropriate drive and directory. As you work through the remaining exercises in this chapter, you'll be reminded when it's important to include the correct path.

The Browse button in the Program Item Properties box is a handy tool–it lets you locate the .EXE and .COM files in your system. The Browse dialog box has the same features as the Open dialog box you learned about in Chapter 7. This exercise will step you through its use; if you need more information, refer to Chapter 7.

8

Note

Although .EXE and .COM files are generally selected in the Browse dialog box to start programs, .PIF files (discussed in Appendix B) and .BAT files (discussed in your DOS manual), can also be selected. In addition, you can list and select an associated document file using the Browse dialog box.

1. From the Program Item Properties dialog box, click the Browse button, or press (ALT)-(B). You'll see the dialog box shown in Figure 8-3.

2. In Figure 8-3, the files in the Windows directory are listed when you first open the dialog box. If you're not sure where your own Windows files are located, here's your chance to find out. The path to these files will be displayed above the Directories list box in your Browse dialog box, and you should write this down for future reference, especially if it is a path other than C:\WINDOWS.

3. In the Directories list box, note the subdirectories that branch from the Windows directory. In this example, you need to access the SYSTEM subdirectory, so look for the SYSTEM subdirectory icon,

Figure 8-3.   *The Browse dialog box is used to locate .EXE and .COM files to assign to program item icons*

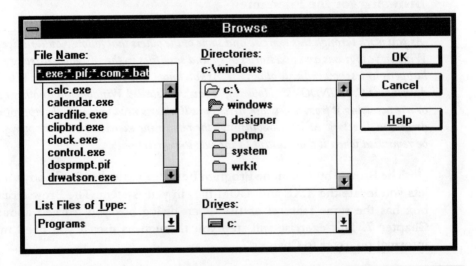

and double-click it with the mouse. This displays a listing of executable files for that subdirectory.

4. Drag the slider button in the File Name scroll bar until you see the filename SYSEDIT.EXE, and click that filename.

5. Click the OK button or press (ENTER). This inserts the path and filename of the SYSEDIT.EXE file into the Command Line field of the Program Item Properties dialog box.

Selecting the Icon

Now choose an icon for the SYSEDIT program.

1. In the Program Item Properties dialog box, click the Change Icon button, or press (ALT)-(I). Here is the Change Icon dialog box:

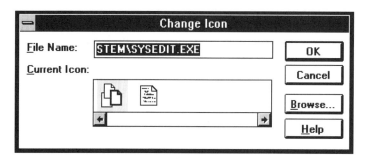

2. Two icons are shown in the display area for SYSEDIT. Double-click the icon on the left. (Later in this chapter, in "Changing Icons," you'll learn more about making different icons available for a program item.)

Later you'll learn how to choose from a larger list of icons.

Note

Completing the Task

There are several other items in the Program Item Properties dialog box that you might need to designate for some programs, but not for SYSEDIT. For example, there is no need to mark the Run Minimized box because SYSEDIT is a utility that you'll normally use as soon as you start it. Also, a working directory is not required because SYSEDIT uses files in the root and Windows directories only.

8

You can add a shortcut key by clicking in the Shortcut Key box and typing S or some other letter.

To complete the creation of the SYSEDIT icon, click the OK button or press (ENTER), and the icon appears in the Main group window. To test your new icon, double-click it with the mouse or press the shortcut key you assigned. Once you've made sure your icon works, you can close SYSEDIT again—you won't need it until a later chapter, when you modify the startup procedure of your computer and Windows.

Creating a Document Icon

A *document icon* is a program item icon that starts an application and loads a document in that application's workspace, in one step. This section shows you how to set up a document icon in the Everyday Tools group; but first, you create a document to associate with the icon, as discussed next.

Creating the Time Log Document

The Notepad accessory has a unique time log that inserts the date in a file every time you open it. You can use this feature to create a time-stamped log of notes or events. Follow the steps here to create the time log file:

1. Activate the Accessories group in Program Manager by double-clicking its icon, or choose its name from the Window menu.

2. Start Notepad by double-clicking its icon.

3. When the Notepad window appears, type **.LOG** on the first line. Do not include spaces or tabs before this entry, be sure to include the period, and use all capital letters for LOG.

4. Save this file by choosing the Save As option from the File menu.

5. When the Save As dialog box appears, type **TIMELOG** in the File Name text box, and make sure the Windows drive and directory are selected in the Directories field. Click OK or press (ENTER) to save the file.

Every time you open the TIMELOG file, the time and date will be inserted after the last line. You can then enter a note or activity record under the time that was inserted. Now add some notes to this "diary" file.

6. Select the Notepad File command and choose Open on the menu.

7. Type **TIMELOG** in the File Name field, and click OK or press ⎡ENTER⎤.

8. Under the date and time entry, type the following text:

   This is an exercise for Windows 3.1 Made Easy.

9. Press ⎡ALT⎤-⎡F⎤ ⎡S⎤ to save the file.

10. Repeat these steps to add a few more lines to the TIMELOG file, and get an idea of how the file will look after you've opened it several times.

Tip

The Notepad time log is an excellent tool for those who need to track their time for billing or record-keeping purposes, or for keeping track of telephone calls. The icon you're about to create will make the file easy to access.

Creating the Document Icon

Now you're ready to create a document icon for the TIMELOG file in the Everyday Tools group window. Follow these steps:

1. Move the Notepad window out of the way for now by clicking its Minimize button.

2. Activate the Everyday Tools group in the Program Manager by clicking it or choosing it from the Window menu.

3. Select the File command and choose New from the File menu.

4. When the New Program Object dialog box appears, select Program Item and click OK. You'll then see the Program Item Properties dialog box (shown previously in Figure 8-3).

5. The blinking cursor will be in the Description text box; type **TIMELOG** as the name to appear under the icon.

8

6. Click in the Command Line box, and type the following command (assuming the file is stored in the Windows directory):

NOTEPAD.EXE TIMELOG.TXT

Note

*Because TIMELOG.TXT is associated with Notepad, you could type just **TIMELOG.TXT**. This example shows how you would type a startup command for a non-associated document. In addition, it is important to enter the command as shown here because you will work with this entry again later in this chapter, in "Changing the Properties of a Group or Icon."*

7. Click OK to execute your entries, and the new TIMELOG icon will appear in the Everyday Tools group window.

The command you typed in the Command Line field first loads Notepad, and then opens the TIMELOG.TXT file. Note that the name of the file is specified as a parameter after the program name. Now try opening the time log again, by double-clicking the TIMELOG icon. You'll see your time log file, with the latest time and date inserted in the bottom line.

Using the Setup Utility to Create Startup Icons

The Windows Setup utility offers yet another way to create startup icons for applications. You may already be familiar with Setup from the installation routine. Another task Setup can do for you is search your hard drive for executable files and create startup icons for those it finds. It will then create a PIF for the program.

Start the Setup utility now by double-clicking the Setup icon in the Main group window of the Program Manager. You'll see a window similar to this one:

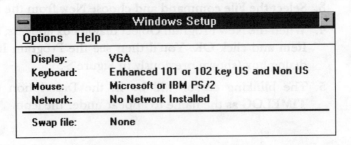

Follow these steps to create a new application startup icon using Setup:

1. Select Options, and choose Set up Applications to display the following dialog box:

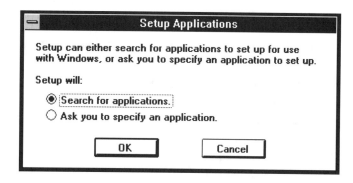

2. Select the button marked "Search for applications," and then click OK.

To create an icon and PIF for a single application, select the button marked "Ask you to specify an application," then specify the path and name for the file.

Tip

Setup now will do all the work of searching for the applications on your hard drive. (The other button in the Setup Applications dialog box works similarly to the Browse button in the Program Item Properties box.) Next, you'll see this dialog box:

8

3. More than one option can be selected. Click the drives to search and/or click Path to search the directories specified on the DOS path.

Note

Searching the path is often the most efficient way to have Setup do a search, but the programs must be on the path.

4. You'll see the Setup Applications dialog box; it will look like Figure 8-4 with a different listing of files.

On the left of the Setup Applications dialog box is a list box containing filenames of applications that are not currently set up as program item icons. (Every system is different, of course, and your list will represent what's available on your computer.) In the list box, choose the programs you want to add to Program Manager. For example, if your system runs with DOS 5, you'll probably see QuickBASIC in the list box, and you can select it. Continue with the program setup process:

5. Click to select the filenames of the applications you want to add to Program Manager, and click the Add button. The applications then

Figure 8-4. *A Setup Applications dialog box*

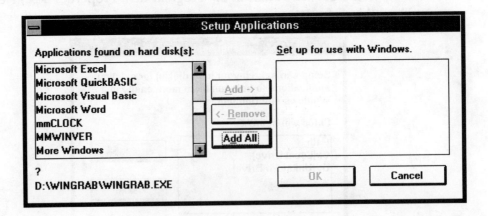

appear in the list box on the right. To select several applications and add them all, click to select them and choose the Add All button.

If you change your mind about selecting an application to be added, click it again to deselect it. If you've already added it to the box on the right, select it there and click the Remove button to replace it in the box on the left.

6. When you are done selecting applications, click OK or press (ENTER).

Windows Setup will create icons for the applications you selected, in the Applications group or the Non-Windows Applications group. You can open these groups now to see where your new application icons appear.

Other Program Manager Options

In this section, you learn how to change the properties of existing groups and program items, how to delete program items, and how to make applications start every time you start Windows.

Changing the Properties of a Group or Icon

The Properties option on the Program Manager File menu is used to change the properties of the selected group or program item icon. You work with the same Program Item Properties box that you use for adding a new group or icon (Figure 8-3). Remember these guidelines:

- To change the properties of a group, it must first be reduced to an icon; otherwise, Program Manager assumes you want to change a program item icon in the group window.

- Group properties that you can change include the group's name and the name of the group file.

- Program item properties that you can change include all those that were available when you created the item, including the item name, command line, working directory, icon, and shortcut key.

8

In this exercise, you change the properties of the TIMELOG icon you created previously.

1. Click the TIMELOG icon in the Everyday Tools group window.

2. Select the Program Manager File command, and choose Properties from the File menu.

The Program Item Properties dialog box is displayed, and includes the information you entered when creating the TIMELOG program item. One property you can change is the command line; in this case you do not need to include the filename NOTEPAD.EXE. Because all .TXT files are associated with Notepad and are loaded into its workspace when Notepad is opened, you can simply use the filename TIMELOG.TXT as the command line. Do the following to change the Command Line field:

3. Double-click the Command Line text box with the mouse.

4. Type **TIMELOG.TXT**. (Make sure you include the .TXT extension; without it, the file will not load.) Press (ENTER) to accept the new field text, but don't click OK yet. Leave the Properties box open for the next exercise.

Creating a Shortcut Key

A *shortcut key* makes it possible to start an icon without selecting it first. Try adding a shortcut key to the TIMELOG icon.

1. In TIMELOG's Properties box, click the Shortcut Key field.

2. Press (T) to make (CTRL)-(ALT)-(T) the shortcut for opening the TIMELOG file.

3. Do not click OK yet; leave the Program Item Properties dialog box open.

Notice that when you press (T), Windows inserts CTRL + ALT + T in the Shortcut Key text box. Shortcut keys use the (CTRL)-(ALT) and (CTRL)-(SHIFT)-(ALT) key combinations to avoid conflicts with other (ALT)-key assignments used by Windows. Write the shortcut key on a list for future use.

Changing Icons

The startup icon suggested for the TIMELOG file is the same icon used for Notepad. However, because in this case you are configuring a document icon to load a specific document (the time log) into Notepad's workspace, you'll want to change the icon to look more like a document. Here's how to change the icon:

1. Click the Change Icon button; this displays the Change Icon dialog box.

In the Change Icon dialog box, the File Name field contains the name of the Notepad executable file. Notice that only one icon is displayed in the Current Icon display area. Most programs written for Windows contain at least one icon, but some provide several. In this case, there isn't much of a selection, but you can "borrow" an icon from another application by typing the application's filename in the File Name field. In the remainder of this exercise, you use the Browse button to find the PROGMAN.EXE file in the Windows directory and borrow an icon from that program's extensive list.

2. In the Change Icon dialog box, click the Browse button to open the Browse dialog box. You'll see a list of files in the Windows directory.

3. Select MORICONS.DLL, and then click OK. The Change Icon window returns, with a large list of icons for third-party applications displayed in its Current Icon display area, like this:

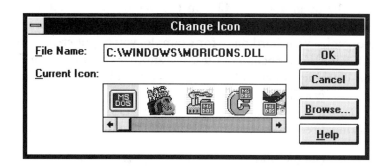

4. Scroll through the list by dragging the slider button right, then left.

5. To see a more generic assortment of icons, click the Browse button again, then click to select PROGMAN.EXE (Program Manager), and click OK. The assortment of icons in the Current Icon display area looks like this:

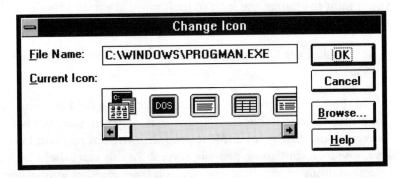

6. Scroll left and right through the display. One excellent use for TIMELOG is to track telephone calls, so select the telephone icon by double-clicking it. The new icon now appears in the lower-left corner of the Program Item Properties box.

7. Click OK or press (ENTER) to save all the changes you have made to the TIMELOG icon in the last few exercises.

Defining a Working Directory

Most of the applications and accessories that come with Windows automatically open and save files in the Windows directory. However, you've learned how saving document files in separate directories is a practical way to organize your hard disk—for example, you might create a directory called DOCS for Write document files, and another called ART for Paintbrush files. The Working Directory field in the Program Item Properties dialog box lets you specify a directory where the application will open and save its files.

To see how this works, let's start the DOS Prompt to see what its default working directory is, and then return to Windows and change that directory.

1. Double-click the DOS Prompt icon in the Main group of the Program Manager. (You may have moved this icon into your Everyday Tools group; if so, click it there.)

2. You'll now see the name of the Windows directory. (If you don't, type **PROMPT PG** at the DOS prompt and press (ENTER).)

When you work at the DOS level, it's likely that you'll want to work in a directory other than Windows. To redefine the DOS Prompt icon so it opens to another directory, do the following:

3. Type **EXIT** at the DOS prompt to return to Windows. The DOS Prompt icon will be highlighted when you return. (If it isn't, click the icon.)

4. With the DOS Prompt icon still highlighted, select the Program Manager File command and choose Properties from the File menu.

5. Click the Working Directory text box and type **C:\DOS** (or type the path of a directory you want to use when you exit to DOS).

6. Click OK or press (ENTER) to save the changes.

7. Double-click the DOS Prompt icon again. When the DOS prompt appears, the DOS directory will be the active directory.

You can make similar changes to your other program items to ensure that files created with those programs are stored in specific directories.

Deleting a Program Item or Group

The Delete option on the Program Manager File menu is used to delete the currently selected group or program item.

Note

A group must be reduced to an icon before it can be deleted.

8

Caution

Deleting a group also deletes any program items within the group. If you want to save any of the items, move their icons to another group before deleting the group.

To delete a program item or group, first reduce it to an icon, and highlight the icon. Press the (DEL) key or choose Delete from the File menu. Windows displays a message box asking if you really want to delete the icon. Answer Yes to go ahead with the deletion, or No if you change your mind.

The Startup Group

The Startup Group has special significance in the Program Manager: any program item copied to this group will automatically start when Windows is started. Open the Startup Group now to see if it contains any program item icons. If you worked through the exercises in "Starting an Application from the StartUp Group," in Chapter 2, the File Manager icon should be in the group. You can use this next exercise to add some other icons to Startup:

1. If the File Manager icon is not included in the Startup group, copy it there now by dragging its icon from the Main group. *Make sure to hold down the* (CTRL) *key while dragging the icon.* This makes a copy of the icon in the Startup group and leaves the original icon in the Main group.

Tip

It's better to copy icons to the Startup group rather than move them there. If you ever need to close an application that started automatically with Windows, restarting the application will be easier when its icon is in a familiar group like Main or Everyday Tools. Typically, you leave the Startup group reduced as an icon during your Windows sessions, so it isn't as readily available.

2. Copy the Clock icon from the Accessories group to the Startup group, pressing (CTRL) as you drag.

3. Copy any other icons for applications you want to start whenever Windows starts, keeping in mind the memory limitations of your system.

Now you need to make sure the applications in the Startup group reduce to icons on the desktop when they start, because it's unlikely you'll need to use all of them immediately.

4. Click and highlight the File Manager icon in the Startup group.

5. Select the Program Manager File command and choose Properties in the File menu.

6. When the Program Item Properties dialog box appears, mark the Run Minimized box.

7. Repeat these steps for the Clock and any other icons you may have copied into Startup.

Chapter Wrap-Up

Now that you've made changes to the Startup group and to other Windows settings, you can try exiting Windows and then restarting it. Before doing so, however, make sure the Save Changes on Exit feature on the Options menu is checked. Then choose Exit Windows from the Program Manager File menu, or double-click the Control button. When you return to the DOS prompt, restart Windows in the normal way. You'll then see all the changes you made, including the Clock and other startup icons added on the desktop.

Notice that the Clock displays the correct time, even when minimized to an icon. You can leave it minimized all the time if you don't mind looking at the time in such a small format. If you can't make out the time, try changing the display by choosing Analog or Digital on the Clock's Options menu. If you still can't read the display, just open the Clock window and resize it to any size you like.

8

9

Managing Files, Directories, and Disks with File Manager

File Manager is a Windows program that displays the drives, directories, and files on your local hard drive or the hard drives of remote network file servers. You can manipulate these files in a number of ways, the most important of which are listed here:

- Copy and move single files or groups of files by clicking and dragging their icons to other drives or directories.

- Delete or rename files or groups of files.

- Start executable program files by double-clicking their icons.

- Open documents by double-clicking their icons.

Of course, File Manager has many more features that you learn about as you read through this chapter and work the examples. You read about some of these features in Chapter 4, but here in Chapter 9 are more thorough explanations. It is assumed you have an understanding of the file and directory concepts discussed in Chapter 7.

The File Manager Window

The first time you start File Manager, it looks similar to the window pictured in Figure 9-1. (If your File Manager screen looks different, don't worry—in a moment you'll get a chance to restore the File Manager default settings.) Like the Program Manager, File Manager holds document windows within its borders, but in File Manager these windows are called *directory windows* because each displays the contents of a single directory. Directory windows have the following features:

- The *drive icon bar* depicts each of the floppy drives, hard drives, RAM memory drives, and network drives available to File Manager.

Figure 9-1. *The File Manager*

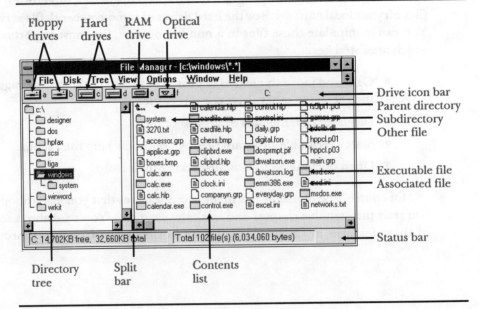

- The *directory tree* depicts the directories on the drive that is currently selected in the drive icon bar.

- The *contents list* shows the files for the directory selected in the directory tree.

- A *split bar* separates the directory tree and contents list. You can click and drag the split bar left or right to enlarge either side of the directory window, or you can remove the split altogether and display only directories or only files.

- The *status bar* displays important information about the selected drive, such as the number of files and their total disk space.

The following steps restore the File Manager default settings for the exercises in this chapter. You'll rename the WINFILE.INI file in the Windows directory, which holds the configuration information File Manager reads every time it starts. This information includes the size of the window, the settings on the Options menu, and the contents of directory windows. When the file is renamed, File Manager won't find it and will thus create a new file using default settings.

1. First make sure the Save Settings on Exit option is not enabled. Open the File Manager Options menu; if the Save Settings on Exit box is checked, click it to turn it off.

2. Select File, and choose Rename from the File menu.

3. When the Rename dialog box appears, type the following in the From text box. (If your Windows directory is on a drive other than C, replace C in the entry with the correct drive letter.)

   C:\WINDOWS\WINFILE.INI

4. In the To text box, type the following, again substituting the appropriate drive letter if necessary.

   C:\WINDOWS\WINFILE.TMP

5. Exit File Manager, and then restart it by double-clicking its icon in the Program Manager.

9

File Manager now creates a new WINFILE.INI file. Because Save Setting on Exit is turned off, Windows re-creates the file with the default settings.

You're now ready to continue with the exercises in this chapter. After you finish the chapter, if you want to restore the previous settings, first delete WINFILE.INI, and then rename WINFILE.TMP to WINFILE.INI using the Rename command on the File menu.

Customizing File Manager

You can customize File Manager in a number of ways. For example, you can change the fonts that display filenames, turn the status bar on or off, or change the way File Manager asks you to confirm your commands. The options discussed in this section are on the File Manager Options menu.

Suppressing Confirmation Messages

When you delete or copy files in File Manager, warning messages appear asking you to confirm your actions. If you feel these confirmation messages are unnecessary, you can use the Confirmation option on the Options menu to turn some or all of them off. Choose Confirmation now to display the following dialog box:

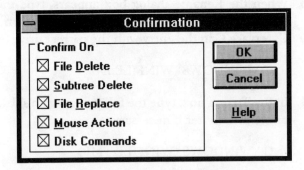

Marking these check boxes controls confirmation messages for the following operations:

Option	Operation
File Delete	Deleting files
Subtree Delete	Deleting directories and subdirectories
File Replace	Overwriting a file that already exists
Mouse Action	Copying and moving files using mouse click-and-drag techniques
Disk Commands	Disk-management commands such as FORMAT

If you are a new user, leave all these options checked until you become more familiar with File Manager operations.

Controlling File Deletions

In some cases, it's advantageous to temporarily turn off a confirmation request. For example, you can disable the File Delete confirmation when you're deleting large groups of files and you're sure it's safe to delete all the files. *Be sure to turn the option back on,* so you'll be cautioned as usual when deleting files in the future.

Another way to control file deletion confirmations is in the Confirm File Delete dialog box. For example, when the File Manager File Delete confirmation option is turned on, you see a dialog box similar to the following when you try to delete a group of files:

You can click the Yes to All button if you're sure the remaining files should be deleted. Or you can selectively delete individual files by clicking the Yes or No buttons as this confirmation box appears for each file. Click Cancel to keep the remaining files and stop the delete command.

9

Changing Fonts

To change the font used to display filenames in directory windows, choose the Font option on the Options menu. You'll see the Font dialog box shown in Figure 9-2.

Here's how to change the font:

1. In the Font list box, use the scroll bars or arrow keys to scroll through, and click the font you want to use.

2. In the Font Style list box, choose a style for the font you want to use.

3. Choose a font size in the Size box. Keep in mind that large fonts reduce the total amount of information you can see in the window.

4. If you prefer uppercase letters, click the Lowercase check box to turn this option off.

5. A sample of your selected font appears in the Sample box at the bottom of the dialog box. To see what the font looks like in the File Manager listing, click the OK button or press (ENTER) to accept your selection.

Figure 9-2.   *The Font dialog box is used to change the file listing text in a directory window to another font, style, and size*

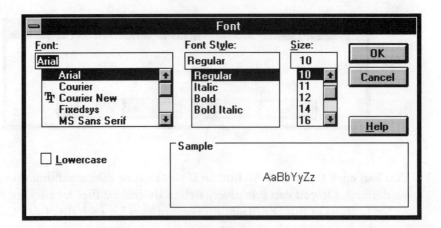

Displaying the Status Bar

The status bar at the bottom of the File Manager window displays the following useful information about disk space and file sizes for the currently selected disk:

- When a directory is selected, you'll see information about the drive at the left of the status bar, and about the directory at the right of the status bar.
- When a file is selected, the status bar tells you the size of the file.
- When multiple files are selected, the status bar indicates the number of files and their total number of bytes.

You can turn the status bar off and on by choosing Status Bar from the Options menu. Turning the status bar off is not usually necessary unless the desktop is so crowded that you need to make the File Manager window as small as possible.

Minimizing File Manager on Use

When the Minimize on Use option is enabled, File Manager reduces to an icon whenever you double-click an application startup file. To see how this works, try the following exercise:

1. Select Options, and click the Minimize on Use option to turn it on.
2. In the File Manager directory tree, click the Windows directory (if it is not already selected).
3. Locate CARDFILE.EXE in the file listing for the Windows directory, and double-click the icon. This starts the Cardfile application and minimizes Program Manager to an icon.
4. Close Cardfile now to save memory.

If you want the Program Manager to minimize in this way whenever you start applications, keep the Minimize on Use option marked; otherwise, click it again to disable it.

9

Save Settings on Exit

When the Save Settings on Exit option on the Options menu is enabled, any settings you make during a File Manager session are saved for the next session. Settings that are saved include the marked options on the Options menu, changes to directory windows and their contents, and the rearrangement of directory windows within the File Manager. You can click this option now if you want to save the settings you make while working through this chapter.

Tip

When the Save Settings on Exit option is on, any windows that are open when you exit File Manager will be reopened in the next File Manager session. Usually, this isn't a problem; however, to avoid screen clutter in the next session, you may want to close any unnecessary windows, or any windows you don't want reopened, before you leave File Manager.

Working with Directory Windows

The first time you start File Manager using its default settings only one directory window is open, and it fills the entire File Manager window. You can open additional directory windows to display files on other drives and directories.

Opening Another Directory Window

Multiple directory windows can be opened to display the contents of several drives and directories. To set up a new directory window, do the following:

1. Choose New Window from the Window menu.

2. Choose Tile from the Window menu to arrange the two windows. Notice the title bar in each window indicates the current directory, but the original window is labeled 1 and the new window is labeled 2.

3. In the upper window, click the DOS directory, or any other visible directory.

A quick way to open a new directory window is to double-click a drive icon in another directory window. A new window for that drive appears.

Tip

The Split Bar

Within the directory window, the split bar divides the directory tree and the contents list. Drag the bar to the left to provide more space for file listings in the contents list, or to the right to get a wider view of the directory tree when necessary. You can also remove the split altogether, and display only the directory tree or only the file listing.

To drag the split bar and change the allocated space for either side of the window, click and hold the bottom of the bar and drag it with the mouse. Note that when the mouse pointer is over the split bar, it changes to a double-headed arrow, as shown here:

C: 4,012KB free, 32,660KB total   Total 87 file(s) (3,651,668 bytes)

In one of the windows you now have open, try moving the split bar to the left so you can see more files in the contents list.

You can also move the split bar by choosing the Split option on the View menu, and then using the (LEFT ARROW) or (RIGHT ARROW) key to move the split bar.

Note

To remove the window split entirely, select the View menu, and choose Tree Only to display only the directory tree, or Directory Only to display only files for a selected directory. Here's an example of a window that displays only

9

the tree; the window has been resized, and all branches of the tree have been opened.

Here's an example of a directory window that shows the file list only:

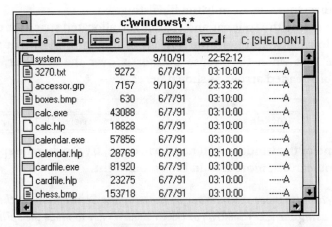

Note that files are listed vertically, along with size and creation date information.

Arranging Windows

When more than one directory window is open, you can rearrange them by using the Cascade and Tile options on the Window menu, or by dragging them with the mouse. You can also minimize them, as shown in Figure 9-3.

Directory window icons take on the name of the directory they list, as well as the type of files listed. The icon itself indicates the view. In Figure 9-3, the left icon lists the root directory tree only, the middle icon lists files only from the Windows directory, and the right icon lists both the directory tree and files from the HPFAX directory.

Windows Refreshment Time

No, it's not time to take a break. The Refresh option on the Window menu is used to update the list of files in a directory window in the following situations:

- When you've performed a file operation outside the File Manager that affects the file list, and the list has not yet been updated in the directory window

- When you restore a minimized directory window and you want to make sure its file list is current

Figure 9-3.   *Minimized directory windows*

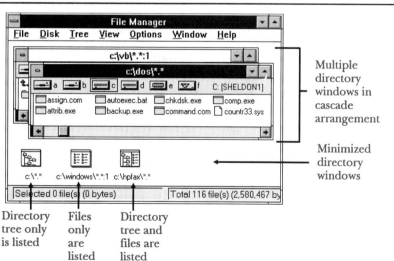

Multiple directory windows in cascade arrangement

Minimized directory windows

9

Directory tree only is listed

Files only are listed

Directory tree and files are listed

- To update the list of files for a floppy disk drive after changing the floppy disk in the drive
- To update network drive file lists

Climbing the Directory Tree

The directory tree displays the directories and subdirectories of the currently selected drive. To select a different drive, click one of the drive icons at the top of a directory window. On a network, some drive icons may represent network drives, which are storage devices on the remote system to which your computer is connected.

To display the list of files in another directory, click that directory icon in the directory tree. Alternatively, if the highlight is in the directory tree, press the arrow keys on the keyboard to scroll through the tree. As each directory is highlighted, its files are listed in the contents list. When a directory has branching subdirectories, use one of the methods described next to access files in the subdirectory.

Expanding and Collapsing Branches

The following exercise demonstrates how the directory tree can be expanded and collapsed. Before you begin, make sure the Windows directory is displayed in a directory window. If it isn't, click the directory window you want to use, or choose New Window from the Window menu. Next, click the icon of the drive that holds the Windows directory, and then click the Windows directory icon.

When a drive contains many directories and directory levels, the entire tree may not fit in the window. By collapsing the directory tree, you display only certain levels of files. You can shrink the tree by collapsing the entire tree or by collapsing specific branches.

1. **Collapse the entire directory tree by double-clicking the root directory icon.**

2. **Double-click the root directory icon again to expand the branch. Now the first level directories branch from the root, similar to the directory tree shown here:**

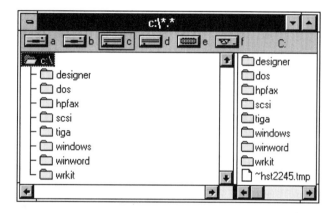

Note that the names of directory folders are displayed along with filenames in the contents list on the right.

3. **Click the root directory icon. To see another way to collapse a directory, press ⊖; then press ⊕ to expand it.**

4. **To display the branching subdirectories of the Windows directory, double-click its directory icon, or highlight it and press (ENTER). The System directory and possibly others appear, depending on your setup.**

5. **Click the System directory icon, or press the (DOWN ARROW) key to select it. The files of this directory are displayed in the contents list on the right.**

6. **Now close the branching System directory. You can do this any of three ways:**

    Double-click the Windows directory icon.

9

Highlight the Windows directory and press the minus (⊖) key.

Highlight the Windows directory, select Tree from the menu bar, and choose Collapse Branch.

7. Now expand the entire directory tree. Select Tree and choose Expand All, or press ⌈CTRL⌉-⊛. When a directory tree is completely expanded, as many branches as will fit in the window are displayed.

8. Try collapsing a few branches by double-clicking the directory at the top of each branch.

Indicating Expandable Branches

Expanding the entire directory tree is a convenient way to see all directories and branching subdirectories for the selected drive. However, this usually means you can't see the entire tree, and you'll need to scroll through it using the arrow keys or the scroll bar.

The Indicate Expandable Branches option on the Tree menu provides another way to view the directory structure. Selecting this option causes a plus sign to appear in the icons of directories that have branching subdirectories, or a minus sign when the directory is already fully expanded. In this way, you don't need to expand every branching subdirectory to know that subdirectories exist. The following exercise demonstrates this feature.

1. Double-click the root directory to collapse it, or highlight it and press the minus (⊖) key.

2. Select Tree, and choose Indicate Expandable Branches from the Tree menu.

3. Double-click the root directory again to display first-level directories. Plus signs appear in the icons of directories that have branching subdirectories.

The Indicate Expandable Branches feature is a remnant of Windows 3.0, and causes File Manager to run more slowly. If you don't need this feature, turn it off.

Tip

Working with the File List

The File Manager lets you select files from a list and then execute commands that affect the selected files. The following sections help you learn how to manipulate the file lists in directory windows. First let's examine the options on the View menu that let you change how files are listed.

Changing the File View

The File Manager View menu lets you change the way files are listed in the contents list. Here is the View menu:

```
View
√ Tree and Directory
  Tree Only
  Directory Only

  Split

√ Name
  All File Details
  Partial Details...

√ Sort By Name
  Sort By Type
  Sort By Size
  Sort By Date

  By File Type...
```

The first four options were discussed previously. This section is concerned with the remaining options on the View menu.

Showing File Details

The Name, All File Details, and Partial Details options on the View menu let you change the amount of information displayed about each file. You can display just the filename in a directory window, or you can also display the following information:

- The size of the file in bytes
- The date the file was created or last modified
- The time the file was created or last modified
- The *attributes*, or "status flags" of a file, which indicate if it can be changed and erased, or if it has been backed up

Let's display some additional information for the files in the Windows directory.

1. Click the Windows directory icon in a directory window.
2. To display detailed information about each file, select View and choose the All File Details option. The file information is listed in rows, like the listing in Figure 9-4.

Figure 9-4.   The All File Details display for files

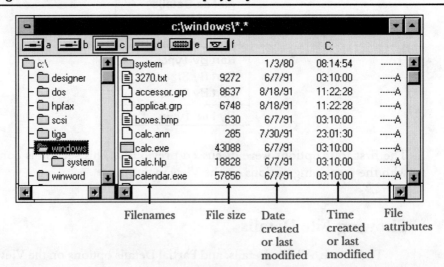

The first column lists the filename and shows its icon. The second column shows the size of the file in bytes. The third and fourth columns list the date and time the file was created or last modified. In the last column are the current attributes of the file, which are flags that designate the read and write status of a file (see "Viewing and Changing File Properties" later in this chapter), and whether it has been backed up.

Customizing the File Details Listing

Typically, the All File Details option is preferred for listing information about files. Sometimes, however, you'll need to make a directory window as small as possible. If so, select the Partial Details option on the View menu to select which file details you want. Choose this option now, and you'll see the following dialog box:

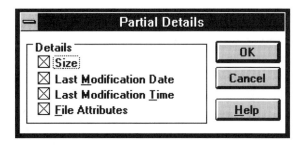

If you previously selected All File Details, all of the options in the Partial Details box will be marked. To turn any option off, click its check box, and then press the OK button. This removes the items from the file list, and you can reduce the size of the window accordingly.

Sorting the File List

The four Sort By options on the View menu change the order in which files are listed. This makes it easier to see and select groups of related files. Here are the Sort By options:

9

- *Sort By Name* is the default option. Files are sorted by the first eight characters of the filename.

- *Sort By Type* arranges files by their filename extension. For example, all executable (.EXE) files are listed together, all Write (.WRI) files are listed together, and so on.

- *Sort By Size* puts files in size order, with the largest file first. This option is useful when you need to find and delete large files to make room on a disk.

- *Sort By Date* lists files together by date; this may be the date they were first created or the date they were last modified. Files with the most recent creation or modification date are listed first, and the oldest files are last. You can scroll to the bottom of the list to see if there are any old files that need to be deleted.

Listing Specific Files

You can use the Sort By Type option to specify exactly which files you want to list, using wildcard characters or special check-box options. Choose the Sort By Type option on the View menu to display the following dialog box:

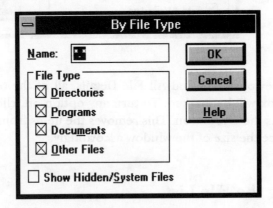

The Name field is highlighted when this dialog box first opens. To see how wildcard characters can be used to display specific file groups, try this next exercise. Before you begin, make sure the Windows directory is still the current directory.

1. In the Name text box, type ***.TXT**, and press (ENTER) to list all files with the extension .TXT.

2. Choose the Sort By Type option again. This time type ***.BMP** in the Name field, and press (ENTER) to list Paintbrush bitmap files.

3. Choose the Sort By Type option once again. Type ***.EXE** in the Name field, and press (ENTER) to list the program files with the extension .EXE.

4. Click the DOS directory icon in the directory tree. Notice that for this directory, too, .EXE files are grouped and listed in the contents list. You can use this trick when you're looking for specific files in various directories: click the directory icons one after the other (or use the Search command).

5. Choose the Sort By Type option one more time, type the wildcard characters ***.*** in the Name field, and press (ENTER). This specifies that all files with all extensions should be displayed.

Now try selecting some of the options in the File Type box of the By File Type dialog box. Each option is defined here:

- *Directories*   Mark this box to include the names of any subdirectories that branch from the current directory in the file listing.

- *Programs*   Mark this box to include executable files with the extensions .EXE, .COM, .BAT, or .PIF in the file listing.

If you want to start applications from the File Manager by double-clicking their icons, you'll need to mark the Programs option so that executable files for the programs are listed.

Note

- *Documents*   Mark this box to include associated document files in file listings. (Recall that associated files are those created by Windows accessories or associated with a Windows application. You can double-click associated files to open the application and the associated file in one step.)

9

- *Other Files*   Mark this option to list all files not included in the previous options.

- *Show Hidden/System Files*   Turn on this option when you want to display files with the Hidden or System attribute. DOS creates these files and typically hides them in directory listings at the DOS level to prevent them from being accidentally deleted by users. Though you can display these files in a directory window, there is little reason to do so since they are rarely changed, moved, or deleted.

Try choosing each of these options, and various combinations of them, in the By File Type dialog box to see how the file list is affected. For example, consider this combination:

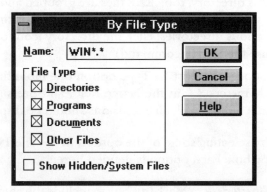

This displays all files with the first three characters WIN. Now choose the Sort By Type option again, and set it as shown here:

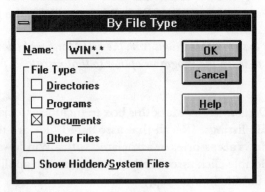

This setting reduces the file list further, displaying the WIN files only if they are also associated document files.

Selecting Files

Before you can execute a File command, you need to highlight files for the command to act upon. In the exercises that follow, you select files in the Windows directory, so begin by specifying the file listing you want, as follows:

1. Select View, and choose Sort By Type.
2. Type ***.*** in the Name field.
3. Mark all the File Type boxes.
4. Click the OK button or press (ENTER).

Keyboard methods for selecting files are not covered in this section. For a list of keyboard selection techniques, select Help and choose Keyboard on the Help menu. Then choose Print Topic on the File menu of the Help window to print the keyboard help information.

Note

Selecting Contiguous Files

Contiguous (adjacent) files are easy to select. Simply click the first file you want to select, hold down the (SHIFT) key, and click the last file. If the last file you want to select is not visible in the window, you can scroll the list. The following exercise demonstrates this selection technique:

1. Rearrange the contents list by choosing Sort by Type from the View menu. Notice that files with the extension .BMP are listed at the top.
2. Click the first .BMP file in the list.
3. Press and hold the (SHIFT) key, and then click the last .BMP file in the list. If you have a long list of bitmap files, it may be necessary to scroll down the list using the scroll bar. Don't worry if the first file you selected scrolls out of sight; all files in between it and the next file

9

you click will be highlighted and selected, as long as you keep the
(SHIFT) key depressed when you click.

  To quickly jump to a file in a list, type the first letter of the file's name.

Tip

Selecting Noncontiguous Groups of Files

When the files you want to select as a group are not listed together, but
scattered throughout the file list, they are referred to as *noncontiguous* files.
Sometimes you can't group these noncontiguous files using the Sort By
options or wildcard characters, but you can still select them as a group. To
do this, hold down the (CTRL) key as you click the icon of each file you want
to select. Try these next two exercises to see how this works:

1. The .BMP files should still be selected from the last exercise. Select
   View and choose Sort By Name to list files in filename order. Notice
   that the .BMP files remain selected, even though they are no longer
   listed contiguously.

2. Select some other files. Hold down the (CTRL) key and click on several
   scattered .EXE files in the list, such as CARDFILE.EXE and
   PBRUSH.EXE.

Selected files remain selected until you click another file without holding
down the (SHIFT) or (CTRL) key. Files also remain selected as you scroll through
the file list looking for other files to select. Try the following exercise to select
scattered executable files.

1. Scroll to the beginning of the list. Click the first .EXE file you see,
   which should be CALC.EXE. Notice that the files you selected
   previously are no longer selected when you click this new selection.

2. Hold down the (CTRL) key and continue selecting other .EXE files, scrolling through the list as needed. Files remain selected as you scroll through the list.

3. Add a contiguous group to the noncontiguous selections you just made. With the .EXE files still selected, hold down both the (CTRL) *and* (SHIFT) keys, and click another file in the list. All files in between are added to the current selection list.

Deselecting Files

If you change your mind about selecting a file, you can easily remove it from the selected group (deselect it), by pressing the (CTRL) key and then clicking the file's icon. Similarly, you can deselect a whole group of selected files by holding down the (SHIFT) key and clicking the files' icons. These techniques are handy because it is often easier to select a large group of files and then deselect one or two that you don't want than it is to select all the files you want individually. Try this method in the following example:

1. Scroll to the beginning of the contents list, and click the first file.

2. Hold down the (SHIFT) key and click the last file you can see in the window. This selects all the visible files in the window.

3. Hold down the (CTRL) key and click some files at random within the selected group. This deselects the files.

4. Hold down both the (SHIFT) and (CTRL) keys, and click a selected file. All files between this and the last file selected are thus deselected.

Using the Select Files Option

The Select Files option on the File menu provides a versatile alternative to selecting files by clicking them with the mouse. Choose Select Files to display the following Select Files dialog box:

9

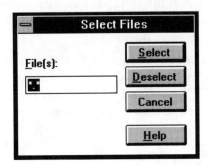

To select files using the Select Files dialog box, type a file specification in the File(s) text box, using wildcard characters. Initially, the specification *.* is suggested in this field, but you can type over it. These next steps help you practice with this dialog box:

1. If files are currently selected in the contents list, deselect them by clicking the Deselect button in the Select Files dialog box.

2. Double-click in the File(s) field, type ***.EXE**, and press the Select button. All executable files in the directory window will be highlighted.

3. You can continue to add more selections. For example, double-click in the File(s) field and type ***.BMP**, then click the Select button.

The Set Selection dialog box can be closed and reopened without losing your current selection of files in the contents list.

Note

4. Click the Close button to close the Set Selection box; the files you selected remain selected.

5. Scroll to the beginning of the list.

6. Now deselect all files that start with C. Choose Select Files from the File menu, type **C*.*** in the dialog box, and press the Deselect button. Filenames starting with C are deselected.

Use the Select Files option whenever you know the filenames or extensions of the files you want to select. Use the mouse selection methods (described in the previous section) when you don't know the filenames or you prefer to scroll through the file list and search for files. You can also combine both selection methods.

Tip

Copying and Moving Files with the Mouse

You can copy and move files with the mouse using click-and-drag techniques. In this exercise, you create a new directory and copy files to it. Keep the following guidelines in mind regarding moving and copying files:

- *Moving Files*   When you click and drag a file icon from one directory to a different directory, Windows assumes you want to move the file, and deletes the file from its original location.

- *Copying Files*   When you copy a file, Windows makes a duplicate of the file in the destination location, and leaves the original file intact. To copy a file, hold down the (CTRL) key while you drag the file icon.

Note

When you drag a selected file icon to another directory on the same drive, Word assumes you want to move the file; but when you drag the file to another drive, Word assumes you want to copy the file. To move a file to another drive, press (ALT) while you drag the file icon.

Follow these steps to create a new directory, select files, and copy them to the new directory:

1. Make sure that the Windows directory is the current directory.

2. Select File and choose Create Directory to display the following dialog box:

Create Directory	
Current Directory: C:\WINDOWS	OK
Name:	Cancel
	Help

9

Since the current directory is Windows, the new directory will branch from it.

3. Type **TEMP** in the Name field, and click the OK button or press ⌜ENTER⌟.

The new TEMP directory icon appears as a branching directory of the Windows directory. Now you can copy files to it using mouse click-and-drag methods.

4. The Windows directory should still be selected. Select View and choose Sort By Type.

5. Select all the .TXT files.

6. Hold down the ⌜CTRL⌟ key, click anywhere in the selection of contiguous files, and drag left. The mouse pointer changes and appears as three overlapping files.

7. Drag the icon to the TEMP directory icon in the directory tree.

8. When a rectangle surrounds the TEMP directory icon, release the mouse. You'll then see the following dialog box:

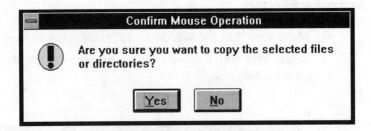

9. Here you must confirm the mouse operation; click the Yes button to confirm the copy.

In the foregoing procedure, you have copied the .TXT files to the new directory. If you want to move rather than copy files, follow the same procedure, but don't hold down the ⌜CTRL⌟ key in Step 6. Move operations are useful when you want to reorganize the files on your drive, because the files are removed from their original locations.

Using the File Menu Commands

The File menu holds a set of commands that you use to manipulate the files and directories you've selected in directory windows. You examine each command as you work through the following sections.

Caution

Keep in mind that some commands on the File menu act on the currently selected directory in the directory tree. For example, if you click the Windows directory in the directory tree, and then choose the Delete option on the File menu, the dialog box will suggest deleting the Windows directory! So be careful as you work.

Opening Selected Directories and Files

File Open does basically the same thing as the (ENTER) key. If you select a directory icon and choose File Open, the directory's branching subdirectories are displayed. If you select an .EXE file in the contents list and choose File Open, the program starts. If you select an associated document and choose File Open, the associated application is started and the document is loaded into its workspace.

Moving and Copying Files

File Move and File Copy are used to move or copy files and directories. Use these commands when you can't click and drag files because the source files or directories are not visible in a directory window, or when the destination directory is not visible in a directory window. The Move and Copy commands have the following advantages over mouse methods:

- If you know the filenames and locations of the files you want to copy or move, you can use Copy and Move to copy or move files without first opening directory windows.

- If the source files are visible in a directory window, but you can't see the destination directory icon or window, you can click the files to copy or move, choose the Copy or Move command, and specify the destination.

9

- When using Copy or Move, you can use wildcard characters to specify the exact files to copy or move. This method may be easier than clicking each file or using the Set Selection dialog box.
- Copy and Move are available even if your mouse is disabled.

First let's look at the Move dialog box:

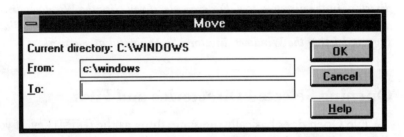

In this dialog box the Windows directory name appears in the From text box, because its icon was highlighted when the Move command was selected. If any files are selected in the directory window when you select Move, their names will also appear in the From field of the dialog box. You can double-click in the From field to specify new parameters or to insert more parameters after the existing path information. In the To text box, type the drive and directory where you want to move the files.

Here is an example of the Copy dialog box:

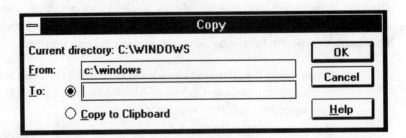

Once again, the current path and any selected files in the directory window appear in the From text box. You can type over the From box contents with your own file specification, by first double-clicking in the field. The following exercise demonstrates how to copy the Paintbrush .BMP files from the Windows directory to the TEMP directory you created earlier in this chapter. Since Copy lets you specify the path where files are located, you don't need to change directories before executing the Copy command.

1. Select File and choose Copy.

2. Type **C:\WINDOWS*.BMP** in the From text box. As usual, you'll want to replace drive C with the letter of your own Windows drive, if it is different.

3. Type **C:\WINDOWS\TEMP** in the To text box.

4. Click OK to copy the files.

When Windows copies the files, notice that it does not display any warning or confirmation messages, because in this situation files are not being overwritten or deleted.

The Copy to Clipboard button in the Copy dialog box is used when linking and embedding objects such as Paintbrush graphic files into a document.

Note

Deleting Files

One of the easiest ways to delete a file or directory is to click its icon with the mouse and then press the (DEL) key. A warning message appears asking you to confirm your deletion request—unless you have turned confirmations off as described in "Suppressing Confirmation Messages" earlier in this chapter.

The File Delete command is used to specify the path and filename of the files or directories you want to delete. In the following exercise, you delete the Paintbrush .BMP files you copied to the TEMP directory.

1. Select File and choose Delete to display the following dialog box:

9

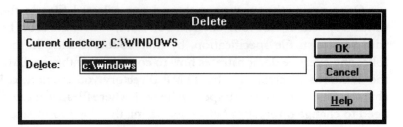

If any files are selected, their names appear in the Delete field.

2. Type **C:\WINDOWS\TEMP*.BMP** in the Delete field. This will delete all files with the extension .BMP in the TEMP directory.

3. Click the OK button to execute the deletion request.

If file deletion confirmations are still enabled, the following dialog box will appear for each file to be deleted:

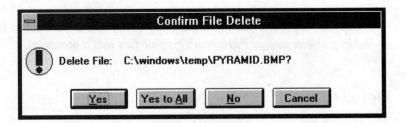

To go ahead with the deletion, click the Yes button; click No to keep the file. To delete all remaining files that match the specification, click the Yes to All button.

 Using the confirmation box as a "control" is a useful method when you want to select a group of files and then delete only some of them.

Tip

Renaming Files

File Rename lets you change the names of your directories and files. If you choose Rename with a directory or file highlighted in the contents list, that path and filename appear in the From text box of the Rename dialog box. In the following illustration, the period in the From field indicates the current directory:

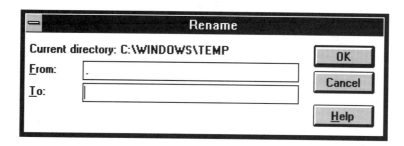

Caution

Don't rename files in the Windows directory.

Renaming groups of files is a little tricky. There must be a common element in the names of all the files. For example, entering the following parameters in the Rename dialog box will rename the two .TXT files listed in the From text box to the same filenames, but with the new extension .DOC:

9

This next example renames the NEWDATA1.DBF, NEWDATA2.DBF, and NEWDATA3.DBF files to OLDDATA1.DBF, OLDDATA2.DBF, and OLDDATA3.DBF:

```
┌─────────────────────────────────────────────────────┐
│ ▬                        Rename                        │
├─────────────────────────────────────────────────────┤
│ Current directory: C:\WINDOWS            ┌──────────┐ │
│                                          │    OK    │ │
│ From:   NEWDATA?.DBF                      └──────────┘ │
│                                          ┌──────────┐ │
│ To:     OLD*.*                           │  Cancel  │ │
│                                          └──────────┘ │
│                                          ┌──────────┐ │
│                                          │   Help   │ │
│                                          └──────────┘ │
└─────────────────────────────────────────────────────┘
```

In this Rename dialog box, the From text box calls for all filenames starting with NEWDATA and having the extension .DBF to be renamed. The question mark holds the place of the eighth character of the filename, which differs for each file in the group. The To text box specifies that OLD will be the first three characters of the new filenames.

Viewing and Changing File Properties

You can display the attributes, or *properties,* of files and directories with the File Properties option. These properties are assigned to files to protect them from unauthorized changes or accidental deletion, or to designate whether the files have been backed up. The properties are discussed in the following sections.

Read Only   Files marked R, Read Only, cannot be changed or deleted unless the Read Only attribute is removed.

Archive   When a file is first created, or when it is altered, its Archive flag (A) is set on. DOS commands such as BACKUP and XCOPY look at the Archive flag to determine if a file should be included in an incremental backup (the periodic backup of files that have changed since the last backup). During the incremental backup, the Archive flag is set off so the file is not included in the next backup. If the file changes in the meantime, its Archive flag is once again set on and it will be included in the next backup.

In most cases, you won't need to worry about the Archive bit (flag). However, there may be times when you want to manually set it to include or exclude a file from a backup. For example, to create a second set of backup disks, it may be necessary to set the archive bit on for files in directories you want to back up.

Hidden Files marked Hidden (H) will not appear in a DOS file listing, and will only appear in directory windows if the Show Hidden/System Files check box is marked in the By File Type dialog box (discussed in "Listing Specific Files" earlier in this chapter).

System Files marked System (S) are DOS files that are hidden in DOS file listings, and only appear in directory windows if the Show Hidden/System Files check box is marked in the By File Type dialog box (discussed in "Listing Specific Files" earlier in this chapter).

To get an idea of how attribute flags work, try the following exercise:

1. Click the Windows directory in the directory tree.

2. Click the file named 3270.TXT.

3. Select File and choose Properties to see this dialog box:

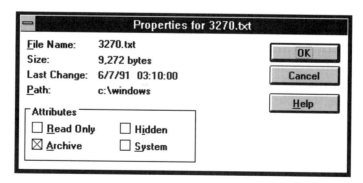

The dialog box displays the file's size, date and time of creation or last modification, and path name. Any attributes set for the file are marked in the Attributes area. For this example, apply the Read Only attribute to the file and see what happens when you try to rename it.

4. Click the Read Only check box in the Attributes area, and then click the OK button or press (ENTER).

5. Back at the File Manager, double-click the 3270.TXT file icon to start Notepad and load the file.

6. Type your name at the blinking cursor; then select File and choose the Save option. The following dialog box appears:

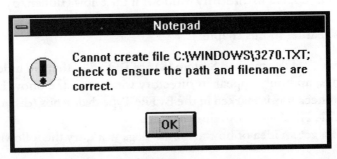

Because you have set the Read Only attribute on for this file, it cannot be saved with the changes you've made. You'll need to save the changes to a new file with a different name to keep the original intact. For now, click OK to close the message box and close the window without saving.

Using the Read Only attribute is how template files are protected from accidental erasure or change. A *template* is a document used to create other documents. For example, a template might contain your company logo and address. The Read Only template file is opened, saved under a different filename, and used to create a letter, while the original template is preserved for future use.

Printing from File Manager

In File Manager, you can print a document by *dragging and dropping* its icon on the Print Manager, but the Print Manager must be running as a window or icon on the desktop for this to work. The exercise that follows shows you how to print a Notepad file without having to start Notepad and load the file in its workspace.

1. The Print Manager must be running before you can drag and drop files on it. To start the Print Manager from the File Manager, double-click the file PRINTMAN.EXE in the Windows directory.

2. Make the File Manager window active; then click the Windows directory icon to make its files appear in the contents list.

3. Select a small text file, and click and drag the file to the Print Manager icon.

4. When the icon for the file is over the Print Manager icon, release the mouse; this causes the file to be printed.

Another way to print in File Manager is with the Print option on the File menu. Click the file you want to print, select File, and choose Print. When the Print dialog box appears, the file you selected is listed in the Text field. Click the OK button to print the file.

Program and Document Associations

As you have learned, associated document files are linked to their creating program by means of the filename extension. For example, when you double-click a .TXT file, its associated application, Notepad, starts in its own window and the file is loaded into its workspace. Other Windows associations include Write and its .WRI files, as well as Paintbrush and its .BMP and .PCX files.

The File Associate command lets you create your own file associations. For example, if you add a new program that creates files with the extension .ZAP, you can use the Associate command to link the .ZAP files with the program. Then you can easily double-click the .ZAP files to quickly open them together with the program. Alternatively, you might want to associate .ZAP files with Notepad.

9

Caution

Be careful not to associate a particular filename extension with more than one application. If you do, the last associated application is started when you double-click the document.

Documents created by Windows applications are already associated. The File Associate command is your tool for linking non-Windows applications with the documents they create, or to change associations. For example, you could remove the .TXT association from the Notepad and assign it to another text editor of your choice.

Assume for this exercise that you want the TIMELOG files that you create with Notepad to have the extension .LOG, rather than the usual .TXT extension associated with Notepad. The following exercise associates the .LOG extension with Notepad. Keep in mind that the .TXT extension also remains associated with Notepad (unless you remove it).

1. Select File and choose Associate from the File Menu to display the following dialog box:

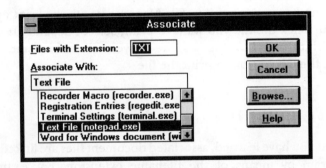

If a file is highlighted in the contents list, its extension is displayed in the Files with Extension text box of the Associate dialog box. You can save a step when associating files by first clicking a filename that has the extension you want to associate.

Tip

2. The cursor will be in the Files with Extension text box; type **LOG** (the period is not necessary) as the extension you want to associate.

3. In the Associate With list box, find Text File (notepad.exe) and click it. (You can also type in the name of the program if you know it, or click the Browse button to search for a program filename.)

4. Click the OK button (or press (ENTER)) to establish the association between the .LOG extension and Notepad.

To remove an association, simply choose None in the Associate With list box (or type it in yourself).

Searching for Files and Directories

The File Search option is used to locate files and directories within your disk filing system. You can search for a file by specifying its full filename, or by specifying a partial name and using wildcard characters. In the following exercise, you look for files with the filename extension .SYS on the current drive.

1. Select File and choose Search; you'll see this dialog box:

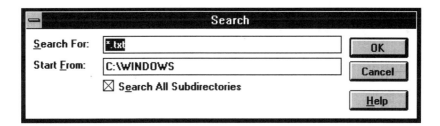

2. Type ***.SYS** in the Search For text box.
3. Type **C:** in the Start From field. (If your Windows directory is on another drive, replace C with the appropriate drive letter.)
4. Mark the Search All Subdirectories box, and click the OK button.

In a moment, you'll see a Search Results dialog box similar to this one:

9

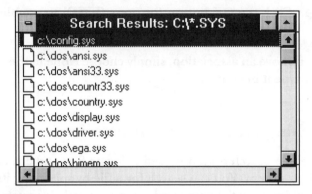

Scan through the list box and note that .SYS files are listed in several different directories, including the DOS and Windows directories. The Search Results window displays files like any other directory window. You can click any file in the list and execute the commands on the File menu or click and drag the files to other drives or directories. In addition, if executable files are listed, you can double-click them to start their programs.

Working with Directories

You can create, copy, and move directories in the File Manager. When copying or moving directories, File Manager can copy an entire directory tree or branches of it to a new directory or disk. It's easy to delete directories as well, but you'll want to use caution when you do, because File Manager will also delete a directory's branching subdirectories unless you specify otherwise.

Creating Directories

The Create Directory option on the File menu is used to create new directories. Before selecting the option, click the directory from which you want the new directory to branch. Alternatively, you can type the full path for the new directory in the Create Directory dialog box.

In a previous exercise, you created the TEMP subdirectory under the Windows directory. In this exercise, you create a new subdirectory that branches from TEMP.

1. Make sure a directory window is open to the drive that holds the Windows directory. Select the directory window that displays files in your Windows directory (or create a new directory window).

2. Double-click the Windows directory icon to display its subdirectories, if they are not visible.

3. Click the TEMP subdirectory.

4. Now you're ready to create the new subdirectory. Select File and choose Create Directory, and you'll see this dialog box:

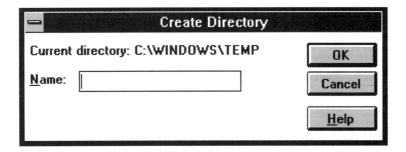

5. In the Name text box, type **LEVEL3** as the name of the new directory. (This name is used as an example only. It has no significance except to indicate that this is a "level 3" subdirectory.)

6. Click OK or press (ENTER). This creates the new directory as a branching subdirectory of the TEMP directory.

Another way to create this level 3 subdirectory is to type its full path name in the Name field of the Create Directory dialog box. For example, in the foregoing exercise, you could skip Steps 1 through 3 altogether, and begin at

the Create Directory dialog box; in the Name field, you would enter C:\WIN-
DOWS\TEMP\LEVEL3.

Copying and Moving Directories

When you copy a directory, Windows makes a duplicate at the new
location. When you move a directory, Windows deletes the original directory
after it is moved to the new location. Copying and moving directories are
useful ways to create a new directory structure on another drive, or to
reorganize a drive. Remember that any branching subdirectories of a directory are copied or moved along with it, unless you specify otherwise.

In this exercise, you practice moving the TEMP directory and its branching subdirectory, LEVEL3, to the root directory. In this way, TEMP will
branch from the root, not from the Windows directory.

1. Click the drive icon for the Windows directory, if it is not currently
   active.

2. If you can't see the Windows directory's branching subdirectories,
   including TEMP, double-click the Windows directory icon.

3. Click and drag the TEMP directory's icon over the root directory
   icon. When the rectangle appears over the root directory icon,
   release the mouse button.

4. A confirmation message asks if you are sure you want to move the
   directory; choose Yes.

In a moment, you'll see the new structure of the directory tree. If you
can't see the LEVEL3 directory, scan down through the list to find it, or
double-click the TEMP directory to open its subdirectory tree.

Typically, you'll move rather than copy directories from one location to
another. Copying creates duplicates of every file, which wastes disk space. In
the instances when you really want to copy an entire directory, hold down the
(CTRL) key and drag the directory icon to the new location.

Note

Directories are copied, not moved, to another disk by default, because Windows assumes you want to keep the original directory in place. To actually move a directory to another disk, hold down the (ALT) key while you drag the directory icon.

Tip

You can also use the File Copy and File Move commands to copy directories. The advantage of using this method is that you can type the exact path where the directory should be copied.

Deleting Directories

In this section, you delete the TEMP directory. You have learned in previous exercises how to copy and move files to it, and to move it to another location. Now it's time to delete this practice directory so it doesn't take up space on your hard drive. To delete a directory, highlight its icon in the directory tree and press the (DEL) key. Alternatively, select File and choose the Delete option; then type the path and directory name.

When deleting directories, you'll want to be aware of the current confirmation settings in your Windows environment. Choose Confirmation from the Options menu now to display the Confirmation dialog box, and note the following settings:

- *File Delete*   If the File Delete confirmation is enabled, File Manager will ask you to confirm your commands to delete files in a directory and its subdirectories. Make sure this option is turned on, because you'll always want to make careful choices about deleting all files.

- *Subtree Delete*   If the Subtree Delete confirmation is enabled, File Manager will ask you to confirm your commands to delete a directory and each of its subdirectories. It is recommended that you always leave this option on so you'll be warned before you complete a deletion that might include a subdirectory you may have forgotten about.

9

Make sure all the confirmation options are set, and then follow the steps here to delete the TEMP directory:

1. Click the TEMP directory and press the (DEL) key. The following dialog box appears displaying the name of the TEMP directory:

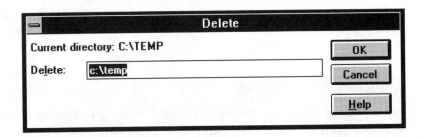

2. Click the OK button or press (ENTER). You then see the following confirmation box:

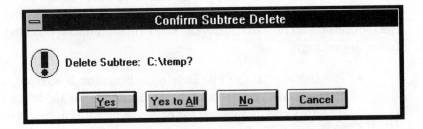

If you click the Yes button in the Confirm Subtree Delete dialog box, File Manager starts deleting files in the TEMP directory, asking you to confirm the deletion of each branching subdirectory. If you click the Yes to All button, File Manager automatically deletes each subdirectory without asking for confirmation. It is recommended that you always choose the Yes button technique.

3. Click the Yes button in the Confirm Subtree Delete dialog box. You'll see a confirmation box similar to this:

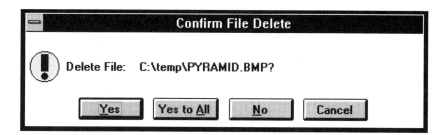

If you click Yes in the Confirm File Delete dialog box, a similar confirmation request will appear for each file to be deleted in the directory. Don't choose the Yes to All button unless you're sure you want to delete every file.

4. In this case, click the Yes to All button in the Confirm File Delete dialog box.

5. The Confirm Subtree Delete dialog box appears for the LEVEL3 subdirectory. Click the Yes button to delete the directory.

All of the remaining files are deleted, and the TEMP directory is removed. You are not asked to confirm the deletion of the files in the LEVEL3 directory because you clicked the Yes to All button in Step 4.

If you want to delete the files in a directory but not its branching subdirectory, click the No button when the Confirm Subtree Delete dialog appears for the directory you want to keep. This leaves the directory structure intact.

Tip

Using Disk and Network Commands

The options on the File Manager Disk menu are used to format, label, and copy floppy disks. In addition, options are provided for connecting to network drives and accessing network resources. The Disk menu options are described in the following paragraphs.

If you are connected to a network, additional options will appear on your Disk menu. See your network administrator for more information.

Note

9

Copy Disk   The Copy Disk option is similar to the DOS DISKCOPY command. It copies the contents of one disk onto another, deleting any files that might be on the destination disk. If your system has one floppy disk drive or two different types of floppy drives, type **A** in the Source In and Destination In text boxes. You'll be asked to switch disks during the copy.

Label Disk   The Label Disk option lets you add or change the electronic name assigned to a disk. Disk labels appear at the top of directory listings and are used by some programs to ensure that the correct disk has been inserted in the drive. To label a disk, place the disk in a drive and click the drive icon. Select Disk, choose Label Disk, and type the new label for the disk.

Format Disk   The Format Disk option lets you format a bootable system disk or a non-bootable disk. You can quick format a disk that was previously formatted. Quick formatting erases previously formatted disks. You can also specify a disk label. Note that a non-bootable disk has more room for files because it does not contain the system files.

Make System Disk   The Make System Disk option copies the system files to a formatted disk, thus making it bootable. If the disk is only to hold data, don't use this option.

Creating Program Manager Startup Icons with File Manager

File Manager provides an interesting way to create startup icons in Program Manager groups. When you add a new application and want to create a startup icon for it, simply locate its .EXE file in the File Manager and drag and drop the file icon on a group in the Program Manager. The file icon supplies Program Manager with all the file property information it needs to create the startup icon, including the path and name of the executable file that starts the program.

Document startup icons can be created in the same way. In the following exercise, you create a document icon for a Calendar file in the Program Manager Everyday Tools group. (If you didn't create this group in Chapter

8, substitute the Accessories group in the following steps.) First you need to create the Calendar file. Here's how:

1. In File Manager, locate CALENDAR.EXE in the Windows directory window and double-click its icon.

2. When the Calendar window opens, select File and choose the Save As option. Type **DAILY** in the File Name text box. Make sure the Windows directory is selected in the Directories list box.

3. Click the OK button. Calendar saves the file with the extension .CAL.

4. You don't need to add appointments now, so close the Calendar window.

Next you need to locate the new DAILY.CAL file in the Windows directory.

5. Click anywhere in the file list of the Windows directory, and type **D**. This places the highlight on or near the DAILY.CAL daily file.

Now you need to arrange the File Manager and Program Manager windows so they are both visible. In particular, the Everyday Tools group icon or window needs to show in the Program Manager.

6. Move the File Manager window to the right, but make sure you can see the icon for the DAILY.CAL file. You may need to resize the window.

7. Move the Program Manager window to the left, and arrange its group windows so you can see all or part of the Everyday Tools group.

8. In the File Manager, click the DAILY.CAL file icon and drag it to the Program Manager. As you drag the icon, notice that it turns into a No symbol (a slashed circle) when it's over areas where the icon can't be dropped.

9. When the icon is over the Everyday Tools group (or the Accessories group), release the mouse button.

9

A Calendar icon appears in the group window. To check its properties, you can click it and choose the Properties option on the Program Manager File menu. You can also double-click the icon to open Calendar and use the daily calendar file.

The Setup utility is probably the best way to install new program icons, but the drag-and-drop method described in the foregoing exercises is the best one to use when you need to create startup icons for document files. In contrast, the next section describes how you can use File Manager (instead of Program Manager) as the place to open all applications and documents in Windows.

Starting Applications from File Manager

The icon-oriented Program Manager provides an excellent means of starting your applications and organizing them into meaningful groups. However, with this method, only the programs and documents for which you have created icons are easily accessible. The File Manager, on the other hand, offers an alternative "launching platform" that provides wider access to the files on your system. For example, to start the Notepad editor from File Manager, you can double-click its file icon in the same way you double-click the Notepad icon in the Accessories group of the Program Manager. In addition, the document files are easily opened by double-clicking their icons in the File Manager file lists. To take advantage of this feature, you can list all your document files in a directory window, as described in the next section, "Establishing Launch Windows."

File Manager also provides ways to organize your programs and files for easy launching. First, files are already organized into directory groups, making them relatively easy to find. If you can't find a startup file or a document, you can use the Search command. Second, files you want to look at can be extracted from directory lists and sorted for easier viewing. For example, you might list all the executable (.EXE) files in a directory and hide all the rest.

Establishing Launch Windows

In this section, you see how to set up File Manager for use as a program launcher to replace Program Manager. The arrangement described here and pictured in Figure 9-5 is only a suggestion, based on the files in the Windows directory. Consider organizing your own system so executable files are in a special program directory, and document files are in one or more special data directories. Here are some suggestions:

- Create a "normal" directory window, containing a directory tree and contents list, that shows all files (*.*) in the selected directory. This will be your "working window"—you can use it to list the contents of other drives and directories when necessary.

- Make a directory window that lists all executable (.EXE) files in filename order.

- Use a directory window that lists documents sorted by their filename extensions to help you easily find files associated with accessory programs.

Figure 9-5. *File Manager directory windows organized for program launching*

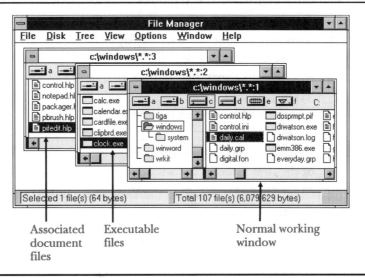

Associated document files   Executable files   Normal working window

The last two windows suggested in the previous list need not be split, since you won't be changing the directory within the windows. When you want to view another directory, you can always use the first "working window." Let's take a closer look at these three window arrangements.

The Working Window

If you're still in File Manager, you should already have a directory window open. Make sure it displays the directory tree and file list; if necessary, choose Tree and Directory from the View menu. You may want to resize the window so you'll be able to have other windows on the desktop as well. Alternatively, you can use the Cascade or Tile option on the Window menu to reorganize all the windows into the desktop arrangement that works best for you.

Creating the Executable Files Window

Here are the steps to create a new directory window exclusively for executable program files:

1. Choose New Window from the Window menu. (You can skip this step if you already have a second directory window open.)

2. Make the second window active (if necessary), and make sure the drive that holds the Windows directory is selected. Then click the Windows directory in the directory tree.

3. Remove the split bar and display only the file list (select View and choose Directory Only).

4. Now list only .EXE files in the window. Select View, choose Sort By Type, and type ***.*** in the Name text box. In the File Type box, unmark and turn off all options except Programs. Click OK or press (ENTER).

5. Choose Name on the View menu to display only the names and icons of the files listed in the window.

6. Choose Sort by Name on the View menu to sort the list in filename order.

You now have an organized list of executable program files. You can resize the window now, if necessary, but later you'll put all three of your new directory windows in the cascade arrangement.

Creating the Documents Window

Now create a window that lists only documents:

1. Select Window and choose New Window. A new window appears that looks like the window you just created.

2. To list documents only, choose Sort By Type from the View menu. Type ***.*** in the Name field. In the File Type box, mark the Documents option and unmark all the other options. Click OK or press (ENTER).

3. Choose Sort By Type from the View menu to organize the listed files by their filename extensions.

Organizing and Saving the Arrangement

Now you can organize the three windows in a cascade arrangement on the desktop. Since the working window has a directory tree and is used to view other directories, place it on top. Click it now to make it active, and then select Window and choose Cascade. You'll get an arrangement similar to Figure 9-5.

Now you can launch applications by double-clicking their icons in the executable files window, or you can open documents by double-clicking their icons in the document window.

To save this arrangement for the next File Manager session, make sure the Save Settings on Exit option is enabled on the Options menu. Then close the File Manager.

The File Manager Run Command

The Run command on the File menu opens a dialog box in which you can type the name of an executable program file you want to start. When the dialog box first opens, the name of the file currently selected in the contents list is displayed in the Command Line text box. After this entry you can specify additional parameters for a command before running it.

In this exercise, you add parameters to a command in the Run dialog box:

1. Click your new directory window that lists executable files in the Windows directory, and highlight the file NOTEPAD.EXE.

9

2. Select File and choose Run. NOTEPAD.EXE appears in the Command Line text box.

3. Type a space after the filename, and then type **TEST.TXT** after the space, as shown here:

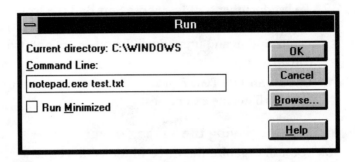

4. Click OK.

5. If the file exists, Notepad will load it into its workspace. If the file doesn't exist, you will see the following message box:

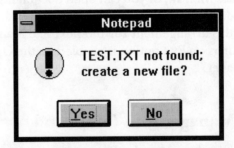

Click Yes to open a new file with the name TEST.TXT.

6. Close Notepad by double-clicking its Control button.

 Some DOS commands use special parameters. You can use the Run dialog box to enter these parameters when executing the commands.

Tip

Drag-and-Drop Procedures

The drag-and-drop method can be used to quickly open documents in File Manager. First start an application, and then open a directory window in File Manager that lists document files for the program. Click one of the document files and drag it to the running program's window or icon. The document then appears in that program's workspace. The following exercise demonstrates how Notepad files can be opened using drag-and-drop.

1. In the File Manager, activate the executable files window.
2. Double-click NOTEPAD.EXE to start the Notepad editor.
3. Minimize the Notepad window so it appears as an icon on the desktop, and make sure you can see the icon.
4. Activate the document directory window in the File Manager.
5. Locate the README.TXT file. Click the file icon, and drag its icon over the Notepad icon on the desktop. The README.TXT document immediately opens in Notepad's workspace.
6. Now click on another document and drag it to the Notepad window. The new document immediately opens in the workspace.

The advantage of this drag-and-drop method, compared to double-clicking the document icon, is speed. With Notepad already in memory, you can quickly load and view a document. Drag-and-drop is also useful when you are trying to identify files by viewing their contents.

You can drag and drop any document that is associated with an application. Remember, too, that you can print any associated document by dragging its icon over a running copy of the Print Manager, as discussed in "Printing from File Manager" earlier in this chapter.

9

10

Printing with Windows

Printing a document in any Windows application is a relatively simple task; typically you choose the Print option from the application's File menu. There may be some slight variation in the way the Print command is listed or used, but its basic operation is essentially the same from one application to the next. There are, however, some behind-the-scenes details about printing that you should know, and they are covered in this chapter.

To use your printer with Windows, you need to make sure Windows knows certain facts about that printer. Windows includes *printer driver files* for a wide variety of printers. These drivers provide Windows with information about printers, such as their graphics printing capabilities, how they handle paper, and which fonts they can use. Driver installation is normally done during Windows Setup, but you can use the Printers utility on the Control Panel at any time to change the way a printer is set up, to add a new printer, or to remove a printer.

This chapter assumes the driver for your printer or printers is already installed. If this is not the case, choose the Printers icon in the Control Panel and install your printer drivers. Return here when your printer installation is complete.

The Printing Process

When you need to change among two or more printers, specify different paper sizes, specify different printing orientations, and so forth, choose Print Setup on the File menu of the application you are working in. The Print Setup dialog box is pictured in Figure 10-1.

To print a document, use the Print command on the File menu of your applications. The Print Manager then appears as an icon on the desktop, as shown here, for the duration of the print job:

Print Manager

Another way to print is to drag document icons from the File Manager and drop them onto the Print Manager while Print Manager is running as a window or icon on the desktop.

Figure 10-1. *The Print Setup dialog box*

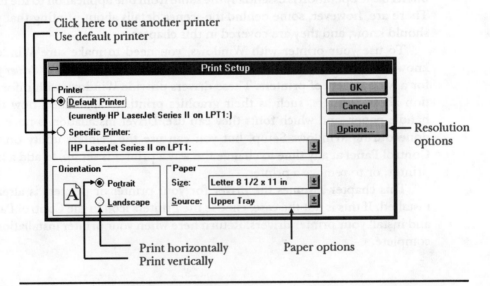

Print Manager sends your document to the printer in the background as you continue working on other tasks. Documents are held in the Print Manager queue until they can be printed. You can view documents in the queue, change their order, or remove them, as long as they haven't yet started to print.

You can disable Print Manager if you don't need it and it slows performance.

Note

A typical Print dialog box is pictured in Figure 10-2. It has options for specifying the range of pages to print and the number of copies to print. In some cases, you can specify the quality of the printout from low resolution for drafts to high resolution for final copies.

You learn about the Print command, Print Setup, and the Print Manager in the following sections. The exercises guide you through the steps of printing a document using Windows Write.

A Word About Fonts

The fonts that appear on character formatting menus of Windows applications are either TrueType fonts, fonts specific to your printer, third-party fonts, or screen fonts. In most cases, you'll want to print with the TrueType

Figure 10-2.   *A typical Print dialog box*

Print
Printer: Default Printer (HP LaserJet Series II)   **OK**
┌ Print Range ┐   **Cancel**
◉ A̲ll   **S̲etup...**
○ S̲election
○ P̲ages
From: 1   To: 1
Print Q̲uality: ▼   C̲opies: 1
☐ Print to Fi̲le   ☒ Collate Copies

10

fonts, which include Arial, Courier, Symbol, and Times New Roman. True-Type fonts are scaleable fonts; that is, you can change their size over a large range. They are also designed to print just as (or better than) they appear on the screen. The character size, character spacing, and line spacing you see on the screen closely match the appearance of the printed document.

Documents with TrueType fonts will have a consistent appearance when printed on any Windows-supported printer, except for differences introduced by the resolution of the printer itself. That means you can send documents to other users to print on their printers, knowing the printout will look similar to your own.

The non-TrueType fonts listed on character formatting menus are usually fonts built into the printer you've installed. For example, in the Font dialog box shown here,

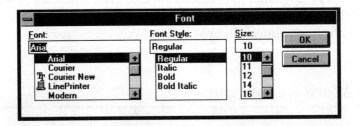

Arial and the Courier New font are TrueType fonts, as designated by the TT icons next to their font names. The other Courier font is a printer font.

When you install and select a PostScript printer, the Font dialog box displays font listings similar to these:

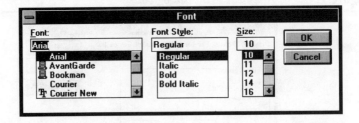

Notice that, in addition to TrueType fonts, PostScript fonts like AvanteGarde and Bookman are available.

Since all Windows-supported printers can print TrueType fonts, this chapter assumes you've activated TrueType fonts. If you haven't, follow these steps before you do the exercises in the chapter:

1. Double-click the Control Panel icon in the Program Manager Main group.
2. Double-click the Fonts icon.
3. When the Fonts dialog box opens, make sure the Use TrueType option is marked. If it isn't, click it and then click the Close button.

Printing a Document

In the next few exercises, you work through the steps of printing a document, but first you need a document to print. Follow these next steps to create a document called FONTTEST that contains a sampling of several different fonts. When you're done, you print this font test to use in the future when assigning fonts to text.

You work with the FONTTEST document again in Chapter 11, so be sure to create it and save it exactly as described.

Note

1. Start Write by double-clicking its icon in the Program Manager Accessories window.
2. When the Write window opens, choose Fonts from the Character menu.
3. When the Font dialog box opens, click Arial in the Font list box. You may need to scroll to the top of the list to see it.
4. Click 12 in the Size box.
5. Click the OK button or press (ENTER).
6. Type the following text in the Write workspace, and press (ENTER) at the end of the line:

   This is Arial 12 point regular

10

Repeat Steps 2 through 6 twice, first for TrueType Courier New and then again for TrueType New Times Roman. In Step 6, be sure to specify the correct name for the font you've selected.

Now add one of the fonts that's specific to your printer by following these steps:

1. From the Write menu bar, open the Font dialog box.

2. Choose a non-TrueType font, such as Roman. (Remember, non-TrueType fonts are not preceded by the TT icon.)

3. Choose a font size of 12, and click the OK button.

4. Type the following text on a new line:

   This is Roman 12 point regular, a non-TrueType font

5. Choose Save As from the File menu.

6. Type **FONTTEST** in the File Name field.

7. Click OK or press (ENTER).

When you are done, the Write window will look similar to this:

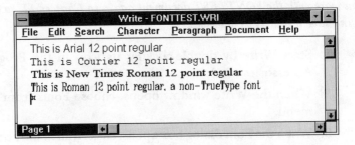

The Print Setup Dialog Box

Before printing a document, you may need to change the settings of a printer or switch to another printer. To do this, choose Print Setup on the File menu to open the Print Setup dialog box (Figure 10-1). Before you try

File menu to open the Print Setup dialog box (Figure 10-1). Before you try printing the FONTTEST document, work through the following sections to learn the features of the Print Setup dialog box.

Choosing a Printer

When you have more than one printer, follow these steps to choose the printer you want to use:

1. In the Printer area of the Print Setup dialog box, click the down-arrow button in the Specific Printer list box until you see the printer you want to use; then click the printer name.

2. You'll make other selections in this dialog box later, but for now click OK to accept the new printer and close the dialog box.

Figure 10-3 shows what the Print Setup dialog box looks like when several printers are available. In Figure 10-3, the HP LaserJet III PostScript printer is attached to LPT1, and the Epson printer is attached to LPT2. In addition, the HP LaserJet III attached to FILE is used to print non-PostScript documents to a disk file, as described in the next section.

Note

It is not uncommon to install multiple drivers for a single printer, as is the case in Figure 10-3. The HP LaserJet III PostScript and HP LaserJet III are the same printer; the first is used when the removable PostScript font cartridge is installed, and the second is used when the cartridge is removed.

Using Print Files   A *print file* contains all the information required to print a document at a later time, even when the application that created the document is not running. You can create a print file with a Windows application, and then send the file to a friend or coworker to print on their printer. To create the print file, you need not have the user's printer, and the user need not start the application that created the file.

To create print files, install the printer driver for the printer on which the document will be printed, and specify FILE as its connection port.

When you print a document to a printer attached to a file connection port, Windows asks for the name of the file where the print information

10

Figure 10-3.   *Several printers available in the Specific Printer list box*

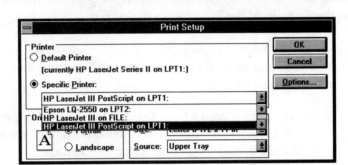

should be stored. Once the file is created, you can copy it to disk and send it to other users. There are three ways the user can print the print file:

- In the File Manager, drag and drop the icon for the print file to the running Print Manager.

- Select the Print command in the File Manager and specify the name of the print file in the text field.

- Use the COPY or PRINT command at the DOS prompt, as described in your DOS manual. For example, the following DOS COPY command prints a file called JANBUDG.DAT to the printer connected to the first parallel port (LPT1):

COPY JANBUDG.DAT LPT1

Setting Print Orientation

The choices shown in the Orientation area of the Print Setup dialog box (Figure 10-1) are for Portrait (vertical) or Landscape (horizontal) printing mode. Clicking one of these buttons changes the paper icon on the left representing the print orientation. Choose Landscape when you are printing wide spreadsheets and tables, or graphics that are wider than they are tall.

Choosing Paper Size and Source

In the Paper area of Print Setup, select the size and source of the paper to print on. Click the down-arrow button on the Size list box to view a list of paper sizes. Make sure you select the correct paper size so that pages will properly eject from the printer.

For Source, choose the paper tray where your printer will get paper, or the method it will use to advance paper as it prints. For a printer that has multiple trays, the list box will present different paper sizes or forms. For example, one tray might hold company stationary and another might contain regular or legal-size paper. When manual feed is selected from the list box, the printer waits for you to insert a sheet of paper or envelope in the manual feed slot.

Setting Other Options

Click the Options button on the Print Setup dialog box to display the Options dialog box. Not all options boxes will be the same. You can click the Help button for details. The following dialog box appears for most printers:

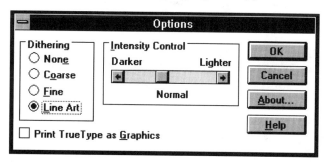

This dialog box is used to adjust the screen resolution when printing graphic images. The options are described in the paragraphs that follow.

After setting the options you want, click the OK button or press (ENTER) to return to the Print Setup dialog box, and click OK there also.

Dithering   The dithering options let you specify the fineness of detail in graphic images when color images are printed on black-and-white printers.

10

The Dithering box choice works in conjunction with the Intensity Control slide bar to control the conversion of colors to gray scale.

You can achieve the maximum number of dots per inch by selecting Fine or Line Art. The Fine and Line Art options work best on high-resolution printers like laser printers. The Line Art option converts some colors to patterns for special effects, so you'll need to experiment with the colors available in your applications when using this option.

Select Coarse to use larger dots, and None to print images with no gray shading at all.

Intensity Control   The Intensity Control slider bar allows you to darken or lighten the dot pattern when Coarse, Fine, or Line Art is selected in the Dithering box. You'll need to experiment to get the intensity that's right for your art. For example, in Paintbrush, yellow is the lightest color, but sliding the Intensity Control slider bar all the way to the Darker end causes yellow to print black. Sliding the bar toward Lighter makes colors that normally print black on black-and-white printers appear in various shades of gray. When Line Art is set, the nondithered colors on the left of the color bar in Paintbrush change intensity.

TrueType Fonts as Graphics   Mark the TrueType Fonts as Graphics option when you want to overlap graphic images onto text. When enabled, it prints TrueType fonts as bitmap graphics.

The Print Dialog Box

This section describes how to print your FONTTEST document once you have chosen your Print Setup settings. The steps listed here help you print the file, and the options on the Print dialog box are discussed in the paragraphs that follow.

1. On the Write File menu, choose Print to display the Print dialog box, shown in Figure 10-2.

The Print dialog box pictured in Figure 10-2 is specific to the Write application. Examples of other Print dialog boxes will be presented later in this section.

Note

2. Make sure All is selected in the Print Range box, to print the entire document.

3. Click the down-arrow button in the Print Quality list box, and then click the highest resolution listed.

4. Make sure the Print to File option is not marked, and that 1 is indicated in the Copies text box.

5. Click OK or press (ENTER) to print the document.

Watch for the Print Manager icon to appear on the desktop. The document is temporarily placed in a Print Manager queue and then sent to the printer. When the document is printed, examine the text to see how the fonts look when printed.

Now let's explore the options of the Print dialog box.

Specifying the Print Range

The Print Range box contains options for specifying how much of your document to print.

- *All*   Choose this to print the entire document.

- *Selection*   Choose this to print the currently selected text in the document. This option is not available unless you have selected some text.

- *Pages*   This lets you print a range of pages. When you choose this option, you can specify the range to print in the From and To boxes.

Choosing Print Quality and Resolution

You set the print quality based on the type of image being printed and how you want it printed. In most cases, you will want to print with the highest

10

quality available; however, if you need draft copies, want faster printing, or just want to save some ink or toner, pick a lower resolution.

In some cases, an image may shrink when you specify a high resolution, and it may be necessary to pick a lower print quality to print the image at a reasonable size. For example, if you create a graphic image at 75 dots per inch (dpi) and print it on a 300 dpi printer, the image may shrink to about a quarter of its original size. This is because the dot size on your screen is larger than the dot size on your printer. So while 75 dots may produce a 1-inch line on your screen, they print only a 1/4-inch line on your printer when printed at the smaller dot size.

Many applications print at the size you intended by scaling images up on high-resolution printers or down on low-resolution printers. However, in some painting and drawing applications (such as Paintbrush), you can set an option called Use Printer Resolution to print an image at the printer's resolution. Thus you can work with an "exploded" view of an image on the screen, and then print it in a smaller, higher-resolution format.

Setting Other Print Options

Here are descriptions of the other options in the Print dialog box:

- *Print to File*   As discussed previously, you can send a document, including its formats and printer codes, to a file for later printing or printing on other systems. This print file can be copied to disk and sent to another user for printing on his or her system.

- *Copies*   Here, you specify the number of copies to print.

- *Collate Copies*   Mark this option to print your document in reverse order on sheet printers that normally stack pages with the printed side up.

The Setup button in the Print dialog box opens the Print Setup dialog box so you can change the printer settings. Clicking this button is the same as choosing the Print Setup option on the File menu.

Note

Print Dialog Boxes in Other Applications

Print dialog boxes for other Windows applications have features related to those applications, or may have common features arranged in a different format. For example, here is the Paintbrush Print dialog box:

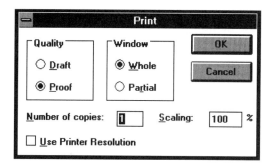

In this dialog box, choose Draft in the Quality box for faster printing, or choose Proof to print the highest quality. To print only part of a picture, choose Partial in the Window box, and then outline the part of the picture to print. The Scaling percentage text box lets you reduce or enlarge the image, and you can mark Use Printer Resolution to match the dot resolution of the image with the printer resolution, as discussed in "Choosing Print Quality and Resolution" earlier in this chapter.

The Control Panel Printer Settings

There are two options available on the Control Panel Printers dialog box of interest here. The first is used to turn Print Manager on or off. The second is used to establish a default printer.

Setting the Default Printer

If more than one printer is connected to your system, one printer can be designated the default printer. When applications are started, they will use the default printer unless another printer is selected in the application's Print Setup dialog box. Here's how to select a default printer:

1. Select the Printers icon on the Control Panel. The Printers dialog box appears, similar to that shown in Figure 10-4.

10

2. In the Installed Printers list box, click the printer you want to operate as the default printer.

3. Click the Set As Default Printer button.

4. Click OK to close the dialog box and accept the setting.

Bypassing Print Manager

The main purpose of Print Manager is to send printing information to your printers while you work on other tasks. However, when you are printing complex graphic images, it may be better to disable Print Manager to improve the printing speed. Print Manager also reduces system performance when in use, but the tradeoff is that you don't need to wait for your document to finish printing before starting other work. To disable Print Manager, follow these steps:

1. In the Control Panel, click the Printers icon to display the Printers dialog box (Figure 10-4).

2. In the lower-left corner of the dialog box, unmark the Use Print Manager check box to turn the feature off.

3. Click OK to close the dialog box and accept the setting.

Be sure to enable Print Manager after printing the graphics.

Note

Figure 10-4.   *The dialog box for the Control Panel Printers icon*

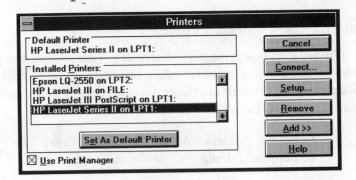

The Print Manager

Print Manager works as an intermediary between your Windows applications and your printer. It accepts print jobs from the applications, places them in a queue, and sends them to the printer in the proper order. You can start working on other tasks almost immediately after sending a document to the Print Manager. Non-Windows applications are not handled by the Print Manager, and instead are printed directly by the application, so there may be some delay before you can continue working.

With Print Manager, it's not necessary to schedule your long and complex print jobs after hours just so you can keep your computer available for important tasks during the work day. For example, if one of your clients calls and needs information, you can quickly access that information on your system even though Print Manager is printing your document. There's no need to stop the print job and finish it or reprint it later. Print Manager can be assigned various priority levels based on how much or little of your processor time you want allocated to printing.

Print Manager holds print jobs in a queue until they can be printed. If the printer is off line or out of service, Print Manager displays an appropriate message and holds the jobs until the printer is again available. If you attempt to exit Windows while print jobs are in a Print Manager queue, a warning message appears and asks if you want to discard the print jobs.

Working with Print Jobs and Queues

You can view the files in the Print Manager queue and change the order in which they will be printed. You can also remove files from the queue. The following exercise gives you a chance to see how Print Manager works:

1. Activate the Write window and make sure the FONTTEST document is open.

2. Take your printer off line or turn it off.

3. Choose Print from the File menu and choose OK to accept the default settings in the dialog box.

10

The Print Manager icon appears on the desktop, along with a message that the file is being printed. Because your printer is off line, the following message box appears:

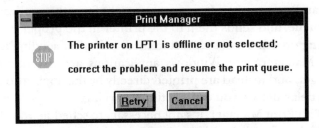

If this message were to appear during a normal printing operation, you would either turn the printer on, set it on line, load paper, or fix any other problem the printer might be having. Then you would choose the Retry button. For the purpose of this exercise, however, let's take a look at how files stack up in the print queue:

4. **Open the Print Manager by double-clicking its icon in the Program Manager, and leave your printer off line. The Print Manager window looks similar to Figure 10-5.**

Figure 10-5.   *The Print Manager with three available printers and a print job waiting in the queue of the first printer*

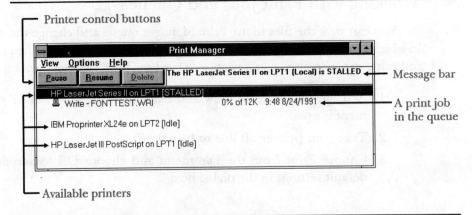

Notice in Figure 10-5 that the message bar says the printer on LPT1 is stalled. Three printers are listed in the work area, and the file waiting to be printed is listed in the queue under the first printer. Your Print Manager dialog box will look different, depending on the number of printers installed. Now send another print job to the Print Manager:

5. Click the Write window, select File, and choose Print.

6. Click OK to print the document. Once again, the Print Manager error message appears.

7. Click the Cancel button in the message box.

8. Repeat Steps 5 through 7 one more time to send yet another print job to the queue. The Print Manager window now looks like Figure 10-6.

9. Click the Print Manager again, and notice that the three print jobs are waiting in the queue to be printed. In the next section you rearrange these print jobs.

Figure 10-6.   *The Print Manager window with three print jobs waiting in the queue of the first printer*

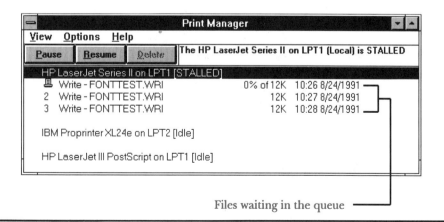

Files waiting in the queue

10

Rearranging Queued Print Jobs

You can rearrange print jobs in the queue. Suppose you want to print the third job before the second job. In this exercise, the queued files have the same name and contents, but you can tell the difference between them by looking at the date and time of each job. The printer icon in front of a print job name indicates that it is ready to print, and therefore can't be rearranged. Let's switch the order of the second and third jobs in the queue:

1. Point to the third print job in the queue, and click and hold the mouse button. The mouse pointer changes to an up-arrow icon.

2. Drag up to the second job, so that a dotted line surrounds it.

3. Release the mouse button to switch the jobs.

Since the filenames are the same, look at the time on the right end of the line for each job to confirm that they have switched positions in the queue.

Deleting Print Jobs from a Queue

Now do the following to delete the second and third print jobs:

1. Click the third print job. The Delete button at the top of the Print Manager window becomes available.

2. Click the Delete button.

3. When Print Manager asks if you want to terminate the print job, click OK.

4. Repeat these steps to delete the second print job.

Resume Printing on a Paused Printer

After correcting a printing problem, you must click the Resume button to resume printing. At present your Print Manager still lists LPT1 as stalled, because you have it set off line. Follow these steps to reset your printer and print the first document:

1. Click the name of the stalled printer. The Pause and Resume buttons become available.

2. Set your printer on line or turn it on.

3. Click the Resume button.

A message informs you that the file in the queue is being printed. Afterward, the printer will be listed as idle.

You've now practiced all the basic Print Manager operations. The next few sections describe some of its other features.

Print Manager Menu Options and Control Buttons

The Print Manager has two important menus. The first is the Options menu, which lets you change the priority and features of the Print Manager. The second is the View menu, which lets you turn the display of file information on or off, and lets you work with network queues.

View Menu Options

Some of the following View menu options may not be available if you are not connected to a network.

- *Time/Date Sent*   When this option is on, the Print Manager window display includes the time and date that the file was sent to the Print Manager queue.

- *Print File Size*   When this option is on, the Print Manager window display includes the file size.

- *Refresh*   When you're connected with a network printer, the Refresh option is used to get the latest list of files waiting in the queue of network printers.

- *Selected Net Queue*   Click this option to see a list of all files waiting in the queue of a network printer. This feature is useful if you're in a hurry to print a job and you need to find a network printer that doesn't have a lot of jobs to print.

- *Other Net Queue*   Click this to display a list of files on other network printer queues.

- *Exit*   This closes the Print Manager window.

The Options Menu

The following sections describe the Print Manager Options menu.

10

Low, Medium, and High Priority   The Low, Medium, and High priority settings let you control how much time Print Manager gives to print jobs in the background as you work with other applications. In any multitasking environment, every running application is given a portion of processor time. The portion you give Print Manager is determined by selecting low, medium, or high priority.

With *low priority,* print jobs are given less processor time as applications are given more processor time. Use low priority when you want to print while you continue to work in a foreground application. This option ensures that your application is given the full complement of processor time when it is working on a task; the print jobs continue printing when the application is not busy.

With *medium priority,* print jobs and applications are allocated processing time somewhat equally. Your application may slow down some when more information is sent to the printer. You might want to start printing with this option enabled, and then switch to low priority if your application is running too slowly or high priority if you need to quickly finish the print job.

In *high priority,* print jobs are given a larger processor share than applications. Choose this priority level for your print jobs when you are working in applications that don't require a lot of processor time—for instance, when typing unformatted text in an application like Notepad.

The print priority setting depends a lot on the type of application you're using. A database application that is sorting a mailing list requires almost 100 percent of your processor time, so printing may pause until the sorting task is complete, depending on the job priority and the application. On the other hand, when working with a word processor, your system will idle every time you stop typing. This idle time can be put to use for printing. If low priority is selected, the idle time is given to the Print Manager, and you won't see much of a slowdown when you resume typing. With high priority selected, you'll see interruptions as Print Manager occasionally sends more text to the printer.

Alert Always   When the Alert Always option is enabled, Print Manager messages are displayed immediately.

Flash If Inactive   Select the Flash If Inactive option if you want the Print Manager title bar or its icon on the desktop to flash when Print Manager needs to display a message. You then open or activate the Print Manager to view the message.

Ignore If Inactive   Turning the Ignore If Inactive option on prevents messages from being displayed if the Print Manager window is inactive or reduced to an icon.

Network   The Network option is available when your computer is connected to a network. It offers two settings. *Update Network Display* lets you turn off or on the status of the network queue. *Spool Net Jobs Direct* lets you send print jobs directly to the network printer and bypass Print Manager.

See your network administrator for more information about using the printers on your network.

Note

Print Manager Control Buttons

Here is a description of the buttons available in the Print Manager window that let you control the printer queue. Some were also discussed earlier in this chapter.

- *Pause*   Click a printer in the list, and then click the Pause button to prevent the printer from printing jobs in the queue. Print jobs can still be sent to the printer, but they won't be printed until you click the Resume button. Use this button if you need to change paper or otherwise adjust a printer.

- *Resume*   Click this button to resume printing on a paused printer, usually after changing paper or correcting printing problems.

- *Delete*   Click this button to delete print jobs from the queue. First select a print job, and then click the Delete button.

10

11

Writing with Windows Write

Windows Write is a word processing program with advanced page-layout and character-formatting features for creating and formatting documents. You can indent the paragraphs of a document in a number of ways, or change their alignment. You can apply fonts and font styles to selected characters. Write also has advanced search-and-replace commands. In addition, you can paste graphic images into Write documents from applications like Windows Paintbrush.

Start the Write application now by double-clicking its icon in the Accessories window of the Program Manager. This opens the Write window shown in Figure 11-1. Before you begin working through this chapter, you will probably want to resize the window, or maximize it to see as much text as possible.

Figure 11-1.   *Elements of the Write window*

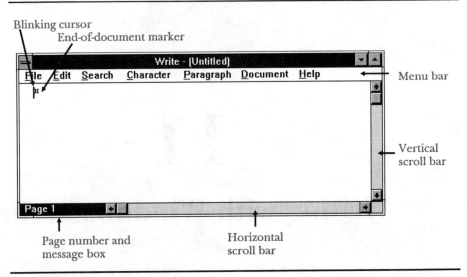

Overview of Write Features and Options

Let's start by taking a moment to look at the options in the Write menu bar. Click each option to look at its menu as you read through the following summary:

- *File*   Use the options on the File menu to start new documents, open existing documents, save documents, and print documents. The Repaginate option separates your document into pages and numbers them.

- *Edit*   These options help you cut and paste text anywhere in a document, among documents, or even between other Windows applications.

- *Search*   You can find specific text in your document, and then replace it if necessary, using options on the Search menu. The Go To Page command lets you jump to a particular page in the document.

- *Character* You assign fonts and styles to selected characters using options on this menu.
- *Paragraph* The options on this menu let you set the paragraph formatting for your document. Most of these options are also available as buttons on the Windows ruler. (You turn on the ruler in the next section.)
- *Document* Use the options on the Document menu to specify how text fits on the printed page, or to define headers, footers, tabs, and margins. The Ruler On option from this menu is discussed next.

The Ruler

After you start Write, display the Windows *ruler* by choosing Ruler On from the Document menu. This option is a toggle, so if the ruler is already on, the menu option will be Ruler Off, and you can leave it as is. When the ruler is on, the Write window looks like the one pictured in Figure 11-2. To

Figure 11-2. ***The Write window with its ruler turned on***

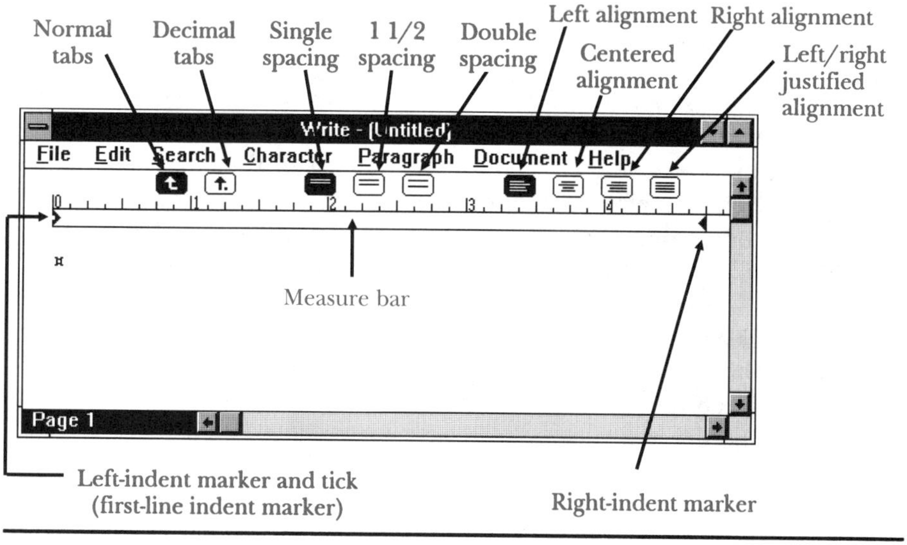
Normal tabs
Decimal tabs
Single spacing
1 1/2 spacing
Double spacing
Left alignment
Right alignment
Centered alignment
Left/right justified alignment
Write - (Untitled)
File Edit Search Character Paragraph Document Help
Page 1
Measure bar
Left-indent marker and tick (first-line indent marker)
Right-indent marker

apply paragraph formatting using the ruler, click a paragraph to select it, and then click one of the spacing or alignment buttons on the ruler.

Keep in mind that each paragraph is a separate entity in Write. To start a new paragraph, press the (ENTER) key. All text within a paragraph is *word-wrapped*, meaning that if a word is too long to fit on the end of the current line, it is automatically "wrapped" down to the start of the next line. Remember—only press (ENTER) when you want to start a new paragraph.

Note

When you click a paragraph, the settings for the paragraph are displayed in the ruler. Here's where you can see formatting elements like the position of indents and tab settings, which are not immediately apparent in the Write workspace as are things like line spacing and alignment.

The Measure Bar   The ruler's *measure bar* helps you to set the indents and position the tabs for paragraphs, and helps you to note the settings of paragraphs when you need to create other similar paragraphs. If you want, you can change the measure bar from inches to centimeters by following these steps. Keep in mind, however, that this chapter is written for a ruler with an inch scale.

1. Choose Page Layout from the Document menu.
2. Point to the cm button in the Measurements area and click.
3. Click OK to accept the change.

The Indent Markers   The measure bar includes a *left-indent marker* and a *right-indent marker*. Click and drag these triangular markers to the left or right along the measure bar to adjust the indents of the currently selected paragraph. There is also a *first-line indent marker,* or *tick*, which appears as a small white square that sometimes overlaps the left-indent marker. Click and drag this marker to change the first-line indent of a paragraph.

The Tab Buttons   The two tab buttons are for setting normal and decimal tabs. The normal tab lets you left-align text at a position on the ruler. The decimal tab is used to align a column of numbers on their decimal point, as shown here:

1.2
12.34
123.456
1234.5678

Decimal tabs are unique because the numbers move to the left as you type. As soon as you type the decimal point (period), any additional numbers you type are placed to the right of the decimal.

The Line Spacing Buttons   The line spacing buttons let you choose a single-spaced, line-and-a-half, or double-spaced format. To set line spacing, click the paragraph you want to format, and click the appropriate line spacing button. Paragraph spacing can also be selected from the Paragraph menu.

The Paragraph Alignment Buttons   The paragraph alignment buttons set the alignment and justification of the selected paragraph. You can align a paragraph flush left or flush right, center it, or justify it so it aligns on the left and right.

Understanding Basic Editing Techniques

Before you read about how to edit text in Write, notice that the blinking cursor and the mouse pointer in the workspace are different than they are in many applications. The blinking cursor serves as the insertion point for new text, and as a marker for other operations. You move it by pressing the arrow keys on the keyboard, or by clicking elsewhere in the document with the mouse.

In Write you'll need to know a few elementary editing techniques so you can correct typing mistakes, insert new text, delete existing text, and so forth. These techniques are described here, and are followed by paragraphs that teach you the basic editing operations.

- Point and click in the text to reposition the insertion point so text can be inserted or deleted.

- The (BACKSPACE) key removes the character to the left of the insertion point. Hold the key down to remove multiple characters.

- Press the (DEL) key to remove the character to the right of the insertion point. Hold the key down to remove multiple characters.

- You can also use (DEL) to remove a block of selected (highlighted) text. As described in "Selecting Text" later in this chapter, text is selected by clicking and dragging through it with the mouse, or using keyboard methods.

- To undo a command, choose Undo Editing from the Edit menu, or press (ALT)-(BACKSPACE). The Undo command reverses the most recent command or keyboard action.

Load a document now and try some of the editing keys. Choose Open from the File menu, type **README.TXT** in the File Name text box, and click the OK button or press (ENTER). Because the README.TXT file is not a Write document, the following dialog box appears:

Click the No Conversion button to load the text without converting it to Write format.

After README.TXT has been loaded, experiment with the editing techniques described previously. Point and click anywhere in the document with the mouse, and then press the (BACKSPACE) and (DEL) keys. Then go ahead and practice the techniques described in the following sections. Don't be concerned about the changes you make to the document, since you can simply close it when you're done, without saving the changes.

11

Navigating in the Document

The horizontal and vertical scroll bars at the bottom and right of the Write window provide one way for mouse users to scroll through documents, but the keyboard techniques listed next often provide a faster and easier way to navigate through documents as you edit and work with them.

Arrow Keys   Press the arrow keys to move the insertion point left or right one character, or up and down one line. Other arrow key methods are listed here:

- Hold down (CTRL) and press (LEFT ARROW) or (RIGHT ARROW) to move left or right one word.

- Hold down (CTRL) and press (UP ARROW) or (DOWN ARROW) to scroll through the text while the insertion point remains stationary.

Page Keys   The (PGUP) and (PGDN) keys move the insertion point up or down one window at a time. To move to the first or last line of the window, hold (CTRL) down while you press (PGUP) or (PGDN).

(HOME) *and* (END)   The (HOME) and (END) keys move the insertion point to the first or last character in the line, respectively. To move to the beginning or end of a document, hold (CTRL) down while you press (HOME) or (END).

Go To   The (5) key on the numeric keypad is the Go To key, and is active when the (NUM LOCK) key is toggled off. Use Go To in combination with the keys listed here, to jump to other parts of the document:

(RIGHT ARROW)	Jump to next sentence
(LEFT ARROW)	Jump to previous sentence
(DOWN ARROW)	Jump to next paragraph
(UP ARROW)	Jump to previous paragraph
(PGDN)	Jump to next page
(PGUP)	Jump to previous page

Take a few moments to practice with the Go To keys.

To print a list of keyboard keys you can post by your computer, choose Keyboard from the Help menu, then Print Topic from the Help File menu.

Tip

Selecting Text

Character formats such as **boldface** and *italic* can only be applied to selected (highlighted) text. Use any of the following methods to select a passage of text:

- With the mouse, click the first character of the text to be selected; then hold down the mouse button as you drag to the end of the selection.
- To select just one word with the mouse, double-click the word.
- The *selection bar* on the Write window provides yet another way for mouse users to select text. As shown here, the selection bar lies between the left window border and the left edge of the text:

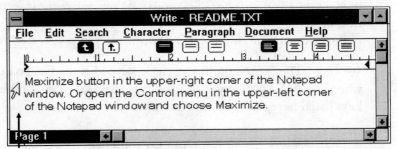

The selection bar

When you move the mouse pointer into the selection bar, the pointer changes to a large arrow pointing to the right. You can then select a line of text by clicking once, or a paragraph by clicking twice. To select the entire document, hold down (CTRL) and click the selection bar.

- From the keyboard, hold down the (SHIFT) key while pressing one of the arrow keys to extend a selection through the words in a passage

11

of text. You can also combine (SHIFT) with other keys to extend your selection. For example, hold down (SHIFT) while pressing (PGDN) to extend a selection one page at a time. Think of the first character as the anchor; as you hold down (SHIFT) and move away from the anchor point in any direction, you select the text between the anchor point and your new location.

Cut-and-Paste Techniques

The cut-and-paste techniques available via Windows's Clipboard have been covered thoroughly in Chapter 4, "Navigating the Windows Environment." Following is a short exercise to remind you of how easy it is to cut or copy text, and then paste it elsewhere in your document. This important feature saves you time and keystrokes.

1. Highlight any portion of the README.TXT file.
2. Choose Cut from the Edit menu, or press (SHIFT)-(X).
3. Move to another area in the text.
4. Choose Paste from the Edit menu, or press (SHIFT)-(V).

Using Prewritten Text

A handy way to use cut-and-paste in Write is when you're using templates that contain "boilerplate" paragraphs or other standard blocks of text that you use a lot. When you're ready to write a new document, open one of your template files and begin typing. The prewritten text blocks move downward in the document as you insert new text and paragraph markers. When you're ready to insert one of the prewritten blocks of text, jump to the part of the document that holds that text, copy it to the Clipboard, and then paste it where it's needed in the document. When the customized document is complete, you can delete any unused blocks of prewritten text at the end of the template, and save it as a document with a new name.

Note

If the document you're creating with the template is long, mark your current editing position before jumping to the end of the document to copy the standard text; then use the Find command to quickly return to the marked spot. A good mark to use is @@@. You'll find additional helpful information about templates throughout this chapter.

Cutting and Pasting from Other Write Documents

Write doesn't let you open multiple document windows, but if you need to cut and paste information from one Write document to another, you can start another copy of Write in another window at any time, and open a document there. To do this, switch to the Program Manager by pressing (ALT)-(TAB) until the Program Manager is highlighted, and double-click the Write icon. When the second Write window opens, choose Open on the File menu there to open a new document. Highlight the text you want to copy, and use Edit menu commands to cut or copy it to the Clipboard. Switch to your other Write document, reposition the insertion point, and paste in the text from the Clipboard.

Designing Documents

Though it's certainly acceptable to begin typing your document as soon as you start Write, you might want to give some thought to planning what your document will look like first. Consider the following when designing your documents; these elements are also the elements of formatting in Write.

- *Document Layout* includes the settings that define how text falls within the boundaries of a page. It includes margins, tab stops, and repeating elements such as headers, footers, and page numbers.

- *Paragraph Elements* fall within the boundaries set by the margins of a document.

- *Character Formats* include the font, style, and size you choose for the text of your document to add emphasis or to make it more readable.

A Word About Templates

Write uses the same margin, tab, paragraph, and character settings every time it starts. You can change these settings by accessing options on the Document, Paragraph, and Character menus, or by changing the settings on the ruler. When you find yourself changing these settings often, and in the same way, you may find it easier to create a special document file that contains only these settings, and save it for future use. Such a document is called a *template*; you can keep a collection of templates ready for use, and they can hold standard or frequently used text (such as your company logo and address), as well as format settings.

When you're ready to start a new document, open the template file. Add to and change the template to create the document, then save it under a different filename so your template is preserved for use with future documents. To further protect template files from being changed or erased, you can set their Read Only attribute in the File Manager, using the Properties command (as discussed at the end of this chapter and in Chapter 9). For now, think about the types of template files you'll need as you learn more about Write's features.

Laying Out Your Document

In this section, you see how to manage the settings and elements of document layout in Write. Before starting, choose the New option on the File menu. This closes the README.TXT file (and any other files) you opened in the previous exercise, and creates a new blank workspace.

Changing Printer Settings

In most cases, the default printer settings on the Printer Setup dialog box are sufficient. The default orientation is portrait (vertical), and the paper selection is letter-size (8.5 by 11 inches). When you do need to change these settings, here's how:

1. Choose Printer Setup from the File menu.

2. Select a printer from the Printer list box if you have more than one printer driver installed.

3. In the Paper Size list box, click the down-arrow button and choose the desired paper size.

4. In the Paper Source box, choose a paper source if your printer has more than one tray or you intend to manually feed the paper.

5. Click OK or press (ENTER) when all the settings are correct.

Setting Margins and the First Page Number

To set document margins, choose Page Layout from the Document menu. You'll see the Page Layout dialog box:

```
┌─────────────────────────────────────────────────┐
│ ─│          Page Layout                          │
├─────────────────────────────────────────────────┤
│                                                   │
│  Start Page Numbers At:  │1│        ┌─────────┐   │
│                                     │   OK    │   │
│                                     └─────────┘   │
│                                     ┌─────────┐   │
│  Margins:                           │ Cancel  │   │
│                                     └─────────┘   │
│   Left:  │1.25"  │     Right:  │1.25"  │           │
│                                                   │
│   Top:   │1"     │     Bottom: │1"     │           │
│                                                   │
│  Measurements:                                    │
│    ◉ inch    ○ cm                                 │
└─────────────────────────────────────────────────┘
```

In addition to setting the left, right, top, and bottom margins, you can also use this dialog box to specify the starting page number for your document. The default is 1, but you may need to specify another number if the document is a continuation of another document, such as a chapter in a book. If the first chapter ended on page 24, you'd type 25 in the Start Page Numbers At text box.

Try the following exercise for setting the page layout options:

1. In the Page Layout dialog box, type a starting page number in the Start Page Numbers At text box (or keep the default of 1).

2. Click the Measurements button for inches or centimeters, depending on the unit of measure you want displayed in the ruler. This setting affects how your values are entered in the Margins text boxes in Step 3.

3. In the four Margins text boxes, type the margin measurement for the left, right, top, and bottom sides of the document. (Press (TAB) to jump from text box to text box.) The values in these boxes are entered in inches or centimeters, depending on the setting you made in Step 2.

4. Click OK or press (ENTER) to accept the settings.

Setting Tab Stops

The tab stops on the ruler determine the movement of the insertion point each time you press the (TAB) key. In Write, default tab stops are set every half-inch, so if you can work within these settings, you'll never need to set custom tabs. Keep the following in mind regarding tab stops:

- Tab stops apply to the whole document. When you change tab settings, all paragraphs that contain tabs are changed. You will usually want to check back through your document and see how it has been affected.

- As soon as you set a custom tab stop, all the default tab stops to its left are removed. Default tabs to the right of the custom tab are retained, until they are affected by other custom tab stops.

- To align columns of numbers on their decimal point, set a decimal tab.

There are two ways to set tab stops. You can either click the tab buttons on the ruler and then click the position on the ruler for the tab stop, or choose the Tabs option from the Document menu and use numeric settings in the dialog box. The following exercises help you get familiar with setting tab stops using various techniques.

Tab Stops on the Ruler

Set a tab stop on the ruler by following these steps. You'll set a normal tab at the 0.75" mark on the ruler.

1. Click the normal tab button on the ruler. (This is the tab button on the left—the one without a decimal point.)

2. Point at the 0.75" position in the ruler, as shown here, and click the mouse:

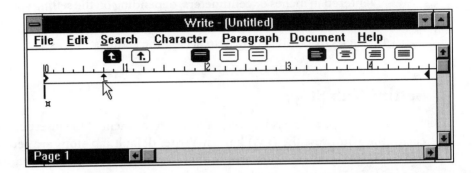

3. Press the (TAB) key on the keyboard several times, and notice that default tabs are still set every half-inch to the right of the custom tab stop you just created.

Now adjust the first tab, add a second tab, and type some text to see how it is affected by the tabs.

4. Point at the tab you set at 0.75" on the ruler; click and drag it to the 1.5" position on the ruler.

5. Add a new tab by pointing and clicking at the 3.5" position on the ruler.

6. Start a new line in the document by pressing (ENTER), and then type the following text at the insertion point. When you see (TAB) in the text, press the (TAB) key.

The first tab is (TAB)here. The second tab is (TAB)here.

Notice that the text jumps predictably to the tab stops you set. Now try positioning the tab stops differently, and see how text can be incorrectly positioned when tabs aren't set right:

7. Drag the first tab marker to the half-inch position on the ruler. Release the mouse, and watch the text immediately reposition itself at the second tab stop, because the tab in the text is now beyond the first tab stop.

8. Reposition the first tab stop to the 2" position on the ruler. Now the first tab point in the text is aligned, but the second one is off, because its text goes beyond the second tab stop.

9. Click and drag the second tab stop to the 4" mark.

The foregoing exercises demonstrate how tabs may need to be adjusted as you create tables in which text lines are longer than you expected. Dragging one tab stop out further on the ruler may correctly adjust the first tab point, but you may then need to adjust other tabs as well.

Create a table of numbers aligned on the decimal point by following these steps:

1. Click the decimal tab button on the ruler; then point at the 1" mark in the ruler and click.

A decimal tab appears on the ruler, but notice that the text is now out of adjustment because it is aligning with the new decimal tab.

2. Click in front of the first occurrence of the word "here," and press (TAB) to adjust the text. Remember that tab stops affect the entire document, so you may need to insert extra tabs in this way to account for the tab settings you've set for other parts of your document.

3. Press (END) to jump to the end of the line, and then press (ENTER) to start a new line.

4. Press (TAB) to jump to the decimal tab, and type **99.99**.

5. Press (ENTER) to start another line. Press (TAB), and type **9999.9595**. Notice how the numbers align on the decimal.

Finally, practice removing a tab stop, as follows:

1. Point to any tab marker on the ruler.

2. Click and drag the marker off to the right or left until it disappears.

Tab Stops in the Tabs Dialog Box

The Tabs option on the Document menu displays the Tabs dialog box (Figure 11-3). Choose this option now, and note that the positions of the tab stops you set in the foregoing exercises are displayed in the box. Use this dialog box for setting tabs when you need to closely control tab positions using numeric values. In the Positions boxes, type the exact ruler position for each tab, and then click the Decimal box if the tab is to be a decimal tab. You can set up to 12 tab stops in this way. Press OK after you've made the settings.

Clearing All Tabs

To clear all custom tabs, click the Clear All button at the bottom of the Tabs dialog box, and then click the OK button. This clears tab stops set with the ruler buttons, as well as from the Tabs dialog box.

Defining Paragraph Formats

A paragraph is a string of text that ends when you press the (ENTER) key. Creating a new paragraph in this way results in a paragraph that has the same formats (indents, spacing, and alignment) as the previous paragraph. To change the format of any paragraph at any time, you can click it and choose

Figure 11-3.   *The Tabs dialog box*

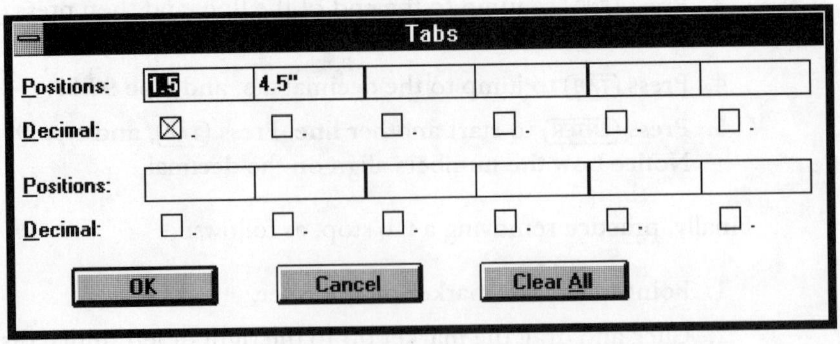

11

new paragraph format options. This section describes paragraph formats and how to apply them. You see how to create bulleted and numbered lists, as well as left- and right-indented paragraphs.

In the following sections, you apply several different formats using the ruler and the Paragraph menu. Do the following to prepare for the exercises:

1. Choose New from the File menu. When Write asks if you want to save changes to the current document, click the No button.

2. Choose Ruler On from the Document menu so that the ruler is visible.

3. From the Character menu, choose Fonts. When the dialog box opens, select Arial in the Font list box and 12 in the Sizes box. Then click the OK button or press (ENTER).

4. Type the following passage from *The Purple Cow* by Gelett Burgess:

    I never saw a Purple Cow, I never hope to see one; but I can tell you, anyhow, I'd rather see than be one.

    and press (ENTER) at the end of the line.

5. Duplicate the poem lines several times. First drag through it with the mouse, and then choose Copy from the Edit menu (or press (CTRL)-(C)).

6. Press the (DOWN ARROW) key to move to a blank line, and press (SHIFT)-(V) several times to paste in several copies of the text.

This creates several new paragraphs that you can use for applying formatting in the following exercises.

Indenting Paragraphs

Figure 11-4 illustrates three different paragraph formats and shows you how the ruler looks for each. The right indents for all three paragraphs were set at the 4" position on the ruler. The left indents for each paragraph were then set using one of the techniques described in the following sections. The

Figure 11-4.   *Three styles of indented paragraphs*

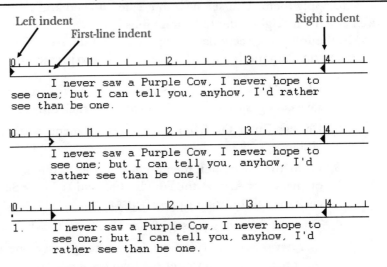

top example in Figure 11-4 is a regular *first-line indent*, and the bottom example is a *first-line outdent*, commonly called a *hanging indent*.

All indents are measured from the margins, not from the edge of the paper.

Note

Applying First-Line Indents

In this exercise, you drag the first-line indent tick mark to the half-inch position on the ruler and create a paragraph like the top example in Figure 11-4.

1. Click the first Purple Cow paragraph.

2. Point to the first-line indent tick mark on the measure bar, click and drag it to the 0.5" position, and release the mouse.

3. Check the indent measurements (this is an optional step when indenting paragraphs). Choose Indents from the Paragraph menu.

The First Line text box should show 0.5", and the other indents should be 0. Click Cancel or press (ESC) to close this dialog box.

Applying Left and Right Indents

In this exercise, you drag the left-indent marker to the right and the right-indent marker to the left, to create a paragraph like the middle example in Figure 11-4. Notice in that example that the first-line indent tick overlaps the left-indent marker when they occupy the same position on the ruler. You must drag the tick out of the way before you can adjust the left-indent marker, and then readjust the tick.

In the following exercise, you move both the tick and the left-indent marker to the same position on the ruler, so that the entire paragraph, including the first line, is indented one inch.

1. Click the second Purple Cow paragraph.
2. Click and drag the first-line tick to the 1" position on the ruler.
3. Click and drag the left-indent marker to the 1" position on the ruler.
4. Click and drag the right-indent marker to the 4" position on the ruler.

Your paragraph will look similar to the middle example in Figure 11-4.

Indenting all lines of a paragraph is a good way to format a quotation, or to emphasize a special paragraph.

Tip

Creating Hanging Indents

In this exercise, you create a paragraph with a hanging indent in which the first line is positioned to the left of the left indent, as shown in the bottom example of Figure 11-4.

1. Click the third Purple Cow paragraph.
2. Click and drag the first-line tick to the 0.5" position on the ruler.

3. Click and drag the left-indent marker to the 1" position.

4. Click and drag the right indent to the 4" position.

5. Choose Indents from the Paragraph menu, and check the indent measurements for this paragraph. Notice that the value in the First Line box is a negative number because the text is positioned to the left of the left indent.

Creating Numbered Lists

Hanging indents are used to create a numbered or bulleted list. To see how this works, make sure you have done the previous exercise, and then follow the steps here:

1. Click at the beginning of the paragraph to which you have just assigned a hanging indent.

2. At the start of the paragraph, type **1.**, and press the (TAB) key.

3. Click at the end of the paragraph and press (ENTER). This creates a new paragraph with the same formats.

4. At the start of the new paragraph, type **2.**, and press the (ENTER) key. Repeat this, typing numbers that increase by one each time, to create as many numbered paragraphs as you want.

Note

If the number at the beginning of a numbered paragraph is too far to the left, move the left indent to the left, or the first-line tick to the right. If you move the left-indent marker to a position without a tab stop, insert one at the new indent position so you can tab to it.

Creating Bulleted Lists

Bulleted lists are created in the same way as numbered lists, except you create bullet characters at the start of the paragraph rather than numbers. The bullet is not a key on the keyboard and must be created as a special character. The following exercise shows you how to do this using the (ALT) key.

1. Create a paragraph with a hanging indent, as described earlier in this chapter in "Creating Hanging Indents."

2. Place the insertion point at the beginning of the paragraph, at the position of the hanging indent.

3. Press the (NUM LOCK) key to toggle on the numbers on the numeric keypad. Hold down the (ALT) key, and type **0183** on the numeric keypad. When you release the (ALT) key, a bullet appears at the insertion point. Press (TAB) to create a space after the bullet.

4. Notice that the bullet character is rather small. Highlight the character by dragging over it with the mouse.

5. Choose Fonts from the Character menu. Click the Symbol font in the Fonts list box, and press (ENTER). The bullet becomes larger.

Tip

Because bulleted lists take a bit more time to create than other kinds of paragraphs, create a bulleted paragraph with no text in one of your template files so you can copy it when you need it.

Tip

You can create other special characters that don't appear on the keyboard by holding down the (ALT) key and typing the code for the character on the numeric keypad. You can use the Character Map accessory discussed in Chapter 14, "Using the Windows Accessories," to view and insert special characters.

Changing Line Spacing in a Paragraph

You can alter line spacing in a paragraph from the standard single-spacing to line-and-a-half or double-spacing. Simply click the appropriate line-spacing button in the ruler, or choose one of the spacing options on the Paragraph menu. Click the second Purple Cow paragraph (the one with a left indent at 1" and a right indent at 4"). Then click each of the line-spacing buttons in the ruler and notice how they affect the spacing of the paragraph.

Changing Paragraph Alignment

The paragraph alignment buttons in the ruler let you change the way a paragraph is aligned within the margins. This element of a paragraph's format can also be controlled with options on the Paragraph menu. Try this:

1. Click in the second paragraph.

2. Click the center-align button in the ruler, and the paragraph is centered. (You can also do this by selecting Centered on the Paragraph menu.)

3. Click the right-align and left-align buttons to see how they affect the paragraph.

Left/Right Justified Paragraphs

In paragraphs that are formatted with the left/right justified button (or the Justified option on the Paragraph menu), Write justifies the lines of the paragraph by adding extra space between words so that the rightmost character is aligned at the right indent. However, if a justified line contains a long word that gets wrapped to the next line, Write inserts excessive space between the words of the line. Thus the paragraph may contain unacceptably large gaps when printed. You can alleviate this problem somewhat by hyphenating words that fall at the end of a line; this technique is explained in "Inserting Optional Hyphens" later in this chapter.

Character Formatting

To apply character formats, first select the text to be formatted. You can click and drag through the text with the mouse, or use the (SHIFT)-key combinations described in "Selecting Text" earlier in this chapter. Once text is selected, you can choose a formatting option from the Character menu, or choose Fonts on the Character menu to open the Fonts dialog box, which provides a more complete set of character formatting options.

Here are a few points to remember about character formatting:

- The three most recent fonts you've selected from the Fonts dialog box appear on the Character menu in numbered order.

- The current font can be reduced or enlarged by choosing the Reduce Font or Enlarge Font option on the Character menu. This is useful for changing font sizes quickly as you're typing text.

11

- The following quick-keys are available for assigning character formatting as you type:

CTRL-B	Bold
CTRL-I	Italic
CTRL-U	Underline
F5	Removes special formats

Create a Font Test Sheet

In the following example, you expand on the typestyle test sheet called FONTTEST that you started in Chapter 10, "Printing with Windows." If you didn't create that document, refer now to "Printing a Document" in Chapter 10 for instructions on creating it. Then return to the following exercise.

1. Select File and choose Open. When asked if you want to save the current document, click the No button.

2. In the Open dialog box, double-click FONTTEST in the file list.

3. Click at the end of the first line, which is the Arial font, and press ENTER to start a new line.

4. Select Character and choose Fonts. In the Sizes list box, click 14, and then click the OK button.

5. On the new line of the FONTTEST document, type the following:

This is Arial 14 point

To add several other font sizes to the font test sheet, repeat the above procedure, with the following changes: In Step 4, choose Enlarge Font from the Character menu. Then in Step 5, substitute another point size. When you're done, your font test sheet will look like the one in Figure 11-5.

The Enlarge Font option on the Character menu increases font size in larger increments than those displayed in the Sizes list of the Fonts dialog box, so you may prefer to set sizes using the Fonts dialog box because it gives you more options.

Note

Figure 11-5.   *Creating text in different sizes for the font test sheet*

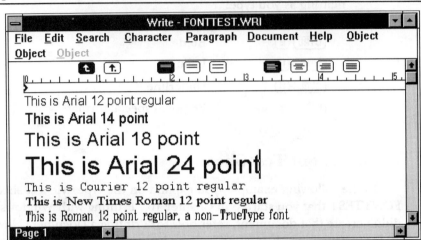

Now let's make a copy of the Arial fonts and apply the italic style to them. This exercise uses the copy-and-paste technique to make building the font test sheet relatively easy. Follow these steps:

1. Highlight all the Arial fonts in the FONTTEST document by clicking in the selection bar and dragging through them.

2. Select Edit and choose Copy, or press (CTRL)-(C).

3. Point to the end of the line for the last Arial font; then click and press (ENTER) to create a new line.

4. Choose Paste from the Edit menu, or press (SHIFT)-(V), to paste in another set of the same Arial fonts.

5. Again choose Paste or press (SHIFT)-(V) to copy yet another set of fonts.

6. Highlight the second set of Arial fonts (the first pasted copy) by dragging through it with the mouse.

7. Open the Character menu and choose Italic.

8. Highlight the third set of Arial fonts, and choose Bold from the Character menu.

You can see how this exercise builds a set of sample fonts using the copy-and-paste techniques and the character formatting commands on the Character menu. For additional practice, insert one more set of Arial fonts and apply bold and italic formatting together. Finally, print the font test sheet and use it as a guide when printing in the future.

Working with Page Breaks

Page breaks in a document cause the printer to eject a page and start printing on a new one. When you print a document, Write automatically repaginates the document and inserts page breaks based on the paper size and margin settings you've established. It also assigns page numbers for any headers and footers you've created.

The Repaginate command on the File menu is used to repaginate the document at any time before printing. Use this command when you want to ensure that pages don't break in awkward places, such as immediately following a section title or in the middle of a table. One way to prevent this is to insert manual page breaks, as discussed next.

Once a document has been paginated, you can jump to specific pages with the Go To Page option on the Search menu.

Note

Creating Manual Page Breaks

Insert manual page breaks while creating a document to start a new section and prevent a table or block of text from being divided over two pages. Page breaks can also be adjusted during a Repagination command to avoid awkward page breaks.

To insert a manual page break, press (CTRL)-(ENTER). When you do so, a dotted line appears across the page to indicate a page break. To delete a manual page break, highlight it by clicking to its left in the selection bar, and then press the (DEL) key.

If you insert manual page breaks after a document has been paginated, this alters all the page breaks (except manual page breaks) that follow your added page breaks. Therefore, you'll need to repaginate your document to reestablish page breaks and page numbers.

Caution

Paginating Documents

When a document is paginated, Write inserts page breaks depending on the paper size and margin settings. Any manual page breaks you've inserted are also taken into consideration. Use the Repaginate command to view and adjust page breaks before actually printing your document.

To paginate a document, choose the Repaginate option on the File menu. You'll see this dialog box:

If you mark the Confirm Page Breaks box and then click OK, Write will show you where it plans to break pages and lets you confirm or move the suggested page breaks. You'll next see this dialog box for the first page break:

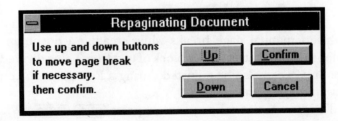

To move the page break up, click the Up button; to move the page break down, click the Down button. After moving a page break up or down, or to keep the suggested page break, click the Confirm button. Write then shows you its next suggested page break so that you can confirm or move it.

Note that, in most cases, page breaks can't be moved down, because Write usually recommends the lowest possible break for a page. Manual page breaks can sometimes be adjusted down, however.

Jumping to Specific Pages

To jump to any page in a paginated document, choose the Go To Page option on the Search menu, or press (F4). When the Go To Page dialog box appears, type the number of the page you want to go to, and click the OK button or press (ENTER).

Keep in mind that documents must be paginated before you can use this option. In addition, if you insert new text or add manual page breaks to existing text, you'll need to repaginate to update the page numbers.

Finding and Replacing Text

The Find option on the Search menu lets you locate a specific word or passage of text. To repeat a search, choose Repeat Last Find from the Search menu; the text of the previous search is used for the new search. To find text and replace it with something else, use the Replace option on the Search menu.

To try the Find and Replace commands, work through the following exercises, using the FONTTEST document.

1. Make sure FONTTEST is still open in the Write workspace. Press (CTRL)-(HOME) to jump to the beginning of the document.

2. Choose the Find option on the Search menu to display the following dialog box:

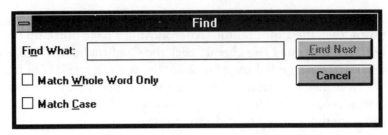

3. In the Find What text box, type **Arial**, and then click the Find Next command button.

Write looks for and highlights the first instance of Arial. The Find dialog box stays open, but becomes inactive so you can work with your document. Click (F3) or the Find dialog box to search for the next occurrence of Arial. Note that the text you entered for the previous search is retained in the dialog box. If you closed the dialog box (by double-clicking its Control button), choose Repeat Last Find from the Search menu to find the next occurrence of the text.

In the Find dialog box, you can mark the following options to customize the Find operation:

- *Match Whole Word Only* causes Find to search for text that is not part of other text. For example, when this option is enabled, a search for "her" would not find "there."

- *Match Case* locates text that matches your uppercase and lowercase specifications. For example, when this option is enabled, a search for "Windows" would not find "windows."

Now return to the Search menu and choose the Replace option. You'll see this dialog box:

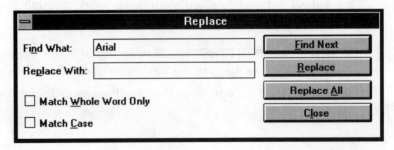

Notice that the text from your last search is in the Find What text box. In this box, too, choose the Whole Word and Match Case options to refine your search.

To practice with the Replace option, try the following exercise with the FONTTEST document:

1. Choose Replace on the Search menu and type **Courier** in the Find What text box of the Replace dialog box.

2. In the Replace With text box, type **COURIER,** in all capital letters.

3. Click the Find Next button, and the first instance of Courier will be highlighted.

At this point, you can click any of the following buttons in the Replace box:

- *Find Next* searches for the next occurrence without changing the currently highlighted text.

- *Replace* replaces the current instance of found text with your Replace With entry. You can then click Find Next to continue searching, or leave the Replace dialog box open (inactive) and continue editing in your document.

- *Replace All* changes all occurrences of the Find What entry. *Be careful with this button.* It's best to first use the Find Next and Replace buttons a few times to make sure you have specified the correct text for the find and the exact replacement you want to use. Once you're sure the Replace settings are correct, you can click the Replace All button to finish replacing through the rest of the document.

- Double-clicking the *Control* button lets you remove the Replace dialog box from the desktop when you don't need it anymore.

Search Variables and Wildcards

The Find and Replace options on the Search menu have a number of variables and wildcards you can use to search for unknown characters, paragraph markers, tabs, spaces, and page breaks. These variables, listed in the following table, are handy tools when you need to search and edit a document after it is written.

Variable	Purpose
?	Used in a search string as a placeholder for unknown characters. For example, use m?n to find all occurrences of man and men.
^w	Represents a space in a find or replace operation.
^t	Represents a tab in a find or replace operation.
^p	Represents a paragraph marker in a find or replace operation.
^d	Represents a manual page break in a find or replace operation.

Next are some examples of find and replace operations using these variables. Suppose you want to insert a blank line between every paragraph in your document. You can replace the single paragraph marker at the end of each paragraph with two paragraph markers as follows:

1. Choose Replace from the Search menu.

2. Type ^p in the Find What text box, to search for paragraph markers.

3. Type ^p^p in the Replace With text box, to replace each occurrence of a single paragraph marker with two paragraph markers.

4. Click the Replace (or Replace All) button to execute the search-and-replace operation.

Here's another example: A common mistake new Write users make is to align text in tables by inserting spaces. When the table is printed, the columns may not align as expected. The trick to aligning tables is to use tabs instead of spaces. Suppose you have a table in which you inserted three spaces to align each column, and you want to redo the table using tabs. The following steps demonstrate how this is done:

1. Highlight the whole table by dragging through it with the mouse. This limits the search to the table.

2. Choose Replace from the Search menu.

3. In the Find What text box, type ^w^w^w to search for every occurrence of three spaces.

4. In the Replace With text box, type ^t to replace the spaces with a single tab.

5. Click the Replace All button to execute the replacement operation all at once.

The table aligns to the default tab settings, or any tabs you may have set yourself. To set custom tabs for the table, click the normal tab button, and then click in the ruler. To adjust the table, drag the tab markers left or right in the ruler until the columns align in the way you want.

Inserting Optional Hyphens

As mentioned earlier in the chapter, you can use hyphens to divide words that won't fit at the end of a line, so they won't be wrapped to the next line. When text is justified, hyphens become critical to the look and readability of your document; they let you have some control over the excess spacing Write inserts between words during the justification process.

An optional hyphen is used to specify where a word should break if it falls at the end of a line. To insert an optional hyphen in a word, press (CTRL)-(SHIFT)-(HYPHEN). The hyphen only appears when the word falls at the end of a line. Optional hyphens can be added to exceptionally long words as you type documents, or you can add them to long words that fall at the end of a line after paginating. Note that you may need to paginate again to "tighten" the text in your document after going through this process.

Working with Pictures in Write

You can copy graphic images created in Windows Paintbrush or in other Windows applications to your Write documents, using the Windows Clipboard. Pictures pasted into Write documents are inserted at the position of the insertion point. You can then resize and move the picture using options on the Edit menu.

Windows's Object Linking and Embedding (OLE) feature provides advanced techniques for placing embedded images into Write documents that maintain a link to the application used to create the object. To edit an embedded object, just double-click it. The application opens with the object in its workspace. If you need this capability, refer to Chapter 16, "Creating Compound Documents."

Before starting the next exercises, choose New from the File menu. Write asks if you want to save the current file. Click the Yes button to save the changes you made to the FONTTEST document.

Pasting a Picture

Begin by capturing a picture in Paintbrush and pasting it into a Write document:

1. Switch to the Program Manager window and start Paintbrush.

2. When the Paintbrush window opens, choose Open from its File menu.

3. Make sure the Windows directory is listed in the Directories box and select BITMAP in the List Files of Type list box. Then choose LEAVES.BMP in the File Name list box and click the OK button.

4. Click the scissors icon in the upper-right of the tool box, as shown here:

5. Move the pointer into the picture, and click and drag to surround some of the leaves with a dotted line.

6. Select Edit and choose Copy to place the image in the Clipboard.

7. Activate the Write window.

11

Figure 11-6. *Pasting a Paintbrush image into a Write document*

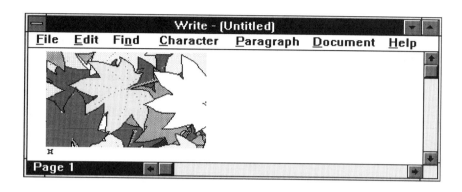

8. Choose Paste from the Edit menu. The Write window now looks similar to Figure 11-6.

In the next exercise, you resize the image.

Sizing a Picture

To resize a picture, first click it; then choose Size Picture from the Write Edit menu. The pointer changes to a square cursor (the handle) that appears on the lower sides or lower-right corner of the picture. Click and drag the handle to resize the image. While sizing, a shadow frame shrinks and grows to indicate the new size for the picture. Try this:

1. Click the picture with the mouse. The picture's colors change to indicate it is selected.

2. Choose Size Picture from the Edit menu. The sizing handle appears.

3. Drag the handle to the lower-right corner. Note that you don't click the mouse button for this procedure. As you drag, notice that the shadow frame indicates the new size.

4. When the shadow frame is the size you want, click the mouse.

5. If you don't like the picture when it appears in its new size, select Undo Editing from the Edit menu and repeat the foregoing procedure.

Note that you can see image sizing information in the lower-left of the Write window (in the status bar); this information lets you size the image proportionally. The image starts out with the coordinates 1x and 1y. To reduce its size by 50 percent, move the mouse until these coordinates are .5x and .5y. To enlarge an image, reverse the mouse direction and double the value of the coordinates to 2x and 2y.

Moving a Picture

To reposition a picture horizontally, choose the Move Picture option on the Edit menu. A shadow frame appears that you can drag left or right to the new position for the picture. When the box is where you want the picture to be, click the mouse. Repeat these steps to refine the position as necessary.

About Headers, Footers, and Page Numbers

You can use headers and footers to print information such as titles, dates, and page numbers at the top or bottom of every page. You can also omit the header and footer on the first page if it is a cover sheet or title page.

To create a header or footer, choose the Header or Footer option on the Document menu. The Write window changes to the HEADER or FOOTER window, as shown in Figure 11-7. Overlapping the window is the Page Header or Page Footer dialog box. You type the text of the header or footer in the window, and select various formatting options in the dialog box. When you're done, you click the Return To Document button.

Before beginning this next exercise, choose New from the File menu and answer No when asked if you want to save your changes. Then follow these steps to create a header with your name and a footer with the page number:

1. In a new document window, select Document and choose Ruler On.

11

2. Choose Header on the Document menu. Click the HEADER window, and type your name as the text of the header.

3. Highlight the text you've entered, open the Character menu, and select a different character format (choose boldface or italic, for example). Then click the center alignment button in the ruler.

4. In the Page Header dialog box, mark the Print on First Page check box.

5. Click the Return to Document command button.

Now create a footer that includes the page number.

6. Choose Footer from the Document menu to display the FOOTER window and Page Footer dialog box.

7. Click the FOOTER window and type **PAGE -** at the blinking cursor.

8. Position the blinking cursor after the dash in the text you just typed, and insert the page number by clicking the Insert Page # button in the Page Footer dialog box. You'll see [page] inserted after your typed entry in the FOOTER window.

Figure 11-7.   *The HEADER window and Page Header dialog box (the FOOTER window and dialog box are similar)*

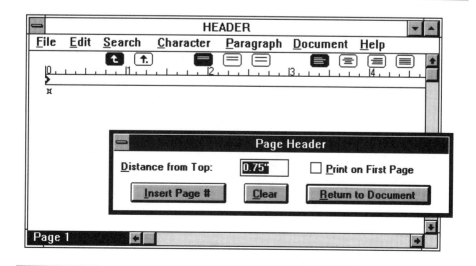

9. Highlight the footer text, open the Character menu, and select a character format as instructed for the header in Step 3. Then click the center align button in the ruler.

10. In the Page Footer dialog box, mark the Print on First Page check box.

11. Click the Return to Document button.

Now print the document to see how the header and footer look on the page. You might want to try adjusting their appearance or position.

Here is additional information to keep in mind about the options of the Page Header and Page Footer dialog boxes:

- *Distance from Top or Bottom*   Enter a measurement to specify the distance between the header and the top of the page, or between the footer and the bottom of the page. In determining this value, remember that laser printers have a nonprinting zone about a quarter-inch from the paper's edge. In addition, take care not to specify too large a distance, or the header or footer text might overlap the main text area.

- *Print on First Page*   Mark this option to print the header or footer on the first page. If your document has a title page or cover sheet, don't check this option.

- *Insert Page #*   Click this button to insert a page number code, which appears as [page] in the HEADER or FOOTER window. You can apply character and paragraph formats to this marker. (Remember that the initial starting page number is set by choosing Page Layout from the Document menu.)

- *Clear*   Press the Clear button to clear the HEADER or FOOTER window.

- *Return to Document*   Click this button to save any changes you made to the header or footer and return to the document.

Saving and Printing Your Write Documents

This section explains how to save and print documents. You should save your documents as often as possible in order not to lose your valuable work in the event of a power failure or other problem. And don't forget to make floppy disk backups to protect yourself from hard-disk failure.

How Write Saves Files

Write saves your document files using its own format. Should you ever need to save files without this format (when you need to share files with other users who don't have Write, for example), you can. Many word processors, though, can read Write files directly.

When you save a file for the first time, choose Save As from the File menu, and type a name for the file in the File Name text box. Once the file has been saved, use the File Save option to periodically save the file as you work with it, or you may need to use the Save As option again to store a copy of the file under a different filename. All Write files are saved with the filename extension .WRI to indicate that they are in Write format; you can save the file in a different format by making a selection in the Save File as Type list box on the Save As dialog box, as described here:

- *Word for DOS Files (*.DOC)*   Select this option if the file is to be edited in Microsoft Word. All character and paragraph formats are saved in the file, for use by either Word for DOS or Word for Windows. The file is saved with the .DOC extension.

- *Word for DOS/Text only (*.DOC)*   Choose this option to save a file for use with Word, but also strip all the character formatting codes from the file. The file is saved with the .DOC filename extension.

- *Text Files (*.TXT)*   Files saved in the text-only format are stripped of formatting codes and given the filename extension .TXT.

Mark the Make Backup check box to tell Write to save the last version of the file, before your most recent changes, as a backup file with the same filename and the extension .BKP. This file is overwritten the next time you save the file with Make Backup enabled. You can use your backup copy to recover from significant editing errors, or as a separate file to be renamed.

Saving a Template

You've already learned how a template file contains document layout information and standard text you use on a regular basis. You might only need one template with a few items, or several templates that each apply to a specific type of document. Templates can be saved as protected files with the Read Only attribute, so that any changes to a template must be saved with a different filename, leaving the original template available for reuse.

Here is a suggested procedure for creating template files:

1. Open a Write document. Select Document, choose Page Layout, and create custom margin settings and a starting page number as desired.

2. Choose Header or Footer from the Document menu to include headers and/or footers in the template. Type the text and specify the format for the headers or footers.

3. Click in the ruler to insert needed tab stops.

4. Create preformatted paragraphs. First, press (ENTER) a few times to add blank lines. Then highlight a line and apply the character or paragraph formats you want to use for the template. Also create paragraphs for tables. Type a single word in the paragraph that describes its formatting, such as "normal" or "table" or "quote." Later, when you type your documents, you can copy and paste these paragraphs where needed.

5. Create paragraphs with special characters, like bulleted lists.

6. Type and format standard text that you use often, such as your name and address, contract terms, letter openings and closings, or special notices. This creates a glossary of frequently used information at the end of the template.

11

Once you've created a template, you need to save it and assign it a Read Only attribute to protect it from unintended changes or accidental deletion. Follow the steps here to do so:

1. Save the template as you normally do, assigning it a helpful filename. Do not save it in another format, such as text-only, as this will remove all your formatting.

2. Open the File Manager, and locate and click the file in a directory window.

3. Choose Properties from the File menu to open the Properties dialog box.

4. Click the Read Only option in the Attributes area.

5. Click the OK button.

The file is now protected from accidental erasure or change. If you ever do want to make changes to a Read Only file, remove the Read Only attribute using the File Manager Properties command, and then make your changes and restore the attribute.

Printing Your Write Documents

To print a Write document, select the Print command from the File menu. In the Print dialog box, choose the number of copies in the Copies text box. You can print all pages of the document, or a specific range of pages by typing the starting and ending page numbers in the From and To text boxes. To print a draft, select a lower resolution in the Print Quality box (this has no effect with some printers).

Remember, to choose a different printer, paper size, or paper source, you need to use the Print Setup option on the File Menu.

12

Paintbrush

Windows Paintbrush is a *painting* program that offers a full set of painting tools and a wide range of colors for creating and printing business graphics, company logos, illustrations, maps, and many other types of pictures. As you work through this chapter, enjoy yourself and experiment with Paintbrush as much as you want. The exercises teach you the Paintbrush techniques you need, but creativity comes from you—so have fun!

Startup and Overview

Start Paintbrush now by double-clicking its icon in the Accessories group window of the Program Manager. The Paintbrush window opens, as shown in Figure 12-1. The Paintbrush window consists of a workspace or *canvas* where pictures are created. At the left of the canvas is the Toolbox, which contains a set of painting tools identified in Figure 12-2. At the bottom of the canvas is the Color Palette, from which you select the colors you paint with;

Figure 12-1.   *The Paintbrush window*

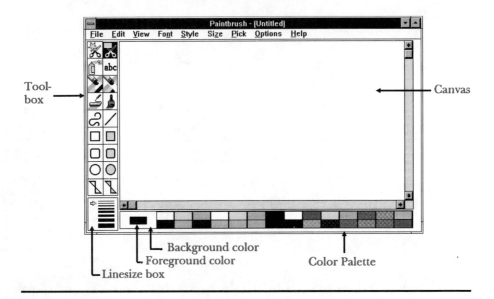

Figure 12-2.   *The Toolbox tools identified*

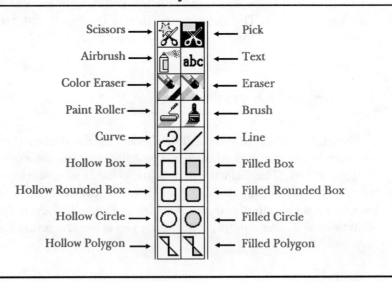

12

at the bottom of the Toolbox is the *Linesize box,* where you select the width of line to paint.

Once you select a tool, color, and line width for a painting session, you just point to the canvas, click and then drag the tool around in the canvas. The following exercises familiarize you with how Paintbrush works. As you work through the chapter, you learn the fine points of each step you execute here.

1. Click the Hollow Box tool in the Toolbox. (Figure 12-2 will help you locate this tool.)

2. Click red in the Color Palette, and notice that the foreground color box shows red.

3. Point to the canvas; then click and drag to create a box. When you release the mouse button, a red box appears.

4. In the Linesize box, click a wider line size; then create another box on the canvas.

5. Hold down the (SHIFT) key, and click and drag to create yet another box. Notice that holding (SHIFT) *constrains* the Hollow Box tool to painting squares only, as opposed to rectangles of any shape. (You learn more about painting with constraint in "Painting with Constraint," later in this chapter.)

6. Click the Circle tool, another line size, and another color. Then click and drag in the workspace. Before releasing the mouse, press the (RIGHT ARROW) key several times. Pressing the arrow keys moves the painting tool in small increments, which is often too hard to do with the mouse.

7. Select part of the drawing (so you can move and copy it in later steps). Click the Pick tool; then click and drag in the workspace so that an object you've drawn is surrounded by a dotted-line box. If the object is not completely surrounded, click and drag again until it is.

8. When the object is surrounded, click inside the dotted-line box and drag to move the selected object, or *cutout,* to a different location in the canvas.

9. Create a copy of an object on the canvas. Repeat Step 7 to select an object; then hold down the (SHIFT) key, click the selected object, and drag a copy of the object off the original.

10. Click the Eraser tool and choose a wide line in the Linesize box. To erase, point in the workspace and then click and drag. Hold down the (SHIFT) key to erase along a straight line, or press the arrow keys to erase in small increments.

11. Erase the entire painting by double-clicking the Eraser tool.

Now you can continue experimenting on your own. Believe it or not, you've just learned about 80 percent of what you need to know to use Paintbrush effectively. The remainder of this chapter explains each feature in detail and shows you some advanced tricks and techniques.

Working with the Color Palette

The Color Palette is the strip of color boxes at the bottom of the Paintbrush window. When a color is selected, it appears at the left of the Palette in the color selection box. If you click a color with the left mouse button, it appears in the foreground color box. If you click a color with the right mouse button, it appears in the background color box.

The Background Color and the Canvas

The background color and the canvas color have an important relation-ship. When you erase a color with the Eraser tool, the color of the canvas shows through unless you've selected a new background color. To see this relationship, try the following exercise:

1. In the Color Palette, click yellow with the right mouse button.

2. Choose New from the File menu, and answer No when asked if you want to save the current canvas.

The Paintbrush canvas is now yellow instead of white. Notice that the background color in the Color Palette is also yellow.

12

3. Choose red as the foreground color by clicking red in the Palette with the left mouse button.

4. Click the Airbrush tool; then click and drag on the canvas to paint red all over the yellow canvas.

5. Click the Eraser, and click and drag it in the canvas. Notice how the yellow canvas shows through when you erase red.

Now let's see what happens if you choose another background color.

6. Click white in the Color Palette, with the right mouse button; then click and drag in the canvas. As you erase, the Eraser changes the areas it touches to white instead of to the canvas color.

You can see that it's important to make sure the background color is the color you want before erasing.

Note

7. Now let's restore the white canvas. Make sure white is still the background color in the Color Palette.

8. Choose New from the File menu, and answer No when asked if you want to save the current canvas. The canvas converts to white.

Foreground/Background Colors and the Fill Tools

Most tools paint with the foreground color; however, when you paint filled boxes, circles, and polygons, the background color becomes the border, and the foreground color becomes the fill. Try this now.

1. Click yellow with the left mouse button.

2. Click red with the right mouse button.

3. Click the Filled Box tool.

4. Point in the canvas; then click and drag to create a filled box.

5. Click a different line size, and then repeat Step 4.

When you're creating filled objects, if you can't remember which mouse button is used for the border and which one for the fill, think of the foreground/background color box as a filled object itself. Notice how the box mimics the color arrangement of the box you painted in the foregoing exercise.

Tip

Foreground/Background Colors and the Color Eraser

Foreground and background color choices are especially important when you're using the Color Eraser, which replaces the foreground color with the background color. Try the following to see how this works. For this exercise, yellow should still be the foreground color, and red the background color.

1. Click the Color Eraser.

2. Point in the canvas, and notice the size of the Color Eraser's point. Click a different line size to make it larger or smaller.

3. Position the Color Eraser over a yellow area of the canvas; then click and drag. Wherever you drag the Color Eraser point, yellow changes to red.

4. Make red the foreground color and blue the background color.

5. Click and drag on the canvas with the Color Eraser to change red to blue.

Understanding the Toolbox

The Toolbox contains a full set of tools for painting in the workspace. Simply click a tool, point to the canvas, and start painting by clicking and dragging the mouse. Most tools paint with the current colors of the Color Palette and the line width selected in the Linesize box.

Here is a summary of the Toolbox functions:

- *Scissors* selects irregularly shaped cutouts.
- *Pick* selects rectangular cutouts.

  These first two tools, Scissors and Pick, are used to define cutouts, which are selected parts of the drawing that can be moved, copied, or deleted.

Note

- *Airbrush* sprays a dot pattern in the currently selected foreground color.
- *Text* types text for captions and titles.

- *Color Eraser* erases the foreground color and changes it to the background color.
- *Eraser* erases by converting all colors to the canvas or background color.
- *Paint Roller* fills a closed area with the foreground color.
- *Brush* is a freehand painting tool.
- *Curve* is a freehand painting tool for creating curved shapes.
- *Line* creates lines.

The remaining Paintbrush tools come in pairs. The tool on the left is used to create a hollow object that is outlined with the current foreground color. The tool on the right is used to create an object filled with the current foreground color and outlined with the current background color. Select the line width for the object *before* painting. To paint symmetrical shapes, hold down the (SHIFT) key while dragging the mouse.

Tip

To create a filled object without a border, select the same color for both foreground and background.

- The *Box* tools create square or rectangular shapes.
- The *Rounded Box* tools create squares or rectangles with rounded corners.
- The *Circle* tools create circles or ellipses.
- The *Polygon* tools create irregularly shaped triangles, boxes, and other multisided objects.

Getting to Know the Paintbrush Menus

As you read the following descriptions of the Paintbrush menu options, open each menu to become more familiar with its contents.

File   The File menu has the standard options for opening, saving, and printing files.

Edit   The Edit menu has the standard Clipboard Cut, Copy, and Paste options. In addition, the Copy To option lets you save a cutout portion of a painting to a disk file, and the Paste From option recovers a cutout file.

Tip

Edit Copy To provides a way to save files using a minimum amount of disk space. Be sure to read the section "Copying, Moving, and Saving Cutouts" later in this chapter for more information.

View   The View menu has a Zoom In option for magnifying part of the picture, and a Zoom Out option for viewing an entire painting. View also includes commands to remove the Toolbox and Linesize boxes when you need to increase your view of a picture in the canvas. The Cursor Position option displays a small window containing the coordinates of the cursor for detail painting.

Font   The Font menu contains font choices for typing with the Text tool.

Pick   Options on the Pick menu are used to flip, invert, size, and tilt cutouts. These features become available after you select a cutout with the Scissors or Pick tool.

Options   The Options menu has commands for changing the specifications of the painting, the shapes used by the Brush tool, and the colors in the Color Palette.

Painting Techniques

This section offers you a few techniques for improving the quality of your pictures and the efficiency of your painting methods.

Making Corrections

To erase part of what you've just painted, press the (BACKSPACE) key. An eraser with an X appears on the canvas; you can drag this eraser over the object you just created to erase it. This technique works with most of the drawing tools; try it in the following exercise:

1. Click on the Line tool.
2. Click and drag in the canvas to draw a line.
3. Press the (BACKSPACE) key to display the eraser.
4. Click and drag to erase part of the line. Leave half of it for the next step.
5. Paint a new line over the remaining part of the existing line.
6. Press the (BACKSPACE) key, and click and drag over the line. Notice how only the most recent line is erased, but not the previously created line.

Note

The backspace eraser only erases parts of the painting you've created with the current tool. All other parts of the canvas you drag over are left unchanged.

Another way to make corrections in the canvas is by choosing the Undo command on the Edit menu. Use this method after pasting an object you don't want, or after making radical changes to an object—like tilting or inverting it—that didn't work out.

Caution

When you use Undo, all changes you've made with the current tool are undone. For example, if you draw three boxes and choose Undo, all three boxes are removed, not just the last box drawn.

Working with the Cursor

The mouse pointer shape is an arrow when you're selecting menus, tools, and colors. When on the canvas, however, it changes to one of the following shapes, depending on the current tool:

- With the cutout tools (Scissors and Pick), Line tool, and all hollow or filled tools, the cursor is a cross-hair.

- With the Text tool, the cursor is an I beam.

- With the Eraser and Color Eraser, the cursor is a box that matches the size of the current line width. Be sure to choose a line size appropriate for what's being erased.

- For the Brush tool, you can select a "tip" for the pointer by double-clicking the tool. You'll see the following dialog box, where you double-click on the brush shape you want to use. (You can also change the width of the line in the Linesize box.)

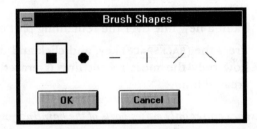

Viewing Cursor Positions

The Cursor Position box is used to view the x and y coordinates of the cursor on the canvas. The upper-left corner of the canvas is position 0,0. Each point represents a pixel or dot on the canvas. Choose Cursor Position on the View menu to display the following Cursor Position dialog box:

The coordinates displayed in the Cursor Position box are useful in the following cases:

- To create objects with an exact size. In "About Image Resolution," later in this chapter, you see how to determine how many pixel elements (dots) there are per inch on your monitor. You can then create objects that print with accurate ruler measurements.

12

- To create objects that match in size. For example, you can create boxes that have the same width or height by matching the coordinates in the Cursor Position box.

- To align objects such as boxes or circles. For example, to align two boxes horizontally or vertically, you note the coordinates for the first box, then start the second box on one of those coordinates, based on whether the alignment is vertical or horizontal.

- To move objects with precision. You can watch the coordinates change as you move the object, for more accurate placement.

Using the Arrow Keys for Precision

An important technique when painting with any tool is to use the arrow keys on the keyboard for precision movements and straight-line movements. For example, you can point the Eraser over an area to be erased, and then position it more precisely with the arrow keys before clicking to erase. You can also hold down an arrow key to continue erasing in a straight line. This is useful when erasing along the edge of a box or line. Try this:

1. Click the Filled Box tool. Then click green with both the left and right mouse buttons. This lets you create a solid box, by making the border (background color) and fill (foreground color) the same color.

2. Click the canvas and drag to create a small rectangle.

3. Choose the Eraser tool, and change the size of its tip by choosing a medium-sized line in the Linesize box.

4. Change the background color to white; otherwise, the Eraser will make everything it touches green.

5. Erase the top quarter of the box by positioning the Eraser at the top-left of the box, and then clicking and holding the mouse button while pressing (RIGHT ARROW), as demonstrated here:

Eraser tip

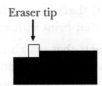

This next exercise shows you how to use the arrow keys to precisely position an object after it has been moved into the general area in which you want it.

1. Select the Pick tool, and position it over the upper-left corner of the green box you just painted.

2. Click the mouse and drag to the lower-right edge of the object. Release the mouse. This surrounds the box, making it a cutout.

3. Point inside the cutout.

4. Press the (SHIFT) key, and click and drag the box. This creates a copy of the cutout that you can drag below the original. After the cutout has started to move, you can release the (SHIFT) key.

5. When the copy is below the original, press the arrow keys until the edges of the two boxes touch.

6. Release the mouse to place the object.

Note that the object remains selected, so you can move it again if necessary. To remove the selection from the cutout and "paste it down" on the canvas, click elsewhere on the canvas or select another tool.

Painting with Constraint

Though the title of this section may suggest a frustrating way to paint, the technique described here is essential to creating pictures that have an orderly appearance. To paint circles rather than ellipses, and paint squares rather than rectangles, hold down the (SHIFT) key while you drag with the mouse. When the Line or Polygon tool is selected, holding (SHIFT) restricts mouse movements to 45-degree increments, as illustrated here:

Try the following exercise to practice using the (SHIFT) key:

1. Click the Line tool; then select a color and a narrow line size.

2. Point in the canvas, and draw a line while holding down the (SHIFT) key.

3. Continue to hold down both the mouse button and the (SHIFT) key, and drag the mouse in a circular motion on the canvas.

You can see how the line is restricted to the 45-degree increments. Repeat the above steps using the Circle and Box tools to see how they are affected by constraint.

Zooming In for Detail

Whereas the arrow and (SHIFT) keys help you paint more precisely, the Zoom In command on the View menu lets you magnify a part of the picture so you can change the *picture elements* (*pels* or *pixels*) or bits that make it up. When you zoom in, you can change the color of individual elements by clicking them with the mouse. To see how zooming works and to see how Paintbrush colors are formulated, follow the steps here:

1. Select the thickest line in the Linesize box.

2. Click the reddish-brown color at the top-right corner of the Color Palette.

3. Click the Brush tool.

4. Paint a wide horizontal line on the upper-left corner of the canvas. If you're a perfectionist, hold down (SHIFT) to constrain the line.

5. Select dark brown and repeat Step 4. Continue selecting colors and painting strips in this way until you get to the lavender shades in the palette. (The lavenders and all colors to their left are solid and not of use for this discussion.)

Now zoom in to take a look at the components of the colors, by following these steps:

6. Select Zoom In from the View menu. A rectangular cursor appears. Position it over the top strips of color in the canvas, as shown here:

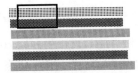

7. Click the mouse to zoom in on the area inside the zoom-in rectangle.

The area selected for zoom is now displayed on the canvas, similar to that shown in Figure 12-3, letting you see and work with the pixels that make up the picture and its colors. Note that these pixels correspond to the x and y coordinates in the Cursor Position box. They form a grid with a width and height dependent on your screen resolution or chosen size. Notice the box in the upper-left corner shows the normal (unmagnified) view of the colors.

8. Click the vertical slider and drag down, watching the colors scroll in the box. When another set of colors is visible, release the mouse button.

9. Repeat Step 8 until you've scanned all the colors. Note that these colors are mixtures of the solid colors on the left side of the Color Palette.

Now you can try changing the individual elements of the colors by following these steps.

10. Scroll back to the top colors. In the Color Palette, click black with the left mouse button, and white with the right mouse button.

11. Click the red pixels and watch the view box in the upper-left corner to see how the picture changes in normal view.

12. Click with the right mouse button to erase pixels.

13. Choose Zoom Out from the View menu to return to normal view mode.

12

You have now completed the basic steps for using the zoom view mode. Typically, you paint in normal mode, and then zoom in to add detail or erase colors you don't want.

The Paintbrush Canvas

The canvas is your painting area. You can change its color, change its size, and zoom out to see the entire canvas.

Figure 12-3.   *The zoomed area displayed on the canvas, with the normal view box in the upper-left corner*

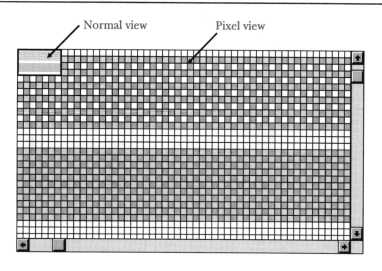

You can make the canvas any color by clicking a color with the right mouse button, and then choosing New from the File menu.

Using the View Picture Mode

When you need to see the picture on the canvas in full screen mode, without the borders, Toolbox, and Color Palette of the Paintbrush window, choose the View Picture option from the View menu. Then stand back and look at your masterpiece—remember, however, that you can't do any editing in this mode. To return to normal mode, click anywhere in the picture or press (CTRL)-(C).

Changing the Canvas Attributes

To change the size of the canvas, the unit of measure, and the type of palette to use, choose Image Attributes from the Options menu. You'll see a dialog box similar to the one pictured here:

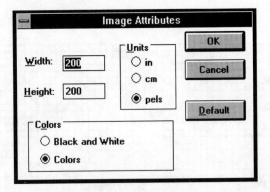

Its options are explained in the following paragraphs. To return to Paintbrush's default canvas settings, choose the Default button in this dialog box. This changes the measures in the Width and Height fields.

Units   Click the button for the unit of measure you want to work with on the canvas (inches, centimeters, or pels). Note that pels are the picture elements or bits you see when you choose Zoom In from the View menu. They are most commonly referred to as pixels.

Width and Height   The width and height for the canvas are changed by entering new values in the Width and Height fields. Be sure to use the same measurement unit you chose in the Units field.

Initially, Paintbrush establishes a default canvas size that matches the pixel width and height of your screen, but if you're low on memory, the canvas may be smaller. To gain more workspace, close any other applications you're not using; then click the Default button in the Image Attributes dialog box and click the OK button. A new, larger canvas will open if you have freed enough memory.

Keep in mind that the smaller the width and height settings, the less disk space is required by the image file when it is saved. (Even white space is saved to disk.) However, don't feel you need to work on a small canvas all the time just to save disk space. You should initially work on a large canvas so you can freely move cutouts around or place them at the bottom of the canvas for later use. Then, when you're ready to save the picture, use one of the cutout tools to surround just the part of the canvas you want to save, and then choose Copy To from the Edit menu to save only the cutout. The canvas size of the saved cutout is smaller and takes up less disk space.

Colors   Normally, you'll work in color, but you can use black-and-white mode to paint with specific dot patterns that may look better when printed on your printer. For example, click the Black and White button on the Image Attributes dialog box and click OK. Notice how the Color Palette changes to various dot patterns and shades. Using these shades makes it easier to discern exactly how an image will appear when printed on a black-and-white printer.

About Image Resolution

If you need to use exact measurements when creating pictures, you first need to find out how many pels there are per inch or centimeter on your screen. Here's how to do this:

1. Choose Image Attributes from the Options menu.

2. Under Units, click the button for inches or centimeters.

3. In the Width text box, type **1**.

4. Return to the Units area and click the button for pels; make note of the value in the Width box.

5. Click Cancel to close the Image Attributes box.

Now you can use the value you found in Step 4 to paint objects that conform to the inch or centimeter scale. The following steps assume you're using inches:

6. If the Cursor Position is not visible, choose Cursor Position from the View menu. Then drag the Cursor Position box to a convenient location on the desktop.

The value in the Cursor Position box is the current location, in pels, of the pointer. The top-left corner of the canvas is coordinate 0,0.

Note

7. Click the Hollow Box tool and choose a narrow line size. Then position the pointer at the 100,100 position on the canvas. (Remember to use the arrow keys if you have trouble positioning the pointer with the mouse.)

8. Use the pels value to draw a one-inch-square box. Add the pels-per-inch value of your monitor to the starting coordinates of 100. For example, if your monitor displays 96 pels-per-inch, drag out to the 196,196 coordinate on the canvas. Watch the Cursor Position box as you click and drag to create the box.

9. When you release the mouse, a one-inch square is created, even though it may not appear that way on your screen, depending on its resolution.

10. Print the picture on your printer, and measure the box to verify that it is one inch square. When you choose the File Print command, make sure the Use Printer Resolution box is *not* checked, as explained next.

12

The Use Printer Resolution feature in the File Print dialog box has an important effect on your drawing when it is printed. When this feature is enabled, the pixels on your screen are matched, one to one, to the dots on the printer. Since the dots on high-resolution printers are much smaller than the dots (pixels) on your screen, the image is printed at a reduced size. When the Use Printer Resolution option is not enabled, Paintbrush instructs the printer to fill in the empty space between pixels with extra dots, so the size of the printed image is close to its size on the screen. For more information, see "Printing Pictures" later in this chapter.

Clearing the Canvas

You can clear the canvas at any time to start a new painting or remove unwanted art, by using one of the following methods:

- Double-click the Eraser tool. If the current image has been edited since it was last saved, you'll be asked if you want to save it before it is erased.
- Choose the New option on the File menu.
- Select one of the cutout tools (Scissors or Pick) and surround the image you want to clear. Then choose Cut from the Edit menu.

When you choose New from the File menu, the canvas becomes the color of the currently selected background color. So be sure to select a white background (or the color you want for your canvas) before opening a new document.

Remember

When You Need More Room

Canvases that are larger than your screen size will not be completely visible in the Paintbrush window; however, you can use the scroll bars to bring other parts of the picture into view, or you can try one of the following techniques:

- Temporarily remove the Toolbox and Linesize boxes by choosing Tools and Linesize from the View menu. The option toggles off and can be restored by selecting it again.

- Temporarily remove the Color Palette boxes by choosing Palette from the View menu. The option toggles off and can be restored by selecting it again.

Tip

Select the tool and color you need before removing the Toolbox and Color Palette.

- Choose Zoom Out from the View menu. In this mode, the entire canvas is visible, but at a reduced size. Use this mode to paste large objects or move objects that are too large to be selected in the normal view. Choose Zoom In to restore the normal view. Zoom Out techniques are explained in "Pasting Large Objects," later in this chapter.

Securing Cutout Objects on the Canvas

Cutout objects you've selected with the Scissors or Cutout tool are not secured or "pasted down" on the canvas until you click another Paintbrush tool or click elsewhere on the canvas. Until then, you can move them elsewhere, or remove them altogether by pressing (CTRL)-(X) (Cut). Be careful—in some cases, changes to a painting may be accidentally removed when you scroll or select a zoom mode. Always click another tool or click elsewhere on the canvas after pasting or moving an object.

Copying, Moving, and Saving Cutouts

The Scissors and the Pick tools are used to create cutouts, as shown in the following illustration:

The star on the left is surrounded with the Scissors tool, since using the Pick tool would select part of the middle star in its rectangular selection area. The star on the right can be selected with Pick because it is positioned well away from the other objects.

Once you've defined a cutout, you can move it, copy it, and save it to disk, as described in the following sections.

Making a Transparent Copy

You've already seen how to move and copy a cutout: simply click and drag to move the cutout, or hold the (SHIFT) key and click and drag to copy the cutout. One thing you may not have noticed is that cutouts copied in this way are *transparent* and allow underlying art to show through. Try the following exercise to see how this works:

1. Start a new drawing by choosing New from the File menu.
2. Select the Line tool and paint a starburst pattern (or any pattern you choose).
3. Choose a different color, and paint another starburst pattern on another part of the canvas.
4. Select the Pick tool and surround the second starburst.
5. Click and drag this cutout over the first cutout. Notice that the underlying starburst shows through.

You can see that you don't need to do anything special to make transparent copies of cutouts; this is the default result when dragging cutouts elsewhere on the canvas.

Making Opaque Copies

You can make *opaque* copies of cutouts, too, by clicking with the right mouse button and dragging. The entire area within the cutout border, including the canvas color, is copied, and the copy overlaps or covers up existing art and does not allow it to show through. Try the following:

1. Using the Scissors tool, surround any piece of art on the canvas.

2. Click the cutout with the right mouse button, drag it over another image on the canvas, and release the mouse button. Notice that the cutout covers up the existing art.

Tip

When copying opaquely, the entire area of a cutout is copied, including any portion of the canvas within the cutout area. To eliminate as much of the canvas as possible from your cutout, use the Scissors tool and outline as close to the edge of the object as possible.

Saving Cutouts

Cutouts that you use often can be saved to disk files, as follows:

1. Define a cutout with the Scissors or Pick tool.

2. Choose Copy To from the Edit menu.

3. Type a name for the cutout in the Copy To box and click OK.

The cutout will be saved in a file with the .BMP extension, unless you specify another extension. The canvas size of this file will be the size of the cutout you defined, which saves space and is useful when creating desktop wallpaper and tiles.

Tip

It's best to use Copy To to save your paintings for future use—in this way, you can define just the most essential part of the drawing and reduce the amount of disk space it requires for storage.

To paste a cutout from another file into your current picture, use the Paste From command on the Edit menu. Once the cutout is pasted into the workspace, it can be copied or moved anywhere on the canvas like a normal cutout.

Using the Painting Tools

This section gives you more specific instructions for using the painting tools: the Eraser and Color Eraser; the freehand painting tools (Airbrush, Brush, and Paint Roller); the Text tool for including text in your drawings; the Line and Curve drawing tools; and the paired Box, Circle, and Polygon tools.

The Eraser Tool

As you've seen, the Eraser erases by replacing everything in its path with the background color currently selected in the Color Palette. In most cases, you'll want to make the background color the same as the canvas color before erasing. To erase small areas, choose the narrowest line in the Linesize box; to erase large areas, choose a wider line.

Finer, precision erasing is accomplished by moving the Eraser to the approximate area to be erased and then adjusting its position by pressing the arrow keys. Click when the eraser is positioned correctly and drag the mouse to erase, or for more precision, press the arrow key while holding down the mouse button.

Tip

To erase small details, choose Zoom In from the View menu and remove individual color bits.

The Color Eraser Tool

The Color Eraser erases by replacing the foreground color with the background color. You can drag the Color Eraser on the canvas, or just double-click it to replace all instances of the color in the visible canvas. Try this:

1. Select red in the Color Palette. Then select the Brush tool and paint a few random lines.

2. Select blue, and paint more random lines.

3. Click the Color Eraser, and then click green with the right mouse button. (Blue is still the foreground color.)

4. Double-click the Color Eraser, and all the blue on the entire canvas is converted to green.

Only the visible part of the canvas is converted when you use the double-click method. To erase on a canvas larger than the window, you must scroll other parts of the painting into view and double-click the Color Eraser again.

Note

Airbrush Techniques

The Airbrush sprays a dot pattern of the current foreground color onto your painting. Simply point, click, and drag to paint with the Airbrush. Here are some additional guidelines:

- To spray straight along a line, hold down the (SHIFT) key as you use Airbrush.

- To change the width of the sprayed pattern, select a different line width in the Linesize box.

- The speed of the cursor across the screen determines the density of the spray. For a dispersed impression, drag quickly over an area many times.

- For an interesting effect, switch colors and spray again over previously painted areas. If a color becomes too concentrated, try spraying over it with white or with the current canvas color.

- Spray with one of the mixed colors at the far right of the Color Palette, for variation. You can then remove one of the elements of the mixed color using the Color Eraser.

Brush Techniques

The Brush lets you paint in a freehand style using different brush shapes and sizes. Double-click on the Brush to open the Brush Shape dialog box, or

12

choose Brush Shapes on the Options menu. Click any one of the brush shapes, and paint with it in the canvas. A few examples are shown here:

Here are some guidelines for the Brush:

- Be sure to select a color in the Palette *before* you begin painting with the brush.
- Try different line widths as you paint with the Brush.
- You can erase with the brush by selecting white as the foreground color.
- To constrain Brush strokes, hold down the (SHIFT) key as you paint.

Paint Roller Techniques

Use the Paint Roller when you want to fill a closed area with the foreground color. (A closed area is one that is completely surrounded by a border, such as a box or circle, or a solid color surrounded by another color.) Point the Roller tip into the closed area and click, as demonstrated here:

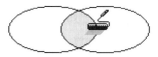

If the color spills out of the closed area, choose the Undo command. Small openings in an enclosed area may cause this to happen, as shown in this next illustration, which is magnified using the Zoom In command on the View menu:

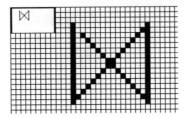

To close up an area like this, click the pixels of the opening, and then use the Paint Roller again to fill the space.

Adding Text

The Text tool lets you add captions and other text to your paintings. You click the tool and then select a font and font style from the Font menu. As long as the Text tool is still selected, you can make font and style changes to the text you've typed. When you choose a different font, all the text in the current selection changes to that font. You can also change colors while using the Text tool.

Once you click another tool, the text is pasted down and cannot be edited without erasing and starting over. Pasting the text converts it to a graphic image on the canvas. Try the following exercise to see how this works:

1. Click the Text tool.
2. Point and click the canvas; a blinking insertion point appears. Type some text.
3. Choose the Fonts option on the Text menu.
4. In the Fonts dialog box, click a font, font style, and size; then click the OK button.
5. Click elsewhere on the canvas to paste the text down.

The text is pasted to the canvas and can no longer be edited. Unlike a word processor or text editor, you cannot click in the text with the I-beam pointer to insert new text. For example, try clicking the Text tool again, and then click anywhere in the text you just typed. Type some more text, and it will overlay the existing text instead of being inserted in it.

Here are some Text tool guidelines:

- Use the (BACKSPACE) key to edit text you are typing while the Text tool is active.

- The Text tool uses the currently selected foreground color.

- Text can only be painted in solid colors, not in the mixed colors at the right of the Palette. If you choose a mixed color, Paintbrush will select the next solid color.

- TrueType fonts do not print correctly in Paintbrush because they are converted to graphic images. The jagged edges you see on the canvas are not resolved when the image is printed, as they are in Write or other applications.

Drawing Lines and Curves

The Line tool and the Curve tool are used to paint lines using the current color in the Palette and the current line width in the Linesize box.

- To constrain a line using the Line tool, hold down the (SHIFT) key as you draw.

- The Curve tool is one of the most interesting tools in Paintbrush. It paints curves using a simple "anchor-and-pull" technique. You'll want to experiment with the Curve tool to get familiar with it—think of the tool as a rubber band stretched between two posts. First you designate the location of the posts, and then you stretch the line like a rubber band out from the posts. A curve is then formed from those coordinates.

Try the following exercise to paint some curved lines:

1. Select the Curve tool, a foreground color, and a line width.

2. Move the pointer to the canvas, and click where you want to locate the first post.

3. Hold down the mouse button, and drag to create a line. Release the mouse to create the second post.

4. Click and hold above or below the line. The line bows out to form a curve, as shown here:

5. Drag the mouse around on the canvas; then release the button to set the curve.

6. You can add one more curve to the current line. Click below the line, as shown here, to create an "S" curve:

7. Drag the mouse around until the curve is the way you want; then release the mouse button.

Now try drawing an enclosed curve that has a teardrop or airfoil shape. For this technique, you don't need to hold the mouse button and drag a line to the second post. Follow these steps:

1. Click on the canvas to create the first post.

2. Click elsewhere on the canvas to create the second post.

3. Click at a third location on the canvas, and then hold and drag the mouse to reshape the curve, as shown here:

4. Release the mouse when you're done shaping the curve.

Using the Box, Circle, and Polygon Tools

Boxes, circles, and polygons drawn with the Toolbox tools can be either hollow or filled, and take on the current color and line width. Recall that filled boxes are filled with the foreground color and have borders of the background color. You've already had some experience creating boxes and circles, so try the following steps to create a polygon shape:

1. Click the Hollow Polygon tool in the Toolbox.

2. Click on the canvas, and drag to another point to draw the first line.

3. Click at another point on the canvas to create another line that connects with the first line.

4. Continue clicking at random points to draw more lines and expand the polygon (or create an object of your choice); then click again at the exact position of the original starting point.

Clicking again at the starting point closes the polygon to form an enclosed space or spaces that can be filled by using the Roller tool. You must click exactly on the original starting point for the polygon to "close up." To make a filled polygon, choose the Filled Polygon tool and repeat the steps above, creating several sides for the polygon. End by clicking at the starting point, and all enclosed spaces created by the polygon are filled with the foreground color. Here is a five-pointed star with the tips filled by using the Filled Polygon tool:

Special Techniques

Use the following techniques to manipulate and enhance objects created with painting tools.

Pasting Large Objects

It is possible to move and paste objects that are larger than the canvas, using the Zoom Out option on the View menu. When you choose Zoom Out, the entire canvas is displayed in miniature within the window. You can then use the Edit Paste command to place large objects on the canvas, and the Pick tool to position them. To move an existing large object, select it with the Pick tool in Zoom Out mode, and then move it. Here's an example:

1. Click white in the Color Palette with the right mouse button to prepare for a new, white canvas.

2. Choose Image Attributes from the Options menu, click the Default button, and press (ENTER). A new canvas appears.

3. Click the Hollow Box tool and paint several images, enough to fill the visible portion of the canvas.

4. Choose Zoom Out from the View menu.

5. With the Pick tool, select the group of hollow boxes you created in Step 3. Notice that in the Zoom Out mode, the selection line appears solid rather than dotted (see Figure 12-4).

6. From the Edit menu, choose Copy and then Paste. The pasted object appears as a cross-hatched shadow, similar to that shown in Figure 12-5.

Figure 12-4. *Working in Zoom Out mode*

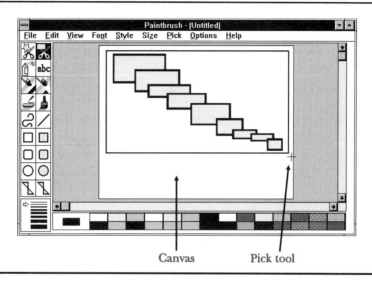

Canvas   Pick tool

Figure 12-5. *A pasted object shown as a cross-hatched shadow*

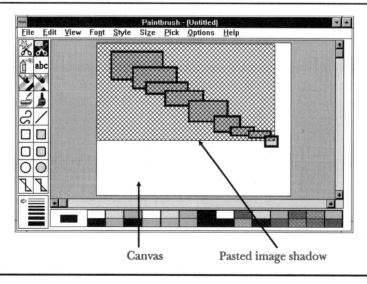

Canvas   Pasted image shadow

7. Click and drag the pasted object to another part of the canvas, and release the mouse button.

8. Remember that the object must be secured before you can zoom back to normal view. To paste it down, click a part of the canvas not covered by the pasted object, or click the Pick tool in the Toolbox.

9. Choose Zoom In from the View menu.

Use this technique whenever pasting objects that are larger than the visible canvas. If you attempt to paste a large object like this without first zooming out, and the object doesn't fit, the edges that don't fit are cropped. Zoom Out mode is the only way to paste such objects on your canvas.

Sweeping a Cutout

You can *sweep* a cutout across the screen, leaving a trail of the cutout in the mouse's path. Try this:

1. Create an object with any Paintbrush tool.

2. Cut out the object with the Scissors or Pick tool.

3. Click the selected object, and hold down the (SHIFT) key while dragging.

Tip

Quickly sweeping the mouse creates a trail of cutouts that are farther apart, as shown at the top of the following illustration. Slowly sweeping the mouse creates a continuous trail of the cutouts, as shown at the bottom of the illustration:

Tip

To make a transparent trail of cutouts, hold the left mouse button as you sweep; to make an opaque trail of cutouts, hold the right mouse button.

The Pick Menu Options

When a cutout is selected, the options on the Pick menu become available.

Shrinking and Enlarging a Cutout

Use the Shrink + Grow option to resize the cutout. If you want to replace the original cutout with the resized cutout, choose the Clear option. Try the following exercise to resize an object:

1. Paint an object on the canvas with any Paintbrush tool.
2. Select the object with the Scissors or Pick tool. The Pick menu options become available.
3. Choose Shrink + Grow from the menu.
4. Point to a blank area of the canvas, and drag out a small frame with the Pick tool. Release the mouse, and the selected object is resized within the frame; the original cutout remains intact.
5. The Shrink + Grow option remains active until you click it again on the Pick menu or select another tool, so let's try another version of this technique. Choose Clear from the Pick menu; this will cause resized objects to replace their originals.
6. Repeat Steps 2 through 4, trying several resizing operations. Because you are now replacing the original objects with the resized ones, you won't clutter up the canvas with all your experiments.

Tip

You can maintain the proportions of a resized object by holding the (SHIFT) key while selecting and resizing the cutout.

Note

A resized object may become distorted. It may be necessary to use the Zoom In option on the View menu to "clean up" areas that have become jagged or out of proportion.

Tilting Objects

Use the Tilt option on the Pick menu to tilt an object horizontally. Like Shrink + Grow, Tilt stays active until you click it again on the Pick menu to turn it off, or until you select another tool. With Tilt, you can also use the Clear option on the Pick menu; in this case, it clears the most recent attempt at tilting the cutout. Clear keeps the canvas from becoming cluttered so you can tilt the object several times until it is the way you like. Here's an exercise using tilting:

1. Paint an object, and then cut it out with the Scissors or Pick tool.

2. Choose both Tilt and Clear on the Pick menu.

3. Click elsewhere on the canvas. Then click and drag the mouse to the left or right to tilt the object, and release the mouse button.

4. Repeat Step 3 until the object is tilted the way you want.

5. When you're done, click another tool to deactivate the Tilt feature.

Flipping Cutouts

You can *flip* (turn) an object several ways, using the Flip Horizontal and Flip Vertical options on the Pick menu. First cut out an object with the Scissors or Pick tool, and then choose one of the Flip options. Note that you can flip an object four ways by combining the horizontal and vertical versions of the Flip options. The best way to learn how Flip works is to experiment. Type some text with the Text tool, select it, and choose each flip option to see what happens. Then try some combinations.

Inverting Cutouts

The Inverse option on the Pick menu lets you *invert* the colors of an object. One practical use of this feature is to change black text to white text with a black background. Inverting also gives you a way to quickly make copies of cutouts look different by just changing their colors.

When you invert, black changes to white, and vice versa. Dark gray changes to light gray, and vice versa. Other color changes are as follows:

- Reds invert to light blues and vice versa
- Yellows invert to dark blues and vice versa
- Greens invert to lavenders and vice versa

Parts of the canvas included inside the cutout area are also inverted, so it may be necessary to use the Eraser (or Zoom In mode) to remove unwanted colors around an object after inverting it.

Creating Custom Colors

You can create (mix) your own colors for use in Paintbrush. When special colors are created, they replace the colors in the Color Palette. Entire custom color palettes can also be saved to disk, so you can define several palettes for use in different painting situations.

Editing Colors

To open the Edit Colors dialog box, double-click the color in the Color Palette you want to change, or choose Edit Colors from the Options menu. You'll see the following dialog box:

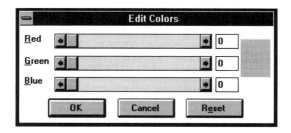

In this dialog box you'll see numeric values representing the proportion of red, green, and blue making up the color you clicked. To design a custom color, click and drag the Red, Green, and Blue slider bars to adjust these color components until the color you want appears in the sample box on the right. If you know the values of a color you want to create, enter its numeric color values, between 0 and 255, in the text boxes. When you have the color you want, click OK or press (ENTER). The new color then replaces the original color in that box of the Palette.

Saving and Retrieving Color Palettes

To save the Color Palette after you've made changes to it, choose the Save Colors option on the Options menu. When the Save Colors As dialog box appears, type a name for the Color Palette file. Paintbrush recommends using the .PAL extension for these files. To load a customized palette at any time, choose the Get Colors option on the Options menu.

Saving Your Work

Use the Save or Save As command on the File menu to save your Paintbrush canvas to a disk file. To save cutouts, choose the Copy To option on the Edit menu, as explained in "Saving Cutouts," earlier in this chapter.

When saving a file, Paintbrush automatically saves files in the .BMP (bitmap) format. You can also choose one of the following other formats by marking it in the Save File as Type drop-down list box on the Save As dialog box.

- *PCX Paintbrush*   Choose this file format when you need to transfer your pictures to an application that supports the .PCX format, but not the Paintbrush .BMP format.

- *Monochrome Bitmap with .BMP Extension*   Select this format to save pictures without colors. Files saved in this format use less disk space.

- *16 Color Bitmap with .BMP Extension*   This is the default Paintbrush file format that supports 16 colors.

The other options in the Save File as Type drop-down list box are not relevant when saving Paintbrush files. They are used when importing pictures from other applications.

After you've picked a file format, type a name for the file in the Filename field, and click OK or press (ENTER) to save it to disk.

Printing Pictures

The Print and Page Setup options on the File menu are used to print your Paintbrush artwork.

The Print dialog box is illustrated here:

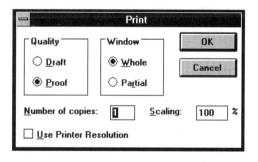

Its options, and the Page Setup options that let you enhance your printed paintings, are explained in the paragraphs that follow.

Printing Part of a Picture   To print a selected portion of a picture, click the Partial button in the Window box, and then click the OK button. The entire image becomes visible. Click and drag over the portion of the painting you want to print; when you release the mouse button, the selected portion is sent to the printer.

Printing Draft or Proof Copies   To change the quality of the printed picture, select the Draft or Proof button in the Quality box. Draft mode is a low-quality, high-speed print mode available with some printers.

Printing Multiple Copies   To print multiple copies of a picture, type a number other than 1 in the Number of copies text box.

Printing Reduced or Enlarged Pictures   You can scale pictures up or down by entering a percentage value in the Scaling box. For example, to print a picture at half its normal size, type 50% in the Scaling box. To double the size of a picture, use 200%. Pictures can even be scaled to a size that is larger than the paper size; in this case, the image is printed on several sheets that can be pasted together.

Using Your Printer's Resolution   Mark the Use Printer Resolution box if you want your painting to print at the resolution of your printer rather than at screen resolution. This sets up a one-to-one relationship between the pixel on the screen and the dot resolution of your printer. On low-resolution printers, the image may print larger than that on the screen; on high-resolution printers, the image may print smaller than that on the screen.

Note

Since colors are converted to dithered patterns on black-and-white printers, try adjusting the intensity controls on the Print Setup dialog box, as discussed in "Controlling Color Output on Black-and-White Printers," later in this chapter.

Page Setup Options for Printed Paintings   You can include a header and footer on the printout of your painting. Select File and choose the Page Setup option. Type the header or footer in the appropriate text box. You can include the following codes to print the date, time, page number, filename, and other information in the header or footer:

Header/Footer	Function Code
&d	Inserts the current date
&t	Inserts the current time
&p	Inserts a page number
&f	Inserts the current filename
&l	Aligns the text with the left margin
&r	Aligns the text with the right margin
&c	Centers the text (the default)

12

For example, the following would print the date and time on the left, the filename in the middle, and the page number on the right:

&l&d&t&c&f&r&p

The Page Setup dialog box also has options for setting the margins on the printed page. The margins are measured from the edges of the paper.

Tips and Tricks for Paintbrush

Now that you're familiar with the features of Paintbrush, read through the following tips and tricks to improve your painting skills.

Controlling Color Output on Black-and-White Printers

When pictures are printed on black-and-white printers, colors are converted to dot patterns that simulate various shades of gray. The dot pattern may be coarse or fine, depending on your printer and the settings of the Printer Setup dialog box. You can control the way colors are converted to grays by adjusting the Intensity slider in the Printer Setup dialog box. The steps listed next show you first how to print the Paintbrush Color Palette box so you can see how each Paintbrush color prints on your printer, and then how to adjust the Intensity control to change the ways the colors are printed.

1. Open Paintbrush and make its window active. Then press (ALT)-(PRINT SCREEN) to capture the Paintbrush window on the Clipboard.

2. Select View and choose Zoom Out. Then select Edit and choose Paste, and click the Pick tool to paste the image down. Voila–the image of the Paintbrush window appears within Paintbrush! Your screen will look similar to Figure 12-6.

3. While still in Zoom Out mode, use the Pick tool to surround the Color Palette; then choose the Copy command on the Edit menu.

4. Select View again and switch to the Zoom In mode. Then choose New from the File menu to open a new canvas.

Figure 12-6.   *The captured Paintbrush window pasted into the Paintbrush*
workspace

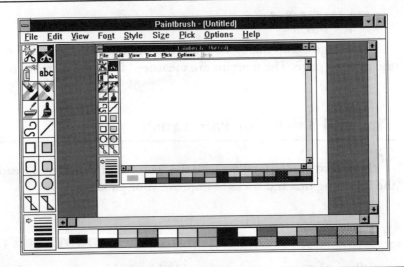

5. Select Edit and choose Paste to paste the Color Palette on the canvas.

Now print the Color Palette to see how each of its colors looks when printed on your printer. To do this, you first need to open the Print Setup Options dialog box and change the Dithering option to produce the best-looking gray scales. In addition, you may need to adjust the Intensity Control slider so that colors are appropriately converted to gray scales. Follow the steps listed here to print the first copy, then print additional copies with different intensity settings if necessary.

6. Select File and choose Printer Setup.

7. Make sure the correct printer is selected; then click the Options button to display the following dialog box:

12

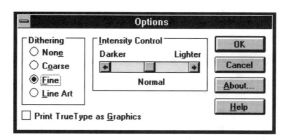

8. Click Fine as the Dithering setting, and then OK to close the Options dialog box. Click OK again to close the Printer Setup dialog box.

9. Choose Print from the File menu to print the image.

Look over the printout of the Color Palette, and compare it to the Color Palette on the Paintbrush window. If some colors are too dark or too light, choose File Printer Setup Options again and adjust the Intensity Control slider to lighten or darken the palette.

To see the full range of intensities, print the palette with the Intensity Control at its darkest and lightest settings, and at several settings in between.

To make these changes the new default, open the Printers utility in the Control Panel, click the appropriate printer, click Setup, click Options, then make the changes. Try to position the intensity slider to the exact position as you set it in Paintbrush's option box. To be exact, count how many times you click the right or left arrow button to move the slider button all the way to one side of the slider bar. Use this number to set the slider in the Printers box or to reset the box at any time in the future.

Creating High-Resolution Pictures

There are two ways to create pictures with high resolution. One method is to draw the picture as large as possible on the screen, and then scale it down when you print it. Any jagged edges you see on the screen are then smoother when printed. Another method, if you have a high-resolution printer, is to

Figure 12-7.   *Work with large images for accuracy, then scale them down when*
                  printing

create images using Zoom In mode, and then print the images at your printer's resolution, as explained in "Using Your Printer's Resolution," earlier in this chapter. These two techniques produce the same results, but provide a different way of looking at the relationship between the resolution of your screen and printer.

The following exercises create a one-inch-square company logo as an example.

The Paint Big, Print Small Method

Painting big on the screen gives you plenty of room to work and to manipulate the fine details of a picture. You can even zoom in for detailed work. You then print the picture at a reduced scale, 25 percent for example, using the Scaling value in the Print dialog box. Let's create a one-inch-square logo, by setting the canvas size to four inches by four inches, and then reducing the image to 25 percent of its original size when printing. Follow these steps:

1. Choose Image Attributes from the Options menu. Click the inches button in the Units box, type **4** in both the Width and Height boxes, and click the OK button.

2. When the new canvas opens, paint a logo large enough to just fit within its borders, remembering that it will be scaled down when it's printed. An example is shown in Figure 12-7.

3. To print the logo, choose Print from the File menu, and enter **25%** in the Scaling box.

Painting at Your Printer's Resolution

Painting at the printer's resolution is equivalent to manipulating the dots of the printer itself. You first determine the dot resolution of your printer, and then define a work area in Paintbrush to match that resolution in pixels. To create a one-inch-square logo on a 300-dot-per-inch laser printer, you need to create an image that is 300 by 300 pixels. Try the following if you have a high-resolution printer (if you don't, try settings that match your printer):

1. Choose Image Attributes from the Options menu. Click pels in the Units box, type **300** in the Width and Height boxes, and click the OK button.

2. When the new canvas opens, paint an image within the boundaries of the canvas, or choose Zoom In to work at the pixel level.

3. When you're ready to print, choose Print from the File menu, and in the dialog box mark the Use Printer Resolution box. Also, set the Scaling value back to 100%.

Remember that each pixel in Zoom In mode has a one-to-one relationship to the dot-resolution of your printer. Since the printer's dots are much smaller, your printed image will be smaller than you drew it on the screen, but will have high definition.

Creating Desktop Tiles

You will recall that various graphic images in Windows can be repeated on the desktop in a tiled formation. Paintbrush is used to create the graphic, and the Desktop utility in the Windows Control Panel is used to install it on the desktop. Put on your artist's beret now and settle into a creative mood; let's design an image and tile it.

1. Open a new canvas by choosing New from the File menu.

2. Draw a picture on an area of the canvas that is approximately two inches square. Don't worry about being exact. Remember that tiled images are placed directly next to one another, so as you work consider how the objects and their colors will look when placed side-by-side in the tiled arrangement. Here's an example of a group of stars:

Tip

To create groups of objects like these stars, copy objects you've painted and then use the Flip Horizontal, Flip Vertical, Shrink + Grow, and Tilt options on the Pick menu. Use the Color eraser to change the objects' colors.

3. When you're done painting, choose the Pick tool and select only the part of the image you want tiled.

4. Choose Copy To from the Edit menu, and save the cutout in the Windows directory with the filename extension .BMP.

5. Open the Control Panel and choose the Desktop utility.

6. In the Wallpaper box, select the file you just created; then click the Tile option and press the OK button. Your image is tiled on the desktop.

Creating Desktop Images

Desktop images can be created in the same way as tiled images, except that you paint one image that fills the entire screen and choose the Center option in the Wallpaper box of the Desktop utility. Here are the steps:

12

1. Choose Image Attributes from the Options menu.
2. Click the Default button and press OK. This creates a new canvas that is the size of your screen.

If the canvas is smaller than the screen size, you don't have enough memory available and should not install Wallpaper.

Caution

3. Paint the image you want to appear on the desktop. You might also import a picture from a clip-art package you have purchased, or use a scanned image.

If you have a scanner, you might scan pictures of your kids or pets, and then add captions underneath, such as their names, birthdays, or an important achievement.

Tip

4. Save the image, using the Save As option on the File menu. Be sure to save the file in the Windows directory with the filename extension .BMP.
5. Open the Control Panel and choose the Desktop utility.
6. In the Wallpaper box, select the file you just created. Click the Center option and then the OK button. Your image becomes the desktop wallpaper.

If you're creating wallpaper that contains text like dates or phone numbers, here's a trick. Type the information in a word processor, such as Notepad, so you can use all of the word processor's editing features. Fit all the text within one screen. When done editing, take a snapshot of the screen by pressing (ALT)-(PRINT SCREEN), then paste that image into Paintbrush. Now erase the window borders and add your own borders. Save the file as a .BMP file, then use the Desktop utility to install it on the desktop. This method makes it easy to update your desktop information since the text is in a word processor that provides easy editing.

13

Terminal

Windows Terminal is a *communications* program used to connect your system with other (*remote*) systems over phone lines, or with another system via a directly connected cable. Once connected with another system, you can have on-screen dialogs with other users, transfer files to and from other systems, and access remote information. Terminal opens up to you the powerful world of *electronic bulletin boards* (BBSs), such as those available through Compu-Serve, and electronic mail services like MCI Mail.

This chapter is divided into three sections. The first part describes basic Terminal setup and dialing procedures, and leads you through the process of connecting to another system. The second section discusses activities you can perform while online with another system, such as sending and receiving files. Finally, you learn about some additional Terminal features that can make your communications sessions more efficient.

Required Equipment

Before you can connect to a remote system, a *modem* must be attached to your computer. A modem is a device that converts digital computer signals to the analog signals used in telephone communications equipment. You then need to find out what parameters the remote system uses to communicate, and set Terminal's parameters the same way. If you plan to connect with an online information service such as Compuserve, you need to get a subscription, login name, and password. Subscription forms are often packaged with modems, or you can buy membership packages off the shelf in computer software stores.

You can also use Terminal to connect two systems together in order to transfer and use common files. For this arrangement, both machines must be running Terminal. You also need a *null modem cable*, which provides the correct wiring to connect two systems and is available at most computer and electronics stores. Be sure the cable's connectors match the connectors on the back of each system; the connector that attaches to your modem is almost always a 25-pin male connector, and the connector that attaches to your computer is either a 9-pin or 25-pin female connector.

Establishing a Communications Session

To start Terminal, double-click its icon in the Accessories window of the Program Manager. The first time you start Terminal, the following window appears:

Click the name of the serial communications (COM) port to which the modem is attached on the back of your system, and then click the OK button. Next you'll see the Terminal window shown in Figure 13-1.

The Terminal workspace displays the text of your session as it progresses. Initially, you'll see dialing information and connection messages. Once you connect with a remote system, the workspace displays messages from the remote system as well as the text and commands that you type. If a person is working at the other system, the same information is displayed in the remote's workspace, and the two of you can communicate by reading and typing messages on your respective screens. If the remote system is a bulletin board or online system, you can issue commands that are executed by the remote system.

To prepare for a communications session, you need to know the communications parameters of the computers with which you plan to connect. The settings of your system and the remote system must be the same; otherwise you'll see illegible characters on the screen or the connection will fail altogether. Typically, the speed of transfer is the most important parameter,

13

Figure 13-1.   *The Terminal communications program workspace*

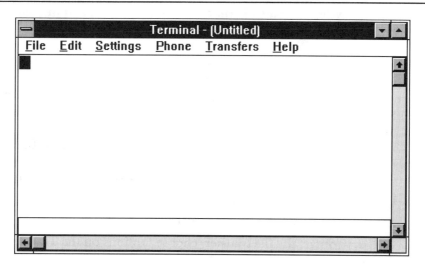

and most of today's modems automatically determine the best transfer speed, or *baud rate*. Baud rate refers to the number of signal changes per second that occur during a data transfer. How signal changes are used to encode characters with a particular modem determines the number of characters that can be sent per second.

A Typical Communications Session

Here's how a typical session works: Let's say you need to transfer a file to a friend's computer. The first thing you do is call your friend and agree on the settings you'll use for the communications session, as follows:

- Decide on the baud rate. If you're not sure what it should be, choose the highest rate possible and let the two modems synchronize when the connection is made.

- Determine the type of file to be sent and the method of transfer, known as the transfer *protocol*. This is the technique used to exchange information with as little error as possible.

- Decide which system will call and which will answer. The calling system executes Terminal's Dial command, and the remote system is placed in auto-answer mode.

Once you've agreed on these settings, you can begin your communications session. Here's what happens when your computer calls your friend's computer (you learn more about each step of this process as you work through the chapter):

1. Select the Terminal Phone command, and choose Dial from that menu to dial the number of the remote system. Terminal dials the number entered in the Phone Number option on the Settings menu.

2. After a successful connection, you can exchange messages with your friend using Terminal's workspace.

3. To start the file transfer, choose Options on the Transfers menu.

4. Once the files are transferred and you're ready to end the session, choose Hangup on the Phone menu.

The settings you've established for a communications session can be saved for future use. Save them in a file with a helpful name, using the Save option on the File menu.

Tip

13

Basic Communications Settings

The following paragraphs describe the settings for a communications session. Keep in mind that you need to set these parameters before you actually dial the remote system. You can try the default settings first; if they fail to give you a proper connection, try some of the other settings recommended here. To avoid problems, however, always try to match the settings of the remote system whenever possible.

Session Timer

Before you begin a session, you may want to activate the session timer. This helps you keep track of how long you are logged on to the remote system.

To see the timer, you need to turn on the function key display. To do this, select Settings and choose Show Function Keys from the menu. A set of ten boxes appears at the bottom of the screen. The lower-right box contains the system timer.

Initially, the timer shows the current time. To begin timing a session, choose Timer Mode on the Settings menu. This toggles the timer from a normal clock to a session timer. To toggle the timer off, select Timer Mode again.

Toggling the Timer Mode on and off does not reset the timer clock.

Note

Phone Number

The next option to set before establishing a communications session is the telephone number you want to call. Choose the Phone Number option from the Settings menu to display the following dialog box:

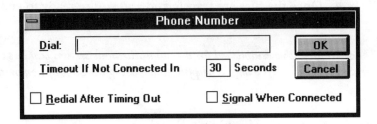

In the Dial text box, type the number you want Terminal to dial. Parentheses and dashes in the phone number are optional, but you may have to type commas to provide time delays, depending on your phone system. For example, if you must dial 9 first to get an outside line, insert a comma after the 9 to introduce a two-second pause (if you need more time, type two or more commas). In the following example, there is a four-second pause (two commas) after the 9 is dialed:

9,,1-234-567-8910

The remaining options on the Phone Number menu are explained here:

- *Timeout If Not Connected In*   Enter the number of seconds you want Terminal to wait for a response from the remote system. If the remote system does not respond within this interval, it may be busy or disconnected.
- *Redial After Timing Out*   Mark this check box if you want Terminal to continue redialing the number if it fails to connect.
- *Signal When Connected*   Mark this check box if you want the computer to beep when a connection is made.

Modem Commands

The Modem Commands option on the Settings menu is used to select a modem. If you have a Hayes-compatible modem and a touch-tone phone, leave the settings in the Modem Commands dialog box as shown here:

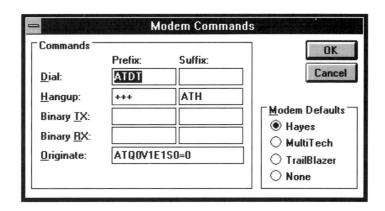

You only need to make changes to the Modem Commands options in the following situations:

- If you have a dial phone and a Hayes-compatible modem, change the command in the Dial Prefix box from ATDT to ATDP. This initiates pulse dialing.

- If you have a MultiTech, TrailBlazer, or other non-Hayes modem, mark the appropriate button under Modem Defaults. When you choose MultiTech or TrailBlazer, the correct modem settings are made automatically. If you choose None, you need to establish these settings according to the modem's instruction manual.

Terminal Emulation

Because of the diversity of computer systems, online services and remote systems usually treat your system as though it is a DEC VT-100 ANSI terminal. This lets the remote system interact with your system without having to define any special features. Services you connect with usually provide a list of key commands you can use while connected.

Select Terminal Emulation from the Settings menu to display this dialog box:

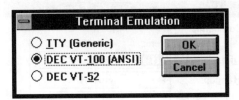

Leave the Terminal Emulation setting at DEC VT-100 unless the remote system specifically requests DEC VT-52 or TTY (TTY is an abbreviation for teletypewriter). Choosing TTY causes Terminal to emulate a no-frills "dumb" terminal that displays text only; special commands that change the screen color or other features are not supported. Use TTY only when you are connecting to systems that do not support the other modes.

Terminal Preferences

The options on the Terminal Preferences dialog box let you designate how you want your system to perform during a communications session. You can control sound, line wrap, and other features. Choose Terminal Preferences from the Settings menu to display a dialog box similar to the one shown in Figure 13-2.

Usually, most of the settings in the Terminal Preferences dialog box can be left the way they are. (You might want to change the font in which text is displayed in the Terminal workspace, by selecting a different font in the Terminal Font list box.) Refer to the section "Terminal Preferences" later in the chapter if you need more details about these settings. For now, note the following:

- If the remote system is sending lines longer than your system will display, mark Line Wrap in the Terminal Modes box.

- If you can't see the characters you type in the Terminal window, mark Local Echo in the Terminal Modes box. If you see duplicates of everything you type, turn Local Echo off. (Duplicate characters may be displayed if the remote system is echoing back the characters you send, for verification.)

- If text types over existing text after each carriage return instead of starting on a new line, the line feed part of a carriage return signal is missing. If this occurs on your system, mark the Inbound check box under CR -> CR/LF to add a line feed. If the remote system has this problem, mark the Outbound box.

• If you are communicating with systems in other countries, you may need to choose a different country in the Translation box.

The Communications Option

Select the Communications option on the Settings menu to display the Communications dialog box shown in Figure 13-3. Except for the Baud Rate and Connector options, the default Communications settings shown in Figure 13-3 will work in most cases. Choose a baud rate that matches the capabilities of your modem, and then choose the port it is connected to in the Connector list box. Other settings in this dialog box are covered in "Communications Options" at the end of this chapter.

Figure 13-2.   *The Settings Terminal Preferences dialog box*

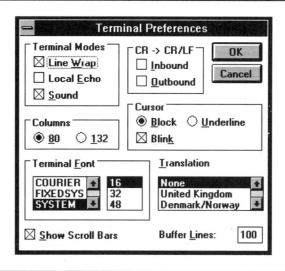

Figure 13-3.   *The Settings Communications dialog box*

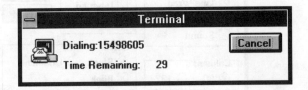

Now You're Ready to Dial

After making the appropriate settings, you're ready to dial the remote system. Choose Dial from the Phone menu to display this dialog box:

If you decide you don't want to make the call, click the Cancel button.

Note   *If you checked Redial After Timing Out in the Phone Number dialog box, the timer counts down and then redials (when necessary). Redialing is continuous until you click the Cancel button.*

When you log in to a service (such as CompuServe), you need to use the commands specific to that service in order to access its features. When you're connected with another user, you can simply type text into the Terminal workspace for the remote user to read. Similarly, any text typed at the remote computer will be displayed on your screen.

The results of a typical dial-up and login session to CompuServe are shown in Figure 13-4. Notice that the modem dial commands are displayed at the top of the screen. The message "CONNECT 2400" indicates a connection has been established at 2400 baud. The CompuServe login procedure then takes over and asks for a user name and user identification.

13

Logging Out and Hanging Up

Caution

*To end a communications session with an online service like CompuServe, **be sure to log off before hanging up**. Logging off is important because you are usually charged for every minute of connection time. If you just hang up or turn your system off, the service may not be able to determine immediately that you are disconnected and may continue to charge you for service.*

Figure 13-4.   *The early part of a typical communications session dialog*

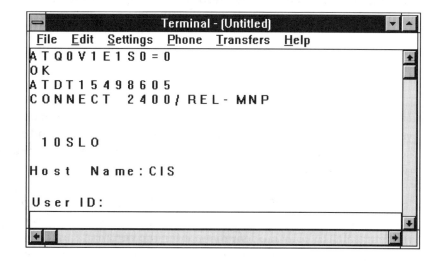

Typically, you type **BYE** to sign off. The system then hangs up on you and displays a message that you are no longer connected.

Once you've logged off, Choose the Hangup command from the Phone menu to ensure that the connection is terminated.

Saving the Settings

If the connection is successful, you can save the settings you used, including the phone number, for future sessions. Here's how:

1. Make sure all the Settings options are still the way they should be. Open the Phone Number and Communications dialog boxes to check. (If you just ended a successful session, you can skip this step.)

2. Choose Save As on the Terminal File menu.

3. When the Save As dialog box appears, assign a meaningful filename appropriate for the session (for example, COMPSERV for Compu-Serve settings, or MCIMAIL for the settings used to connect with the MCI Mail system).

Terminal settings files receive the filename extension .TRM. Later, when you want to make the same connection, you simply load the file from within Terminal and choose the Dial option on the Phone menu to begin.

Auto-Answer Mode

You can arrange to have remote users or systems call your computer to save yourself some long-distance charges. To do this, set Terminal and your modem to auto-answer mode. The auto-answer command for Hayes-compatible modems is ATSO=1; type it in the Terminal workspace and press (ENTER) to initiate auto-answer mode.

This sequence sends the auto-answer command to your modem, instructing it to answer the phone on the first ring. (The 1 after the equal sign indicates the ring count; change it if necessary.) If you have a non-Hayes compatible modem, refer to your modem manual for the command used to place it in auto-answer mode. When the remote system calls you and the connection is made, you may see "RING" displayed on the screen. With your system set to auto-answer, the connection to the calling system is made automatically.

Overcoming Connection Problems

In this section are suggestions for handling some problems that may occur when you are trying to connect with a remote system.

If you have trouble making a connection to the remote system, first make sure your modem is getting the dial signals from Terminal. Turn the volume up and listen for the dial tones. If the modem is not dialing, you may have it connected to the wrong communications port. Try switching the cable to another port, or specify the port it is currently connected to in the Connector list box of the Communications dialog box.

When the modem is dialing, but the connection to the remote system isn't being made, the remote system may simply be busy or offline; you may need to call the remote site by telephone and request assistance.

If your connection looks OK, but the messages on the screen are illegible, choose Communications from the Settings menu and make sure you've selected the same baud rate as the remote system. Or try changing the data bits, stop bits, and parity bit settings in that dialog box. Here are the most common setting combinations for those parameters:

- Data bits=7, Stop Bits=1, Parity=Even
- Data Bits=8, Stop Bits=1, Parity=None

When you connect to an online service, various login or welcome messages are sent to your system. If they appear normal and readable, the connection is good. To verify a good connection with a user-operated remote system, type some text, such as **HELLO**, into the workspace; the remote user should then respond by typing some text back to you. You can then get on with the business of your communications session.

In some cases, a communications session appears to be going well until you start to transmit data. You may discover that the transmission speed is too fast and the lines are noisy. Try reestablishing the connection at a lower baud rate.

Now let's take a look at some typical online tasks and activities.

Online Activities

Once you are properly connected to another system, you can transfer files, chat with other users, and engage in other online activities. This section covers methods for transferring files, and examines some of the other options on the Transfers menu.

Receiving a file from another system is called downloading the file. Sending a file to a remote system is called uploading a file.

Note

Types of Files and Transfer Methods

Terminal separates files into two categories: standard text files and binary files.

- *Text files* contain standard ASCII characters. (ASCII is an industry-wide standard of numerical codes representing numbers and letters of the alphabet.) Almost every computer system recognizes ASCII characters, so you can use Terminal to send text files just about anywhere. Notepad and many other Windows and non-Windows applications create text files.

- *Binary files* are typically program files, or document files with special formatting and control codes. Binary program files usually have filename extensions like .COM and .EXE, and contain executable code that does not conform to ASCII coding schemes. You must send binary files using binary protocols.

In most cases, you can transmit all your files, including text files, using binary transfer methods. These provide several advantages over text transfer methods. For example, errors are more thoroughly tested and corrected in binary protocols. In addition, document files containing formatting codes (such as those created with Windows Write) can be sent to other users with the formatting intact.

File Compression Utilities

File compression utilities are a boon to users who need to send large files or multiple files over modems. Although Terminal does not come with a file compression utility, several good ones exist that you will want to keep in mind. The most popular, PKZIP, is discussed here; it is a shareware product, easily obtained as described later in this section.

A file compressed with PKZIP requires only half the disk space of an uncompressed file. In addition, PKZIP will group and compress multiple files into a single file for transmission, thus eliminating most of the work and half the time involved in a multiple-file transfer.

Note

The remote user receiving the compressed file must have a copy of PKUNZIP in order to uncompress the file.

PKZIP and its companion product PKUNZIP are available from PKWARE in Glendale, Wisconsin. You can obtain these utilities over most bulletin boards like CompuServe. In fact, most files you would download from an online service are already compressed with the PKZIP utility and have the filename extension .ZIP. If you download the utilities and use them, you are asked to make a modest contribution to PKWARE for maintenance and upkeep of the software. For more information on PKWARE, write

PKWARE, Inc.
7545 N. Port Washington Rd.
Suite 205
Glendale, WI 53217

Transmitting Binary Files

Terminal provides two protocols for sending and receiving binary files. Use the XModem/CRC protocol unless the remote system uses the Kermit protocol. Once you've decided on a protocol, choose Binary Transfers from the Settings menu. You'll see this dialog box:

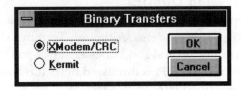

Select the protocol method you want to use, and click OK or press (ENTER).
Then you can begin sending or receiving files as described next.

Sending (Uploading) Binary Files

Here's how to send a binary file:

1. Make sure the remote system is ready to download a file from your system. If you're on a BBS, you need to issue an upload command for the remote system, which will then wait for you to send the file.

2. Select Transfers, and choose Send Binary File. The Send Binary File dialog box appears, which follows the familiar Windows dialog box format for opening and saving files.

3. In the Filename box, type the name of the file you want to send. Click OK or press (ENTER) to start sending the file.

Receiving (Downloading) Binary Files

To receive a binary file, follow these steps:

1. Make sure the remote system is ready to send the file. If you're on a BBS, issue the command that initiates the file transfer.

2. Select Transfers and choose Receive Binary File.

3. In the Filename box, type a name for the file to be received. Click OK or press (ENTER) to start receiving the file.

Transmitting Text Files

If the remote system is incapable of transmitting binary files, you may need to transfer a text file using a text transfer protocol. To do this, select Transfers and choose Text Transfers. You'll see the following dialog box:

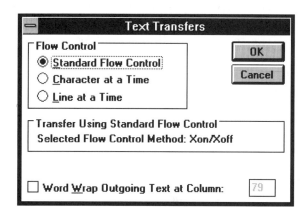

13

Choose a Flow Control method based on the criteria described in the next sections.

Standard Flow Control   Select Standard Flow Control to use the same flow control currently selected in the Settings Communications dialog box.

Character at a Time   Select Character at a Time to send text files as slowly as possible, when there are line problems or the remote system can't keep up with the transfer. When you choose this method, these additional options become available:

- *Delay Between Characters*   Turn on this option to transmit at a slow, even rate, without verification. If you still have problems with the transmission, increase the delay rate.

- *Wait for Character Echo*   Turn on this option if you want to verify the transfer of each character. Terminal sends the character to the remote site, and receives it back to verify accuracy.

Line at a Time   Select Line at a Time to send text files one line at a time. This method is faster than Character at a Time, but if the file is not sent properly, you may need to revert to Character at a Time anyway. When Line at a Time is selected, these additional options appear:

- *Delay Between Lines*   Turn on this option to transmit at a slow, even rate without verification. If you still have problems with the transmission, increase the delay rate.

- *Wait for Prompt String*   Turn on this option to wait for a response from the remote system before sending each subsequent line.

Sending Text Files

Follow these steps to send a text file:

1. Make sure the settings in the Text Transfer dialog box are correct, as discussed in the foregoing section.

2. Select Transfers and choose Send Text File.

3. In the Filename text box, type the name of the file to send.

4. Set the carriage return (CR) options. Choose *Append LF* to add a line feed to the end of each line of text, or *Strip LF* to remove extra line feeds from the text that may have been added by the remote system.

5. Click OK or press (ENTER) to begin sending the file. As the file is sent, it scrolls in Terminal's workspace.

Note

The control buttons that appear at the bottom of the screen during the session can be used to pause, resume, or stop the transmission of data during a file transfer session.

Receiving Text Files

Follow these steps to receive a file:

1. Make sure the settings in the Text Transfers dialog box are correct, as described in "Transmitting Text Files," earlier in this chapter.

2. Select Transfers and choose Receive Text File.

3. In the Filename text box, type the name of the file to be received.

4. Set these options, as necessary, to refine the disposition of the received text file:

   - *Append File*   This lets you append the incoming text to an existing file. You must specify the name of the existing file in the Filename box.

   - *Save Controls*   If formatting codes are being transmitted with the file, such as font or type style changes, turn on this option to save the codes. Not all formatting can be transmitted.

   - *Table Format*   Turn on this option if you want Terminal to replace two or more consecutive spaces with a tab.

5. Click OK to begin receiving text. The file will scroll onto the Terminal workspace as it is received.

You can print incoming file data by choosing Printer Echo from the Settings menu.

Tip

Viewing a Text File

The View Text File option on the Transfers menu allows you to look at a text file before sending it or after it has been received. Select Transfers, choose View Text File, and type the name of the file you want to see. You can ask for line feeds to be added or removed by marking the Append LF or Strip LF box. Click OK or press (ENTER) to view the file.

Other Terminal Options

The following options are used to customize Terminal or set it up to handle special situations.

Terminal Preferences

Select Settings and choose Terminal Preferences to see the choices in the Terminal Preferences dialog box (look again at Figure 13-2). These options let you change the way Terminal looks and operates. You have worked with some of the options already in previous sections of this chapter.

Terminal Modes   Select Line Wrap in the Terminal Modes field if the remote system sends lines that don't fit on your screen. Turn on Local Echo if you don't see the characters you type, and turn it off if you see double characters. Select the Sound option to turn on the bell or beep at the remote computer.

CR -> CR/LF   The CR -> and CR/LF options let you include a line feed in text being sent or received. Mark the Inbound check box if text received from the remote computer is typing over itself. Mark the Outbound check box if the same thing is happening in the data received from your system at the remote computer.

Columns   In the Columns field, choose a button to designate the number of columns of text to display on your monitor. Do not select more columns than your monitor can display.

Cursor   In the Cursor field, select either a block or underline-style cursor, and then mark the Blink check box if you want the cursor to flash on and off.

Terminal Font   In the Terminal Font field, choose a font from the list box for use with text displayed in the Terminal workspace.

Translation   To send and receive data in another language, specify the country in the Translation list box.

Show Scroll Bars   Turn Show Scroll Bars on or off, depending on whether you want scroll bars in the Terminal workspace. Scroll bars let you scan up and down through the text you've received. In text that is wider than your screen, enable the scroll bars so you can scroll horizontally.

Buffer Lines   In the Buffer Lines text box you can specify how many lines of incoming data to save in the communications buffer, which is a memory area that holds data until it is full. When the buffer is full, the oldest data is discarded to make room for new data. You can specify from 24 to 400 lines of buffer storage, depending on the free memory available in your system.

13

Communications Options

Take another look at Figure 13-3 to see the Settings Communications dialog box. The default settings of this dialog box are usually sufficient, as you have learned earlier in this chapter, but you may need to change them as described in the following paragraphs.

Baud Rate   Select a baud rate that matches your modem and that of your remote connection. If your telephone lines are subject to problems, it may be necessary to set both systems at a lower baud rate.

Data Bits, Stop Bits, and Parity   The communications method used by Terminal does not rely on a timer that allows the sending and receiving systems to separate characters using time intervals. Instead, data bits that represent a character end with a parity bit and stop bit. The number of data bits and the type of stop bit and parity bit must be the same for both sender and receiver, to prevent communications problems.

Flow Control   The Flow Control buttons let you specify how the flow of data is managed. The normal setting, Xon/Xoff, is a software method that signals the remote computer when Terminal has received more information than it can handle; the remote system stops transmitting until Terminal can catch up. The Hardware option is used when this type of flow control is accomplished by signals generated by the serial interface port. Use Xon/Xoff unless the remote system specifically requires another option.

Connector   In the Connector field, select the COM port that your modem is connected to. This is usually set the first time you start Terminal.

Parity Check   Mark the Parity Check box when you need to diagnose information that has been corrupted in a transmission. Normally, a question mark is displayed when a character is not received properly. Turning on this option displays on the screen the byte where parity errors occur.

Carrier Detect   When Carrier Detect is enabled, Terminal uses the carrier detect signal to determine when a connection is made. Otherwise Terminal detects a connection by looking at the modem response string. If you have problems connecting, mark this check box and try again.

Working in the Terminal Workspace/Buffer

You can type messages in or paste information from the Clipboard into the Terminal workspace to send to the remote location. To send the contents of the Clipboard, choose Paste from the Edit menu. The pasted information is then sent to the remote site. You can also type text in the workspace, highlight it, then choose Send from the Edit menu to send it to the remote site.

The Terminal screen is really a large buffer that lets you scroll to and use the text and messages from a communications session. For instance, you can scroll back through the text of incoming communications and use Cut and Copy techniques to put text into the Clipboard, and then paste it into other documents.

Printer Echo

Choosing Printer Echo on the Settings menu instructs Terminal to print all information received during a communication session. After the session is ended, you then need to select the option again to turn it off.

Defining Function Keys

You can define special commands for up to 32 function keys in Terminal. These keys can hold text frequently used in messages, or commands you execute often when logged in to a remote system. For example, a handy thing to assign to a function key is the login key sequence for an online service like CompuServe.

To display Terminal's function key labels, select Settings and choose Show Function Keys. Then you can click on the buttons or press the function keys on the keyboard to execute their assigned operations. The labels on the screen correspond to function keys (F1) through (F8), with the upper-left label being (F1), the lower-left label (F2), and so on. There are four levels that can be accessed by clicking the Level label.

In Figure 13-5, several of the Terminal command buttons have been assigned to help navigate through the CompuServe system. Notice that Login is the (F1) key, and Go Microsoft is the (F3) key.

There are eight buttons visible at a time. Up to four sets of eight buttons can be assigned, for a total of 32 function key assignments. You can make each set available by clicking the Level:(*number*) button.

To assign functions to keys or command buttons, choose Function Keys from the Settings menu. You'll see a dialog box similar to the one shown in Figure 13-6. If function keys have already been assigned, their names and commands will appear in the dialog box. To assign an operation to a function key, just type a name for the key, such as "Login" or "Password," in the Key Name text box; this name appears on the command button in the Terminal workspace. In the Command text box, enter the codes for the commands this button or function key will execute, as explained in "Codes for Defining Function Key Assignments," later in this chapter. If you want the button to type out a text string, simply type the string in the Command text box.

The Function Keys dialog box shows eight key assignments at a time. To work with the next set of eight key assignments, click the 2 button in the Key Level box. If you want the key labels to appear at the bottom of the screen, mark the Keys Visible check box.

13

Figure 13-5.   *Terminal command buttons defined to navigate through the CompuServe system*

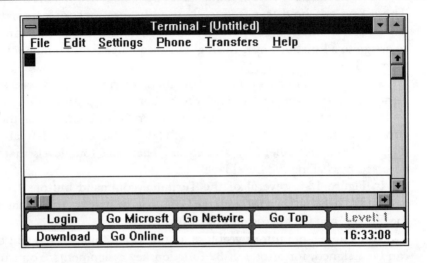

Figure 13-6.   *The Settings Function Keys dialog box*

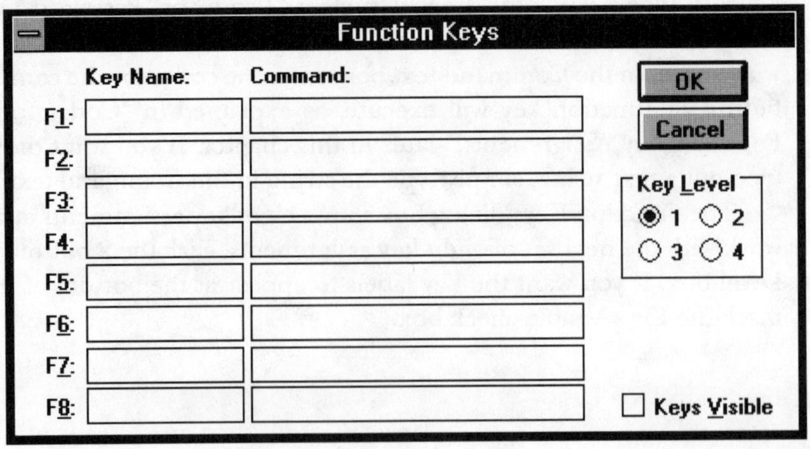

13

Codes for Defining Function Key Assignments

The following codes can be used in the Command text boxes of the
Function Keys dialog box. After the codes, you can enter any text you want
the function key or button to type when pressed or clicked.

Code	Result
^M	A carriage return
^A through ^Z	Sends control codes (A through Z) to the remote computer
^$D<NN>	Causes Terminal to delay the specified number of seconds before continuing
^$B	Causes Terminal to transmit a break code of 117 milliseconds
^$C	Chooses Dial from the Phone menu
^$H	Chooses Hangup from the Phone menu
^$L1 through ^$L4	Changes to another level of function key/command button assignments (sets of eight)

As an example, let's analyze the command shown here:

^M^$D03^M^$D03*ttt*^M^$D03*nnnnn,nnnn*^M

Assigned to the (F1) key, it has all the commands needed to log in to the
CompuServe network after a connection is established.

The first command, ^M, is used to type a carriage return, which is usually
necessary to get attention from the CompuServe system. The $D03 command
causes a three-second wait while CompuServe requests the user's name. The
variable *ttt* in the command would be replaced with the user's name. Another
^M then types another carriage return to accept the user's name, followed by
another three-second wait. The *nnnnn,nnnn* variable would be replaced with
the login identification, and the last ^M types a final carriage return. CompuServe then asks for a password. It is not advisable to keep your password
anywhere but in your own head, so don't include it in login scripts.

14

Using the Windows Accessories

Windows comes with a set of accessory programs that include a calendar, an organizer, and a calculator similar to those you might have on your desk. There is also an electronic card filing system and a macro recorder. You can start these accessories and keep one or all of them handy as icons on the desktop for use during your workday.

Notepad

Notepad is a simple text editor. Though similar to Windows Write in its operations, it doesn't have Write's paragraph and character formatting features.

Startup and Overview

To start Notepad, double-click its icon in the Program Manager Accessories group window. This opens the window shown in Figure 14-1. Take a moment to view each of the pull-down menus in the Notepad window and become familiar with their options and shortcut keys. The following paragraphs contain a brief explanation of Notepad's menus.

File   The File menu lets you open, save, and print Notepad files. Notepad files have the extension .TXT by default, but you can assign other extensions.

Edit   The Edit menu has the standard editing options, including Select All, which selects everything. Use the Time/Date option to insert the current time and date, and Word Wrap to make text wrap automatically at the right-hand window border.

Search   The Search menu lets you quickly locate and jump to specific text in a Notepad document.

Figure 14-1.   *The Notepad window*

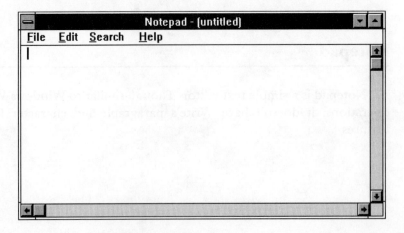

Notepad creates simple text files that do not include the special codes that define character and paragraph formatting; therefore, Notepad is a good tool to use for editing your system startup files (CONFIG.SYS and AUTO-EXEC.BAT). In addition, you can use Notepad to write notes throughout the day, and then copy and paste those notes in almost any application. You don't have to convert the text of the notes to any specific format before pasting them.

Since Notepad requires less memory than a more advanced word processor like Write or Word for Windows, you can leave Notepad open all the time. Also, consider keeping two or more copies of Notepad open so you can juggle blocks of text from one to the other when rearranging or editing documents.

Notepad also has a feature called the time log, which lets you create a file to keep track of activities. Every time you open the time log, it inserts a new date and time, and then allows you to type an entry. The date, time, and text entries can then be saved for the next session.

14

Using Notepad

When you type and edit text in Notepad, you can use many of the same methods that you use in Write. For example, pressing the (BACKSPACE) key removes the character to the left of the insertion point, and pressing the (DEL) key removes the character to the right. Pressing the (TAB) key inserts the equivalent of five spaces; deleting a tab removes all five spaces as a single unit.

The Word Wrap Option

Notepad's *word wrap* feature causes the text you type to "wrap" to subsequent lines, so that lines will fit within the borders of the Notepad window. Text wraps at the right-hand Notepad window border, and when the Notepad window is resized, lines are rearranged to fit within the new borders.

As mentioned earlier, Notepad is not just for keeping notes; it is also an editor you can use to write programs and DOS batch files. When you use it for writing a program, you'll probably want to turn word wrap off so you can see an entire command on one line—although you'll have to scroll to the right to see the entire line when it is longer than the screen width. However, if you're just writing a note or a letter, word wrap is a valuable editing tool.

Try the following now to see how word wrap works:

1. Open the Edit menu and make sure the Word Wrap option is not selected. If it is, choose the option to turn it off.

2. Type the following text in the Notepad workspace. As you type past the edge of the window, notice that the horizontal slider button moves to the right in the slider bar.

   When word wrap is off, text extends beyond the right window border until the Enter key is pressed. When word wrap is on, text wraps at the right window border.

3. Choose Word Wrap on the Edit menu, and watch the text rearrange itself to fit within the window borders. If you print the document, the lines will print as shown in the window, so you can think of the window borders as the margin settings of Notepad.

When word wrap is off, line length in the Notepad workspace is determined by the margin settings you specify in the Page Setup dialog box. Line length will be the width of the paper, less the amount of the left and right margins.

Note

4. Resize the Notepad window. The text again rearranges to fit the new window size, and, if printed, will break as shown on the screen.

Editing and Reviewing Documents

Once you have typed a document in Notepad, you can review it by scrolling up and down through the text. If the text lines are longer than the width of the window, you can use the horizontal scroll bar to see the far end of the lines.

You can use options on the Edit menu to cut, copy, and paste text within the same document, or to and from other windows (using the Clipboard). To select text, drag over it with the mouse, or hold down the (SHIFT) key while pressing an arrow key. You can also select all text in the document by choosing Select All on the Edit menu.

To insert the time and date in your notes or documents, press (F5), or choose Time/Date from the Edit menu.

Searching for Text

The Find option on the Notepad Search menu is used to locate specific text within a document. You can search the entire document or just a selected portion. Try this exercise to search for text:

1. Place the cursor where you want to start searching, or highlight the block of text you want to search through.

2. Choose Find on the Search menu.

3. In the Find What text box, type the text you want to find. If upper- and lowercase letters matter in your search, be sure to use the appropriate case in your Find What entry.

4. Select Match Whole Word Only if you want to find the search text only when it is not part of other words—for example, you may need to search for the word *here*, but not the word *there*.

5. Select Match Case to locate text that matches the upper- and lowercase letters you typed in the Find What box.

6. In the Direction box, choose Up to search to the top of the document, or Down to search to the bottom of the document.

7. Click the Find Next button to locate the next occurrence of the search text.

As you do search tasks, keep in mind the following:

- You can keep the Find dialog box open on the desktop, ready for the next search.

- Notepad remembers the Find What text even if you close the dialog box. To search for the same text again, choose Find Next from the Search menu.

- To work elsewhere in a document but quickly return to your current location, mark your current location with an uncommon string like @@@; then search for that string later to return.

Tip

You can also perform a search-and-replace operation. First type the replacement text into the Notepad workspace; highlight that text, and cut it to the Clipboard. Choose Find from the Search menu, and locate the text you want to replace. When the text is found, it is already highlighted, so you can immediately replace it by pasting from the Clipboard. Since the replacement text stays in the Clipboard, you can continue to search and replace in the document.

Page Layout

The Page Setup option in the File menu lets you set margins, headers, and footers in Notepad documents. Just enter the layout settings you want in the text boxes of the Page Setup dialog box. Type in new measurements for the four margins, if desired. For Header and Footer, you can use the following codes with your header or footer text:

Code	Function
&d	Inserts the date
&p	Inserts the page number
&f	Inserts the current filename
&l	Left-justifies the text that follows
&r	Right-justifies the text that follows
&c	Centers the text that follows
&t	Inserts the time

For example, to include a header with a left-justified title and a right-justified page number preceded by the word *Page*, type the following in the Header text box:

&lThe Title Text &rPage &p

Printing and Saving Documents

To print a Notepad document, choose Print on the File menu. To select a different printer, paper size, or other printer setup option, choose Printer Setup on the File menu.

Choose either Save or Save As from the File menu to save your document. You can select another drive or directory when saving the file. Notepad documents are saved as standard text files with the .TXT filename extension, but you can assign a different extension by typing it in the Filename text box.

Notepad Time Log Feature

Notepad can be used to create a special time log that automatically appends the time and date to the end of the time-log file every time it is opened. You can use a time log to track phone calls or billable activities. To create the file, type **.LOG** on the first line of a new file, and then save the file using any name you want. Every time you open that file, the current date and time is appended to the last line of the file.

Copy your time-log file to the Startup group in Program Manager, so that the time log opens every time you start Windows.

Tip

Calculator

The Windows Calculator comes in two versions, a Standard Calculator and a Scientific Calculator. Use the Standard Calculator for basic calculations; it has a memory feature for storing and accumulating numbers. The Scientific Calculator includes advanced features such as number base conversions, statistical analysis, and trigonometric functions.

Startup and Overview

Load the Calculator by double-clicking its icon in the Program Manager Accessories group window. When the Calculator appears, choose either Scientific or Standard from the View menu. The Standard Calculator is illustrated in Figure 14-2, and the Scientific Calculator is illustrated in Figure 14-3.

The Edit menus of both calculators provide copy and paste options that let you paste numbers to the calculator display from another application, or copy results from the calculator display to other applications.

Using the Keyboard

Though you can click any calculator button with the mouse, you may prefer keyboard methods for quick data entry. Most of the calculators' function keys can also be accessed from the keyboard. All the basic arithmetic operators (+ – * / =) are available on the keypad. (Press the * to multiply, and the / to divide.)

To use the numeric keypad, make sure (NUM LOCK) *is on.*

Remember

Figure 14-2.   *The Standard Calculator is displayed when you choose Standard from the Calculator View menu*

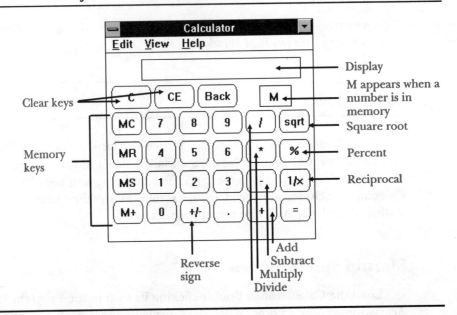

Printing the Function List

The functions of the calculators are extensive. You can print a complete listing and description of their use by following these steps:

1. Open the Help pull-down menu:

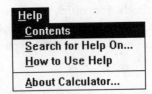

Figure 14-3. *The Scientific Calculator is displayed by choosing Scientific from the Calculator View menu*

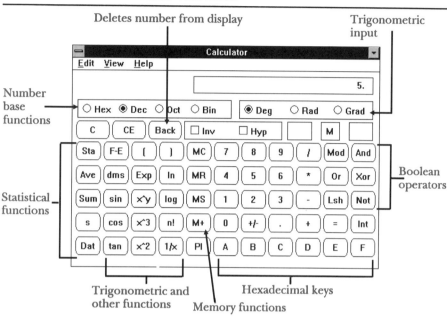

2. Choose Contents to see a list of general topics, or choose Search for Help On and type **keys** to display a list of topics that have keyboard descriptions.

3. When you see the topic you want, choose Print Topic on the File menu.

Calculation Techniques

Calculations are performed on the Windows calculators just as you would on a regular calculator; instead of pressing buttons, you click numbers on the calculator keyboard with the mouse or use the numeric keypad. The following exercise to add two numbers uses the mouse method:

1. Click the first number to add.

2. Click the addition operator (the + key).

3. Click the second number to add.

4. Click the equals operator (the = key) to display the results of the addition.

Clearing the Calculator

To clear the calculator display and memory so you can start new calculations, do one of the following:

- To clear the current calculator entries, click the C (Clear) function or press the (ESC) key.

- To clear the number currently being entered without clearing previously entered numbers, click the CE (Clear Entry) function or press the (DEL) key.

- To remove the most recently typed digit, click the Back function or press the (BACKSPACE) key.

Using the Memory Keys

The calculators' memory keys are used to store numbers for later use or to accumulate totals in a memory location. New values placed in memory either replace the existing value, add to it, or subtract from it. The memory buttons operate as follows:

- The MS (Memory Store) button takes the current value from the calculator display and puts it into memory, replacing any existing value in memory.

- The M+ (Memory Sum) button adds the current value in the calculator display to the value in memory, and stores the new sum in memory.

- The MR (Memory Recall) button displays the current contents of memory.

- The MC (Memory Clear) button clears memory of its current contents.

Number Base Conversions (Scientific Calculator Only)

You can switch the Scientific calculator from its normal (base 10) number system to another number base by clicking one of the following buttons:

- Hex (hexadecimal)
- Dec (decimal)
- Oct (octal)
- Bin (binary)

To convert a value from one number base to another, follow these steps:

1. Click the button of the starting number base (Dec, for example).
2. Enter (type) the value to convert.
3. Click the button of the number base you want to convert to. The value is converted.
4. Using the buttons to the right of the number base buttons, choose a unit of measurement for displaying the results. (These buttons change when you use hexadecimal, octal, or binary.) Click Dword to display the full 32-bit representation of the number, click Word to display the 16-bit representation, or click Byte to display the 8-bit representation. These buttons appear in hexadecimal mode.

The keys A through F at the bottom of the Scientific Calculator are used to enter hexadecimal numbers 10 through 15.

Note

Statistical Functions (Scientific Calculator Only)

The Scientific calculator can perform statistical functions such as averaging and standard deviation. You enter the values for the calculations in a special Statistics Box that appears when you click the Sta button. The Statistics Box can be moved from the calculator onto the desktop, where you can enter a list of numbers or data points. To see how this works, try this exercise:

1. Click the Sta button to display the Statistics Box, shown here:

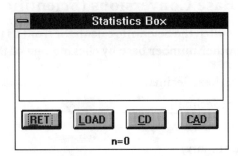

2. Move the Statistics Box to the side. Then click the Calculator and type some numbers, such as 100, 200, 300, and so on, clicking the Dat button or pressing (INS) after each number to insert it in the Statistics Box.

3. To observe the results of statistical calculations on your numbers, click the Ave (Average), Sum, and s (Standard Deviation) buttons. After each result is displayed, click the RET button on the Statistics Box to return to the calculator.

The buttons of the Statistics Box operate as follows:

- *RET* jumps back to the calculator so you can type numbers (you can also jump back by typing numbers).

- *LOAD* copies the highlighted (selected) number in the Statistics Box to the calculator display.

- *CD* deletes the highlighted (selected) number in the Statistics Box.

- *CAD* deletes all numbers in the Statistics Box.

Calendar

Windows Calendar provides a daily or month-at-a-glance view of appointments and schedules. In the daily view, you can add messages and set alarms on the hour, half-hour, quarter-hour, or at any specific time you wish. In the month view, you can click a day of the week to view its schedule.

Startup and Overview

To start the Calendar, double-click the Calendar icon in the Program Manager Accessories window. The Calendar window appears, similar to that pictured in Figure 14-4.

The appointment area contains a list of times. These are initially set in one-hour increments, but you can change the increment to every 30 minutes or every 15 minutes. You can also insert *special times* (specific times in addition to the predetermined incremental times) when needed. The status bar at the top of the appointment area shows the current time and the day being viewed.

Figure 14-4. *The Calendar window*

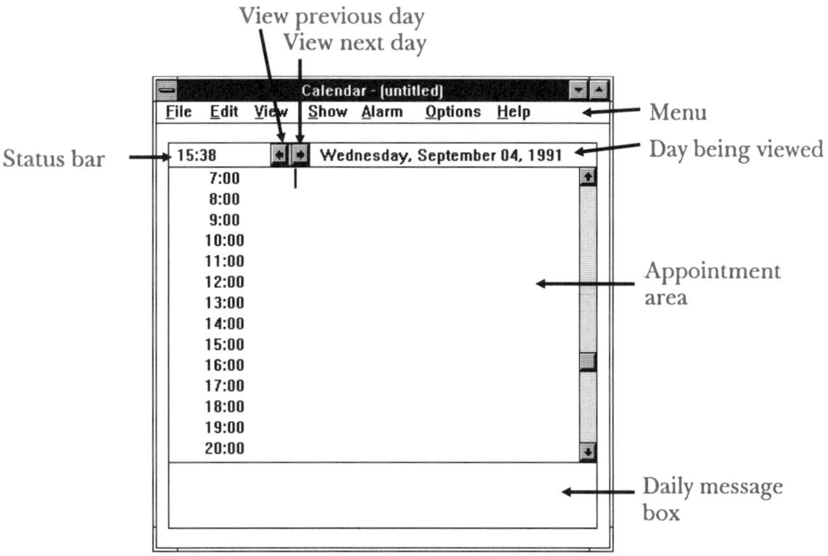

To view previous or subsequent days, click the right or left arrow buttons in the status bar.

The Calendar's date range is from January 1, 1980, to December 31, 2099. The dates are formatted using one of the following schemes:

mm/dd/yy
mm/dd/yyyy
mm-dd-yy

Note

Leading zeros are not required when typing a date.

The Calendar menu options are briefly described in the next paragraphs. As you read through the descriptions, open each menu so you can get familiar with its options and speed keys.

File   Use the options on the File menu to open and save calendar files, and to print out your appointments. You can specify a range of appointments for printing.

Edit   The Edit menu lets you edit your list of appointments, and remove a range of dates from the calendar.

View   As mentioned previously, you can switch between day and month views with the View menu.

Show   The Show menu lets you move back and forth through the days of the calendar.

Alarm   Use the Alarm menu to set the alarm and its controls.

Options   With the Options menu, you can mark days that have significant activities, or change the time increment of appointments.

Using Calendar

When Calendar first starts, the current day is displayed in the status bar. You can move to a future day or a previous day to view upcoming or previous appointments. Once the correct day is highlighted, you can view appointments, add new appointments, or remove appointments. In this section you step through all the Calendar operations.

Calendar Setup

Before you start using Calendar for the first time, you can set some of its features to suit your own needs. For example, follow this next exercise to change the time interval, the time format, and the starting time for each day's appointment area:

1. Select Options and choose Day Settings to display the following dialog box:

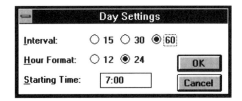

2. Click the time interval you want to use between scheduled appointments. (Keep in mind that special times can be inserted whenever you need them.)

3. To set the time format, click either 12-hour or 24-hour format.

4. Enter a time in the Starting Time text box. This should be the time you normally start your day. It will always appear at the top of the appointment list, but you can still scroll up to earlier times if necessary.

Jumping to a Day or Month

To enter an appointment, you need to select the correct day view. To do this, use any of the following techniques:

- To jump forward or backward among days, click the left or right. arrow button in the status bar.

14

- To move to the appointments for yesterday, tomorrow, or the current day, choose Previous, Next, or Today from the Show menu.

- To view a specific day, choose Date from the Show menu, and type the date you want in the Show Date text box.

- Switch to the month view (shown in Figure 14-5) by choosing Month from the View menu; then double-click a day to get to the day view.

- To jump to a day in another month, choose the Date option from the Show menu and type the exact date to view, or choose Month from the View menu and then click the left or right arrow button to move between months.

Figure 14-5.   *The month view lets you quickly jump to any day or month*

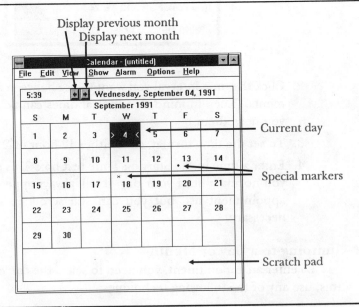

Adding and Removing Appointments and Notes

As you work within the appointment area, use the following keys to navigate around the Calendar window:

- (END) jumps to the end of a line, and (HOME) jumps to the beginning of a line. Use the arrow keys on the keyboard to scroll through the text of a message.

- Use (PGUP) and (PGDN) to move up or down one screen in the appointment list.

- (CTRL)-(HOME) jumps to the first appointment time of the day (as determined by the Starting Time in the Options Day Settings dialog box).

- (CTRL)-(END) moves 12 hours past the day's starting time.

After selecting a day, you can view, add, or remove appointments. It's easy to add appointments—just click the time for the appointment, or press the (UP ARROW) or (DOWN ARROW) key and move the insertion point to the appointment time. (The scroll bars of the appointment area can also be used to scroll through the time list.) Once you've positioned the insertion point, type a description of your appointment, up to 80 characters. The text scrolls to the left if you type past the Calendar window border on the right.

Each daily appointment window has a scratch pad at the bottom of the screen where you can type notes, reminders, or other messages (up to three lines). Click in the scratch pad and then type the text of the note. Or you can press the (TAB) key to jump to the scratch pad, and then (TAB) again to return to the appointment area.

You can remove the appointments for one day or a range of days by choosing the Remove option from the Edit menu. When the Remove dialog box appears, type the first and last dates whose appointments you want to remove in the From and To boxes, respectively, and then choose OK to remove the appointments. The appointments for the selected days are cleared, although the day remains so you can enter new appointments. Use this option to clean out old dates and reduce the size of the file.

Adding Special Times

Special times (specific times not on the list of appointment times) can be inserted in the appointment listing for any day by following these steps:

14

1. Jump to the day for the appointment, using the Month view.

2. Make sure the day view is active by choosing Day from the View menu.

3. Select Options and choose Special Time to open the following dialog box:

4. Type in the special time in the form *hh:mm*, click the AM or PM button, and then click Insert to insert the new time.

To remove a special time in the form *hh:mm*, follow the steps above, but click the Delete button instead of the Insert button.

Calendar Alarms and Messages

You can set an *alarm* to warn you about the arrival or approach of any time in the daily appointment window. When the alarm goes off, Calendar displays a message or alerts you in one of the following ways:

- If the Calendar window is active, a dialog box appears and displays the alarm message.

- If the alarm sound control is turned on, a beep sounds for a few seconds.

- If the Calendar window is open but inactive, the alarm sounds, the Calendar title bar flashes, and the alarm message is displayed when you activate the Calendar window.

- If Calendar is reduced to an icon, the icon flashes. When you select the icon, the alarm message is displayed on the screen but the Calendar window is not opened.

To set an alarm,

1. Move the insertion point to the time for the alarm or add a special time if necessary.

2. Select Alarm and choose Set. A bell appears in front of the time, to indicate an alarm has been set.

You can set an alarm to go off a few minutes ahead of the designated time, and set alarms to go off without making a sound. To set these options, do the following:

1. After you position the insertion point on a time, choose the Controls option from the Alarm menu to display this Alarm Controls dialog box:

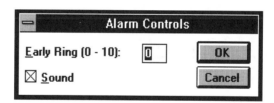

2. In the Early Ring text box, type the amount of time (from 0 to 10 minutes before the selected appointment time) for the early warning.

3. Click the Sound box to turn the alarm sound on or off.

4. Click OK to save the settings.

Marking Dates

Calendar provides a set of five different *marks*, or special characters you can use to call attention to certain dates (in the month view of the Calendar). You can see two of the marks in Figure 14-5.

14

Use the five different marks to represent various types of events. Create a list of what the marks designate on your calendars. For example, the box symbol (Symbol 1) could represent birthdays, and the x symbol (Symbol 4) might represent deadlines.

Here's how to mark a day on the Calendar:

1. Choose Month from the View menu, and click the day you want to mark.

2. Select Options and choose Mark, to display the Day Markings dialog box:

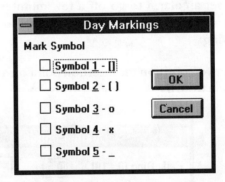

3. Click the mark you want to add, and choose OK.

To mark days in other months, click the left or right arrow button in the status bar and repeat these steps. To remove a mark, use this same procedure; when the Day Markings dialog box appears, click the mark you want to remove.

Saving Appointment Calendars

To save an appointment calendar file, choose Save or Save As on the File menu. Calendar files are saved with the .CAL filename extension unless you specify a different extension. You can maintain any number of Calendar files, and create a special startup icon for each in the Program Manager. For example, you might want a general appointment calendar with one-hour time increments, and also a more detailed schedule with 15-minute increments.

Setting Page Layout and Printing

The Page Setup option on the File menu lets you designate margins, headers, and footers to print your Calendar. Choose Page Setup from the File menu, and you'll see a dialog box with text boxes for entering margin dimension values and header and footer codes and text. Highlight the items you want to change, and type the new settings. The following codes can be used in the Header or Footer field:

Code	Function
&d	Inserts the date
&p	Inserts the page number
&f	Inserts the current filename
&l	Left-justifies the text that follows
&r	Right-justifies the text that follows
&c	Centers the text that follows
&t	Inserts the time

Here's an example of an entry to produce a centered header on a printed Calendar:

&cAppointments for the Week of August 2, 1992

Here's an entry to print a footer with a centered page number:

&cPage &p

Note that the word *Page* will be printed before the page number itself.

To print your appointments, choose the Print option from the File menu. The following dialog box appears:

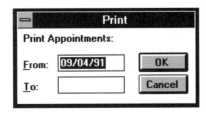

In the From box, type the first date whose appointments you want to print; type the last date you want to print in the To box. Then choose OK to print the appointments. Note that you cannot print the month view.

Cardfile

Cardfile is an electronic index card filing system that is used to store text and pictures. Figure 14-6 illustrates how Cardfile can be used to track the records in a music collection. Each card has a title (a header) that is used for sorting and searching; in the body of the card you can type or paste in additional text and graphics. You can display cards by searching for text either in the header or in the body of the card.

Several sets of index card files can be stored on your system. For example, you might use one to keep a name and address list, a music list, or a household inventory. Cardfile is also an excellent tool for cataloging graphic images

Figure 14-6.   *Cardfile is designed to look and work like an index card filing system*

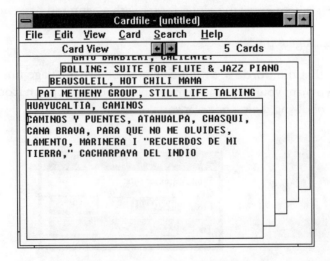

you've created in drawing programs and want to organize for quick retrieval, as described in "Cardfile Scrapbooks," later in this chapter.

Startup and Overview

To start Cardfile, double-click its icon in the Program Manager Accessories window. Take a moment to look over Cardfile's features and menus. The status bar just beneath the menu bar indicates how many cards are in the stack. It also gives the current view, which can be of the cards or of just the index headers. The status bar also includes the arrow buttons used to scroll through the card stack (the left arrow scrolls backward; the right arrow scrolls forward).

The Cardfile menu options are described in the following paragraphs.

File   The familiar File menu includes the usual filing operations common to Windows accessories. In addition to opening, saving, and printing cards in the Cardfile stack, you can also use a Merge option to combine two Cardfile files.

Edit   The Edit menu includes editing options for cutting and pasting text, and for changing index headers on cards.

View   Use View to switch between card view and list view (index headers only).

Card   The Card menu lets you add, delete, and duplicate cards. The handy Autodial option dials phone numbers if you have a modem.

Search   The Search menu is used to locate cards in the stack.

Using Cardfile

When you first start Cardfile, a single, blank index card appears in the workspace. You can add new cards as you need them, using the Add option on the Card menu. When a new card is added to the stack, the index header text is used to place the card in the stack in alphabetical order.

14

Because the index header is used to sort the cards in the stack, use discretion when deciding what to enter. You might want to create a coding scheme in the index header to categorize the information. For example, names in a file of business cards can be coded based on the profession of each person. In this scheme, attorneys' names could be coded with the letter A, and doctors could be coded B.

The following sections explain how to use the Cardfile features.

Adding New Index Cards

Index cards must be added to the stack when you want to catalog new information. To add a new card,

1. Choose Add from the Card menu.

2. In the Add text box, type the index header information for the new card.

3. Click OK to add the card to the stack.

The new card appears at the top of the stack. You can then type information in its text area.

Typing Index Card Text   Once a new card has been added to the stack, you can add text or a graphic image to the body of the card. If necessary, first bring the card to the top of the stack by clicking the card, or by clicking the arrow buttons in the status bar until the card appears on top. The text insertion point will be in the body of the card, so you can begin typing text immediately.

Cardfile wraps the text to a new line as you approach the right edge of the card. You can't type more text than will fit on the card in the window. As you create text, keep in mind that the Search command can be used to locate cards based on words in the body text, so be sure to include important keywords when appropriate.

You see how to add graphics to an index card later in this chapter, in "Cutting and Pasting Graphics."

Duplicating Cards

Another way to add a card is to duplicate one that already exists. This saves time and keystrokes when one card already has much of the information you need for a new card. For example, in a name and address file, you might create a card with a city, state, and zip code, and then duplicate it for use with all addresses in that city. Here's how to duplicate a card:

1. Click the card you want to duplicate.

2. Choose the Duplicate option on the Card menu.

3. Choose the Index option on the Edit menu, and change the header information as needed for the new card.

4. Add to or change the card's body text as appropriate.

Remember that the Clipboard, as well, can be used to copy text and graphics from one card to another.

Tip

14

Moving Among Cards

To edit and make other changes to a card, it must be brought to the top of the card stack. If the card header is visible in the Cardfile window, simply click it with the mouse. Another method is to scroll through the card stack using the left and right arrow buttons on the status bar. Cards are arranged in a circular order, so clicking the scroll buttons repeatedly brings you back around to where you started in the stack. The following keys can also be used to move through the card file:

Key	Function
(PGDN)	Scrolls forward one card in card view, or one page in list view
(PGUP)	Scrolls backward one card in card view, or one page in list view
(CTRL)-(HOME)	Brings the first card to the top of the stack
(CTRL)-(END)	Brings the last card to the top of the stack

Jumping to a Specific Card To quickly jump to a card, hold down the (CTRL) key and type the first letter in the index header of the card. The card will appear at the top of the stack. In many cases, there will be more than one card with that letter at the beginning of the header, so you'll see the first card with the letter. If this isn't the right card, just scroll (using the forward button in the status bar) to the one you want. The cards are arranged in alphabetical order.

The Go To option on the Search menu can also be used to locate a card by its index header information. Choose Go To, and then type the text that appears in the index header of the card you want to see. You only need to type as much text as is needed to differentiate the card from others that begin with the same header text.

Listing Cards

Another way to view and jump to index cards is to choose the List option from the View menu. Each index header in the card stack is listed in alphabetical order on its own line. To view the body information on any card in the stack, click its header in the list view, and then choose the Card option on the View menu. This restores the card view, with the card you selected on top of the stack.

Editing Cards

Use the normal editing keys (arrows, (BACKSPACE), and so on) to edit cards. You can also use Clipboard options to cut and paste text within the same card or among other cards.

To change the index header text of an existing card, choose the Index option on the Edit menu.

Note

Restoring a Card's Text

Cards can be restored to their original condition after an edit if you change your mind or make a mistake. Choose the Restore option on the Edit menu before clicking another card.

Deleting Cards

To delete a card, bring it to the top of the stack, and choose Delete from the Card menu. You will be asked to confirm the deletion of the card.

If the card has some useful information, you can use the Clipboard commands to move that information to another card before deleting the unwanted one.

Tip

Searching for Text in Cards

You can search for a string of text in the body of index cards, using the Find option on the Search menu. Note that you must be in card view, not list view, to perform a search. Here's how to search for text in Cardfile:

1. Choose Find from the Search menu.

2. When the Find dialog box appears, type in the text you want to look for. (Notice that the other common search options are not available, because Cardfile doesn't distinguish between upper- and lowercase or try to match whole words.)

3. Click the Find Next key. The first card with text matching your search text is placed at the top of the stack.

4. To find the next occurrence, click the Find Next button again, or if the dialog box is closed, choose Find Next from the Search menu.

Saving and Printing Cards

To save a card file (a "stack" of cards), choose the Save or Save As command. Card files are saved with the .CRD extension unless you specify another extension.

There are three options for printing Cardfile records:

- To print just the top card in the stack, choose Print from the File menu. The cards must be in card view, not list view.

- To print all cards, choose Print All on the File menu. You must be in card view.

- To print just the index headers, choose List from the Edit menu, and then choose Print All on the File menu.

Other Cardfile Techniques

You can include graphic images on your cards using Clipboard paste techniques. In addition, you can combine two card files. The Autodial option on the Card menu lets you dial a telephone number listed on a card.

14

Cutting and Pasting Graphics

In some cases, you may want to have a graphic image on an index card. Pasting in a graphic is easily done using the Clipboard commands with which you are already familiar. Follow these steps:

1. Open Paintbrush (or another painting or drawing program) and capture an image to paste using the Copy or Cut command on the Edit menu.

2. Return to the Cardfile window, and bring the appropriate card to the top of the stack (or create a new card).

3. Choose the Picture option on the Edit menu.

4. Choose the Paste option on the Edit menu to paste the picture on the card. It is placed in the upper-left corner.

5. When the picture appears, drag it to any position on the card.

If you want to add text to the card, you need to choose Text on the Edit menu before you can type in any text. When you type the text, it will be positioned underneath the image. You can move the image elsewhere on the card at any time, by clicking Picture then pointing and clicking on the image and moving it as needed. The image overlaps the text.

 Be sure to choose Text from the Edit menu after pasting or moving graphics; otherwise, you won't be able to type any text in the card.

Tip

Cardfile Scrapbooks

You can use Cardfile to create an index card *scrapbook* for storing Paintbrush graphics (or images and drawings created by other programs) that you often use. Scrapbooks can be used to collect text, too. When you need a graphic image or block of text while working in another application, simply open the Cardfile scrapbook, search for the image or text you need, copy it to the Clipboard, and then return to your application and paste it into the file there. Here's an exercise to try this:

1. Start a new stack of cards in Cardfile, and save it with the name GRAPHICS.

2. Open Paintbrush and create an image, such as your company logo. Then select the object and choose Copy from the Edit menu.

3. Switch to Cardfile.

4. Choose Add from the Card menu to add a new card. Give the card a header name that describes the graphic image.

5. From the Edit menu, choose Picture and then Paste to paste the Paintbrush image onto the card.

Repeat the foregoing steps to add more images to the Cardfile GRAPH-ICS scrapbook; then keep the scrapbook available on your desktop during Windows sessions.

To transfer a graphic from Cardfile to a document in your application,

14

1. Make the Cardfile scrapbook window active, then locate the card with the image you need.

2. Choose Copy from the Edit menu.

3. Switch to the application where the image will be pasted.

4. Choose Paste to incorporate the image in the other file.

Try keeping a text scrapbook. You can create blocks of text that are used often in legal documents, form letters, or company memos.

Tip

Merging Card Files

You can combine the cards in one file with the cards in another using the Merge option on the File menu. The File Merge dialog box is similar to the File Open dialog box—it displays a list of card files in the current directory. When appropriate, you can specify another drive or directory that contains other card files.

When two card files are merged, they are sorted alphabetically based on the index header. You may want to save the merged file under a new name, using the File Save As option.

Automatic Dialing

If you have a Hayes-compatible modem connected to your system, you can dial the phone numbers on your index cards by using the Autodial option

on the Card menu. Choose this option, and Cardfile reads the first number
it finds on the index card at the top of the card stack and displays the phone
number in the Autodial dialog box, as shown here:

Autodial	
Number: `967-0413`	OK
Prefix: `9-`	Cancel
☐ **Use Prefix**	Setup >>

To dial the number, just click the OK button. (You may first need to select
Tone or Pulse dialing, or the communications port of the modem. Use the
Setup button to set these options.)

*To use Autodial without error, be sure to always enter the phone number as the first
number to appear on a card. Other pertinent numbers can then be typed after the
phone number.*

Note

Recorder

With the Windows Recorder accessory, you can record a series of keystrokes and mouse movements that accomplish a task you perform frequently,
and then play them back at any time by pressing a single key or key-combination. These recorded key sequences are often called *macros*, and are usually
assigned to key-combinations that include the (CTRL) key, the (SHIFT) key, or
both. For example, you might record the sequence of keystrokes used to
format a paragraph or change a font in Windows Write, and then assign the
macro to the (CTRL)-(X) keyboard sequence; then you would only have to press
(CTRL)-(X) any time you wanted to repeat that formatting task.

This section explains the basic features and functions of Recorder.
Recorder does have some peculiarities. For instance, mouse clicks and drags
can be recorded, but it is almost impossible to play them back correctly,

because the arrangement of windows on the desktop constantly changes. You can never guarantee that the size and arrangement of windows will be the same when playing back a macro as when you recorded it. Therefore, you'll want to limit your macros to recording keyboard commands in most cases. Another tricky situation occurs when you switch windows while recording a macro, so it's best to limit each macro to one application.

Macros are usually designed to work in a single application, but you can also create "generic" macros to play back in any application. In this way, you can create a macro that accesses a feature common to many applications, such as the dialog boxes for Print Setup and Fonts. For example, consider a macro that selects a large Arial font from the Fonts dialog box. Since the Fonts dialog box is common to many applications, you'll want the macro to be, also.

Sets of macros are saved in files. In this way, you can create a group of macros for use with Write and another for Paintbrush, for example. On the other hand, you'll want to store macros that work in many applications in a "master" macro file and add it to the Startup group in Program Manager so that it opens whenever Windows starts. When you open a macro file, its key assignments are used, and any previous key assignments are discarded.

In addition, you can make one macro run automatically as soon as the Startup macro file is loaded. This lets you create a macro that includes a series of keystrokes you commonly perform at startup; for example:

- Open the Calendar accessory and print your daily appointments.

- Log onto a network and access the day's messages.

- Access an online service such as CompuServe to access e-mail (electronic mail) or examine stock market activities.

These are only a few of the activities that you can automate with Recorder. The following paragraphs describe its features, and then guide you through the process of recording some macros of your own.

Startup and Overview

Start the Recorder by double-clicking its icon in the Program Manager Accessories window. The Recorder window is shown here:

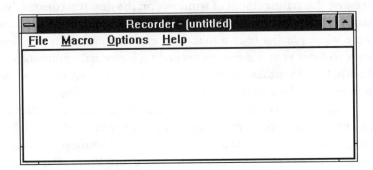

The names of your Windows macros are listed in the Recorder workspace as they are created. You can start a macro by double-clicking its name in the workspace.

The Recorder menu options are described in the following paragraphs.

File   The File menu lets you open and save macros in files for later use. You can also merge macros from other files into your current macro file.

Macro   The Macro menu contains options for recording and running a macro, deleting it, and changing its properties.

Options   The options on the Options menu control the default settings when using Recorder.

Recording a Macro

In the exercise that continues through this section, you will create and play back a macro that formats selected text with the 24-point Arial TrueType font in Windows Write.

Preparing to Record

When you start recording, all keystrokes and mouse movements are recorded. Therefore, you need to prepare your desktop *before* you start recording. Follow these steps to prepare for recording the Write macro:

1. Minimize the windows of any open applications.

2. Start the Recorder accessory if it is not already running.

3. Start the Write accessory, and move its window so you can see the Recorder window.

When it starts recording, Recorder switches to the most recently active window. Do not click any unnecessary windows before executing the Record command.

Note

The Recorder Dialog Box

14

The process of recording a macro starts with the Record Macro dialog box. You type a name and a description for the macro, and assign it a shortcut key, as described here:

4. Select Macro and choose the Record option to display the Record Macro dialog box (Figure 14-7).

Figure 14-7. *The Record Macro dialog box*

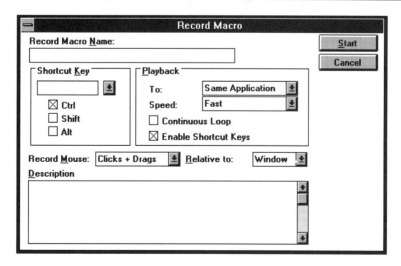

5. In the Record Macro Name text box, type **Arial 24-Point Font**.

6. In the Shortcut Key box, type (F1), or click the down-arrow button and choose F1 from the list. Then mark the Ctrl check box. This assigns the macro to the (CTRL)-(F1) shortcut key.

7. Click the Start button or press (ENTER). (The other items in this dialog box are described in later sections of this chapter.)

Starting now, all your keystrokes will be recorded, until you press (CTRL)-(BREAK) to stop recording.

Recording the Steps of the Macro

When you start recording, the Write window is displayed (assuming it was the most recently active window). Recorder minimizes itself to a flashing icon, indicating that it is in record mode. Now do the following to record the Write macro:

8. Press (ALT)-(C) to select the Character menu.

9. Type **F** to choose the Fonts options.

10. Type **Arial** in the Font Name text box, even if it is already there. (Remember, this dialog box may not look the same when you run the macro later, so type the name instead of selecting it.)

11. Press the (TAB) key twice to access the Size text box; then type **24**.

12. Press the (ENTER) key once to accept your Character menu entries. *Do not click the OK button with the mouse,* because the button may not be in the same place on the screen when you play the macro later.

Stop and Save the Macro Recording

Now you need to stop recording and save the macro.

13. To stop recording, press (CTRL)-(BREAK). You'll see this dialog box:

14

14. To save the macro recording, choose the Save Macro button, and then click OK or press (ENTER).

15. Now restore the Recorder window by double-clicking its icon. The workspace lists the new macro.

Next, save the macro for future use, as follows:

16. Select File from the Recorder menu and choose Save As.

17. Type **WRITE** in the File Name text box, since the macro (and others you may add) are for use with Write.

18. Choose OK or press (ENTER) to save the file.

Recorder saves the file with the filename extension .REC.

Playing Back the Macro

Now you can try executing your new macro by following these steps:

19. Switch to the Write window.

20. Choose another font, such as Courier, from the Character menu; then type some text and highlight it using the mouse.

21. Press (CTRL)-(F1) to execute your new macro, and watch the high-lighted text immediately convert to 24-point Arial font.

Press (CTRL)-(BREAK) *to stop a running macro.*

Note

Another way to play back a macro is to open the Recorder window and double-click the macro name in the workspace. Recorder immediately switches to the most recently active window and plays the macro. Use this method if you can't remember the shortcut key that runs the macro.

Tip

Changing a Macro's Properties

By default, macros play back only within the application where they were recorded. However, some macros are useful in other applications. The (CTRL)-(F1) macro you just created opens the Font dialog box on the Character menu, which is a common task in many Windows applications. Let's change this macro's properties so you can use it in other applications. Follow these steps:

1. Highlight the macro name in the Recorder window workspace.

2. Select the Macro menu and choose Properties to open the Properties dialog box. This dialog box has most of the same features as the Record Macro dialog box shown in Figure 14-7.

3. In the To: list box of the Playback area, choose Any Application.

4. Choose OK or press (ENTER.).

This is one of many changes you can make to a macro's properties after it has been created. You can also change its description, shortcut keys, and other playback options, as described in the sections that follow.

Note

More Macro Recording Options

The features of the Record Macro dialog box (Figure 14-7) are discussed in the following sections. Before recording more macros, read through these paragraphs for additional information. Keep in mind that, although you can always make settings before recording your macros, the Macro Properties dialog box makes it easy to change a recorded macro when you need to.

Shortcut Keys

Shortcut keys are assigned by typing the key name in the Shortcut Key box of the Record Macro or Macro Properties dialog box. (You can also click the down-arrow button to display and select from a list of available keys.) Here are some guidelines for choosing shortcut keys:

- It is recommended that you always assign a key in combination with (CTRL), (SHIFT), and/or (ALT). Avoid using a single key, such as (A) or (F5), because that key then cannot be used for its normal keyboard function.

- Use the (ALT) key sparingly or not at all, because many Windows options are accessed with (ALT)-key sequences.

- Don't assign key-combinations that your application uses, because Recorder's assignments will override them.

- For best results, use a standard pattern for all your macro key assignments, such as (CTRL)-(SHIFT) plus the key name.

The number of assignable keys is practically unlimited if you create multiple recorder files. In this way, you can assign a set of macro keys to Write and another set to Paintbrush. Using this technique also lets you have the same key-combination perform similar tasks in different macro files. For example, a print setup macro can be assigned to (CTRL)-(F2) in both the Write and Paintbrush macro files. To avoid confusion, assign similar shortcut key patterns to similar tasks in all your macro files.

14

The Macro Description

Type a short explanation of the macro, or instructions for its use, in the Description text box.

The Record Mouse Options

As mentioned earlier, most mouse movements should not be recorded in macros. When appropriate, however, you can use the Record Mouse options to set the level at which mouse movements are recorded. Here are descriptions of these options:

- Choose Ignore Mouse to prevent any mouse movements at all from being recorded. The advantage of using this option is that you can use the mouse freely while recording, to make "hidden" changes to windows or other options, without worrying about recording the mouse actions.

- Choose Everything to record all mouse movements. Use this option to record demonstration macros or macros you'll use only once, as described later in this chapter in "One-Time-Only Macros."

- The default option is Clicks + Drags, which only records the position of the mouse when it is clicked. With this setting, not all mouse movements record and play back correctly, but setting the Relative To options (explained next) enhances your chances for accuracy. On the plus side, some mouse movements and actions always play back correctly with this setting, such as dialog box selections or options that need only a mouse click without first positioning the pointer.

The Relative To Options

The position of the mouse can be recorded relative to the borders of your screen, or the borders of a window. Choose Screen if you want to record mouse movements across the entire desktop; choose Window if you want to record only mouse movements in a particular application window. When Screen is selected, the x and y positions of the mouse are measured from the screen border. When Window is selected, the x and y positions are measured from the window border.

When choosing a Relative To option, keep in mind the following:

- The Screen option provides accurate playback of mouse movements among objects on the desktop. However, make sure that objects you select during recording will be in the same place during playback. This is possible after you've established a solid desktop arrangement.

- The Window option replays mouse movements within a window, even if the window is moved around on the desktop. This means you need only be concerned with the size of a window, not its placement on the desktop, when recording or playing back a macro. For example, resizing the Paintbrush window causes the location of the tools to change, so the Eraser might be selected instead of the Brush during playback of a macro.

14

Tip

If you need to record mouse movements in macros that will be played back often, include (ALT)-(SPACEBAR)-(X) *as the first step in the macro. This maximizes the window during recording and playback, to ensure exact positioning.*

When to Record Mouse Movements in Macros

All macros belong to one of three classifications, depending on the use of the mouse in the macro:

- One-time-only macros
- Keyboard-and-mouse macros
- Keyboard-only macros

One-Time-Only Macros

Not all macros are played back over and over again. A *one-time-only* macro performs a task once, and is then discarded. Because the macro is based on your current desktop arrangement, and not a future arrangement, the mouse can be used as much as needed. Once you've recorded the macro, however, the arrangement of the desktop and the size of windows cannot be changed until you're through playing back the macro. Since mouse movements can be used extensively in a one-time-only macro, select Everything in the Record Mouse list box of the Record Macro dialog box.

For example, suppose you want to copy the information from a series of index cards in one Cardfile stack to another. Only some of the cards need to be copied, not the entire stack. Begin by opening two copies of Cardfile and placing them side by side; then load the source and destination card files. Start recording, and execute the necessary commands to select and copy text from a card in the source file. Then execute commands to add a new card in the destination file and paste text in that card. You can then play the macro back for any card you want to copy. Since the macro depends on the current window arrangement, you cannot change the arrangement until you're done copying cards.

Keyboard-and-Mouse Macros

In some cases, it makes sense to use both the mouse and keyboard in a macro. The keyboard is best for selecting options that would be hard to select with a mouse during playback, and the mouse is best for performing actions that are awkward with the keyboard.

When you decide to include mouse movements in your macro, you must keep the placement of objects and windows in mind. In some cases, the position of the mouse when you click it is not critical. For example, in a drawing or painting program, it is sometimes possible to first use the arrow keys to position the pointer relative to the screen border, and then move the pointer with the mouse to create an object. Using the arrow keys to place the pointer solves the positioning problem if the window should be a different size during playback.

Tip

You can guarantee that a window will always be the same size during any playback by maximizing the window as the first step in recording the macro. Press ALT-SPACEBAR-X *to maximize a window.*

When using the mouse in a keyboard-and-mouse macro, choose Window in the Relative To box if the macro is limited to one application, and choose Screen if the mouse is used to select objects on the desktop or in another window. In the Record Mouse list box, choose Clicks + Drags.

Keyboard-Only Macros

Keyboard-only macros are those you play back often in a variety of desktop and window arrangements. Since you can never be sure of the exact desktop arrangement when you run these macros, you should never include mouse movements. Instead, select all options and commands with keyboard commands. In the Record Mouse list box, choose Ignore Mouse.

Options for Playing Back a Macro

Playback options for macros are specified in the Playback box of the Record Macro dialog box. To change these options after a macro has been recorded, highlight the macro in the workspace, and then choose the Properties option from the Macro menu.

The Playback To Options

Some macros are designed for use in a specific application and may produce unwanted effects if run when another application is active. To avoid these problems, you can designate a macro to be for use only in the application where it was created. To do this, choose Same Application in the To list box of the Record Macro dialog box. If the creating application is not open when you play back the macro, windows displays an error message.

When you create a macro that can be used in many different Windows applications, choose Any Application in the Playback To box. The macro can then be played back in the current window. If the current window is Recorder, the macro is played back in the next window, which is the window highlighted when (ALT)-(TAB) is pressed.

Playback Speed

You can opt to play the macro back at Fast speed (the default), or at the speed at which it was recorded. You'll normally use the default Fast speed, so that your macros perform their tasks as quickly as possible. Using the Recorded Speed option to play back a macro is useful for computer demonstrations or training sessions. An example of this kind of macro is presented later in this chapter.

The Playback Continuous Loop Option

Mark the Playback Continuous Loop box if you want the macro to repeat continuously until (CTRL)-(BREAK) is pressed. Set this option when you want to continuously play back a macro for demonstration purposes, or to execute a command repetitively.

The Playback Enable Shortcut Keys Option

To include the shortcut keys of other macros in the macro you are recording, mark the Playback Enable Shortcut Keys box. With this option turned on, you can use other macros (up to five) as you record your macro, so you don't have to record those keystrokes over again.

Other Recorder Options

The following toggle options are available on the Recorder Options menu to use when you record a macro:

- *Ctrl+Break Checking*   Turn this option on to keep Recorder from detecting (CTRL)-(BREAK) during playback. This prevents a macro from being stopped before it finishes.

- *Shortcut Keys*   Choose this option to turn Recorder shortcut keys off. This may be necessary if macros are loaded and you need to run an application that has its own shortcut keys that conflict with the macros.

- *Minimize on Use*   Turn this option on to minimize Recorder to an icon when the macro starts.

Setting Default Preferences

The Recorder Preferences option is used to set default preferences for the options in the Macro Record dialog box. Select Preferences, and you'll see the following dialog box:

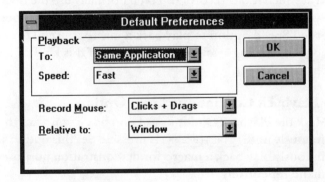

If you record many macros that have similar characteristics and playback requirements, you may want to establish your own set of preferred defaults for the Recorder options. Following the guidelines presented in the foregoing paragraphs, set these options to the choices you prefer for most of your macros. You can easily change these settings for any macro that needs to be recorded differently.

Loading a Macro File at Startup

Once a set of macros is created, you can load it whenever Windows starts, by creating a document icon for the Recorder file and placing it in the Program Manager Startup group. For example, suppose you've created a series of macros, called MAIN.REC, for general use in all of your Windows applications. Follow these steps to create an icon for this file in the Startup group:

1. Open the Startup Group in Program Manager.
2. Choose New from the File menu.
3. In the New Program Object dialog box, choose Program Item.
4. When the Program Item Properties dialog box appears, type **MAIN** in the description field, then click the Browse button to locate the MAIN.REC file in the Windows directory or the directory where it is located. The path and filename are then inserted in the Command field.
5. Click OK or press (ENTER) to create the icon.

The next time you start Windows, the MAIN macro file will be loaded and its macros will be available for use.

Creating a Startup Macro

You can automatically run an individual macro when Windows starts by including the macro's assigned keyboard sequence in the Command Line text box of the Program Item Properties dialog box when you create the startup icon. To represent the (ALT), (CTRL), and (SHIFT) keys from the macro's keyboard sequence, use the following keyboard characters in the Command Line box:

For (ALT), type the % character

For (SHIFT), type the + character

For (CTRL), type the ^ character

Thus, to designate a startup macro that has the assigned key sequence (CTRL)-(F1) from the MAIN.REC file, enter the following in the Command Line text box, as described next:

RECORDER –H ^F1F1 MAIN.REC

The RECORDER parameter is required in the field so that the keyboard sequence can be specified. (In the previous exercise, only the name of the Recorder file was necessary to load the file at startup, so you didn't need the RECORDER parameter.) The –H parameter is required to execute the key sequence of the macro. You then specify the macro key sequence (^F1F1), followed by the macro file to load (MAIN.REC). Specify the path for the macro file if necessary.

To make this change to the definition of the startup icon you created in the last section, follow these steps:

1. In the Program Manager Startup group, click the MAIN icon.

2. Choose Properties from the File menu.

3. In the Command Line text box, type the command described above, **RECORDER –H ^F1F1 MAIN.REC.**

4. Click OK to save the change.

Macro Examples

The following examples are presented to help you become familiar with the macro recording process and give you ideas for your own macros. Create the macros in the MAIN.REC macro file you started in the previous exercises.

A Macro to Open Dialog Boxes

In this example, you create a macro that pulls down the File menu, selects the Open option, and changes the file listing arrangement. The macro can be used in any application that has an Open option on its File menu. To record this macro, you use the File Open option in Notepad but you'll be able to play it back in other applications.

1. Start the Notepad accessory.

2. Start the Recorder accessory, if necessary, or make its window active.

3. Choose Record from the Macro menu.

4. In the Record Macro Name text box, type **List all files on Open boxes**.

5. In the Shortcut Key text box, type **O**; then mark both the Ctrl and Shift check boxes. This assigns the key sequence (CTRL)-(SHIFT)-(O) to this macro.

6. In the To field of the Playback box, select Any Application, to make the macro available for use in any application.

7. Click the Start button. The Recorder window reduces to an icon, and Notepad becomes active.

8. Press (ALT)-(F)-(O) to display the Open dialog box. *Do not use the mouse.*

9. In the File Name field, type ***.*** and press (ENTER). The file list changes to display all files.

10. Click the Recorder icon or press (CTRL)-(BREAK) to stop recording.

11. Click Save Macro and then the OK button.

12. Test the macro by running it in any other application besides Notepad.

14

Your new (CTRL)-(SHIFT)-(O) macro can now be used to list all files in a directory for any application. You can create additional macros that change the drive or directory as well. For example, if you keep all your document files in a directory called DOCS on drive D, you might create a macro that opens the Open dialog box, changes the drive letter to D, changes the directory to DOCS, and types *.* in the File Name field to list all files.

A Continuous Demo Macro

The following macro is of interest to those who need to create demonstrations or tutorials. In this example, you open Paintbrush and record the mouse movements necessary to create a box. You then replay the macro repetitively at the recorded speed.

1. Open Paintbrush.

2. Start Recorder if necessary, or make its window active.

3. Choose Record from the Macro menu.

4. Type **Repeating Demo** in the Record Macro Name text box.

5. In the Shortcut Key box, click the down-arrow button and choose a key from the list. For this example, choose Scroll Lock. Mark both the Ctrl and Shift check boxes, to make the assigned key sequence for this macro (CTRL)-(SHIFT)-(SCROLL LOCK).

6. In the Playback Speed list box, choose Recorded Speed.

7. Mark the Continuous Loop check box.

8. In the Record Mouse box, choose Everything.

9. In the Relative to box, make sure Window is selected.

10. Click the Start button to start recording. The Paintbrush window appears.

11. Press (ALT)-(SPACEBAR)-(X) to maximize Paintbrush. Since you will be using the mouse, this ensures the mouse coordinates will be the same during any playback.

12. Drag the mouse to the Filled Box tool, and click.

Remember

Mouse movements are visible during playback, so use slow, steady mouse movements.

13. Choose foreground and background colors.

14. Click in the workspace and draw a box.

15. Leave the box on the screen for about 5 seconds. Then click the white color box with the right mouse button, and select a wide line in the Linewidth field. Click the Eraser tool, and erase the box.

16. Press (CTRL)-(BREAK) to stop recording, click the Save Macro box, and click OK.

Now you can play the macro back in the open Paintbrush window by pressing (CTRL)-(SHIFT)-(SCROLL LOCK). The macro repeats until you press (CTRL)-(BREAK).

 You can create a similar macro to display a message, such as "I'm out to lunch," across your computer screen.

Tip

A Boilerplate Macro

Boilerplates are stored blocks of text you insert as needed into your documents. In this example, you create a macro that types your company name and address, then centers it and changes the font.

1. Start the Write accessory.

2. Start Recorder if necessary, or make it the active window.

3. Choose Record from the Macro menu.

4. Type **Company Name and Address** in the Record Macro Name field.

5. Choose Caps Lock in the Shortcut Key list box, and mark both the Ctrl and Shift check boxes.

6. Click the Start button. The Write Window becomes active.

7. Press (ALT)-(C)-(F) to open the Fonts dialog box. *Do not use the mouse.*

8. Type **Arial** in the Fonts box. Then tab to the Size box and type **14**. Press (ENTER) to make the changes (do not click OK).

9. Press (ALT)-(P)-(C) (remember, no mouse clicks); this will center the logo.

14

10. On the first line of the Write workspace, type your company name and address, pressing (ENTER) after each line.

11. When you're done, press (CTRL)-(BREAK), click the Save Macro box, and click the OK button to end recording.

You can play this macro back in any Write document. Of course, you can create similar macros that assign other type styles and enter different text. Because boilerplates are so useful, you may want to create a separate macro file to hold the ones you design.

Character Map

The Character Map utility helps you locate and insert special characters, including symbols and non-English language characters, into your documents. You can keep this utility open on the desktop while you write documents in Windows Write, Word for Windows, and other Windows applications. Character Map does not work with non-Windows DOS applications.

To open the utility, double-click the Character Map icon in the Accessories group. You'll see the window shown in Figure 14-8.

The first thing to do is choose the font whose characters you want to see. Click the down-arrow button in the Font field to display a list of fonts, and then select one. Try this now, and select a few different fonts; for each font you select, the large character table (or font map) in the main part of the Character Map screen changes to reflect the characters of the selected font. Compare the Symbols font map to that of a text font such as Courier.

You'll probably use the Symbols font often, because it contains many handy characters not available on the keyboard.

Tip

Figure 14-8.   *Character Map dialog box*

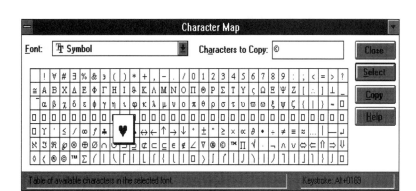

There are two methods for inserting a special character from the selected character table into your document:

- Click the character in the table, and view its keystroke requirement at the bottom-right of the Character Map window. (In Figure 14-8, the heart symbol is selected in the table, and its keystroke is listed.) Then switch back to your application and type the keystroke to produce the character.

- Another method is to use the Clipboard. In the Character Map window, double-click the characters or symbols you want (or click the Select button). The selected characters appear in the Characters box at the top. Click the Copy button to place the characters on the Clipboard, switch to your application, and paste ((CTRL)-(V)) the characters into your document.

Tip

The second method just described is useful when you need more than one character or symbol—for instance, when you are building complex strings or mathematical expressions using the Symbols font.

Tip

When you switch back to your application, be sure to position the cursor before pasting the characters.

Working with Very Small Characters   If a character or symbol is too small to see well, click the character and continue holding down the mouse button, to enlarge it. You can also hold down the button and drag the mouse over the character table; each character is enlarged as the mouse pointer touches it.

Media Player and Sound Recorder

Media Player plays animations, sounds, and MIDI files. MIDI (Musical Instrument Digital Interface) is an industry standard protocol for communicating with electronic musical instruments such as keyboard synthesizers. Other media devices controlled by Media Player include compact disk players and video-disk players.

Sound Recorder lets you record, edit, and play back sounds. This utility records sounds you can assign to system events such as errors and startups; you use the Sound utility in the Control Panel to make these assignments. To record sounds, you need a sound board and a microphone—but even if you don't have this equipment, you can still modify the sounds that come with Windows and assign them to system events. Many other sounds are available through third parties and from computer bulletin boards.

Tip

You can also add sounds to documents using Object Linking and Embedding (OLE), as discussed in Chapter 16.

In order to play back sounds through the speaker inside your computer, the speaker driver must be installed. This driver does not ship with the original release of Windows 3.1; it is available on the Windows Driver Library. Call Microsoft at (800) 426-9400 for more information. You can also play sounds through an external speaker, if you have a special sound board. Sound boards supported by Windows include

Creative Labs Sound Blaster
Media Vision Thunder Board
Ad Lib Gold
Roland LAPC1

Media Player

The Media Player window (Figure 14-9) has push-buttons similar to the controls of a tape deck. You can play, pause, stop, and eject the media. You can display a time scale or a track scale. The menu bar contains options for opening a media file and selecting a device to play. Devices are grouped as follows:

- *Simple devices* start playing as soon as you press the play button; they are not associated with files. An example is an audio compact disc player. If you have a CD-ROM player, place an audio CD in the player, plug in your headphones, and enjoy music while you work—using the controls on the Media Player window. If the CD player is also connected to a sound board, you can connect the sound board to your stereo and listen without headphones.

- *Compound devices* require a device element, which is usually a data file. By choosing a compound device, you can play sounds or MIDI sequences. If you have a sound board with a microphone input, use the Sound Recorder (described in the next section) to record digitized sounds.

To choose a device, select it from the Device menu. If a device is a compound device, its name is followed by an ellipsis (...), and a File Open dialog box appears.

Figure 14-9.   *Media Player dialog box*

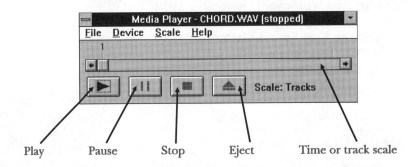

Once a device is selected, click the Play button, and the music, sound, or sequence begins to play. You can press the Pause, Stop, and Eject buttons at any time.

The Scale option provides a useful way to control the media. It shows either a time scale or track scale, selectable from the Scale menu. Use the track scale when playing audio CDs; use the Time scale when playing sounds or sequences.

To quit Media Player, select Exit from the File menu. If a simple device is still playing, it will continue to play after Media Player is no longer active. Reopen Media Player to restore your control of the playing device.

Sound Recorder

To get started with Sound Recorder, double-click its icon in the Accessories group. You'll see the dialog box shown in Figure 14-10.

Using Sound Recorder to record a sound is simple—just click the Record button and talk into the microphone. When you're done, click the Stop button. To listen to the new sound, click the Play button. Once you've got a

Figure 14-10. *Sound Recorder dialog box*

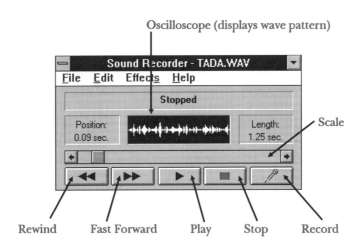

Oscilloscope (displays wave pattern)

Rewind   Fast Forward   Play   Stop   Record

14

sound you like, save it to disk. Then open the Sound option on the Windows Control Panel, and assign the sound to one of the functions listed, or embed the sound in one of your documents. You can also connect sound sources into many sound boards.

About Sound Information

Something to keep in mind is that sound files require a lot of disk space. So make sure you record only the sounds you need, and avoid unnecessary periods of silence when you start recording and when you're done talking.

Sounds are vibrations of air molecules, often represented as an analog (continuous) *waveform*. Sound Recorder captures these waveforms and converts them into digital information. As the sound arrives, its frequency is recorded at intervals, rather than continuously—a process called *sampling*. The digital value at the time of each sample is recorded and saved in a sound file. During playback, these digital values re-create the analog waveform, or an approximation of it, depending on the level of sampling.

You don't need a detailed technical discussion of this process in order to use Sound Recorder, but you should be aware of sampling rates. Sound

Recorder samples sounds thousands of times per second. The sampling rate is determined by the type of sound board you have—the higher the sampling rate, the better the quality of the sound, and the more disk space required.

Another factor that influences sound quality and file size is the amount of information stored every time the sound is sampled. When a sound wave arrives, it has a vertical characteristic defined by the height of the wave. Sound Recorder records this wave as an 8-bit or 16-bit value. Sampling at 16 bits provides the best definition of the wave but, again, requires more disk space.

The following table illustrates the relationship between bit size, sampling rate, and the number of bytes required per minute of sound. Although you can't change the sampling method in Sound Record, this information will let you calculate file sizes based on the sampling method used by your board. Note that kHz (kiloHertz) represents one thousand periods per second; a period is the distance between two consecutive peaks in a waveform.

Sampling Bit Size	Sampling Rate	MB per Minute of Sound
8 bits	11.025 kHz	0.66 MB/minute
8 bits	22.05 kHz	1.32 MB/minute
16 bits	44.1 kHz	5.292 MB/minute

As you can see, there is a trade-off in disk space used in return for the quality of the recorded sound. In some cases, restrictions on your sound board will allow only the lowest quality recording. Check your board manual for details.

Recording Sounds

You can record sounds in a new file, or you can add sounds into an existing file. To record a sound, you must have a microphone attached to a sound board. Here's how it works:

1. On the File menu of the Sound Recorder, choose New to open a new sound file, or Open to open an existing file so you can add more sounds to it.

The following sounds are included with Windows and are already assigned to system events. To increase your sound catalog, you can open these sound files, make changes, and then save them as new sounds.

CHIMES.WAV
CHORD.WAV
DING.WAV
TADA.WAV

2. To add sound to an existing sound, use one of these methods:

   - Click the Rewind button so you can add sound at the beginning.

   - Click the Fast-forward button so you can add sound at the end.

   - Slide the scroll bar to a point in the existing sound wave to insert the new sound. Or play the sound and stop it at the insertion point.

3. Hold the microphone and click the Record button. Start talking, or begin recording a sound. Watch the length values on the screen as you record. Up to one minute can be recorded at a time.

4. When you're done recording, click the Stop button.

5. Click the Play button to listen to your new recording. If it doesn't sound the way you want, choose File New to clear the sound file, and record it again (this will erase the entire sound file).

Inserting and Mixing Existing Sound Files

You can insert, combine, and mix sounds and sound files until you run out of memory.

- *To append an existing sound file to the beginning or end of your current sound,* click the Fast-forward or Rewind button to get to the position in the sound where you want to insert the sound file. Then choose Insert File from the Edit menu, and click the file to insert.

- *To insert new sounds at any location between the beginning and end of a sound,* slide the scroll bar or click its arrow buttons until the insertion pointer is in view. Find the insertion point by rewinding the sound and clicking the Play button. Then listen, and when you get to the insertion point, click the Stop button. Make fine adjustments by using the scroll bar.

- *You can also mix in sounds from a disk file.* When sounds are mixed, they blend together and play simultaneously. First locate the posi-

tion where you want to start mixing in a sound. Choose Mix With
File from the Edit menu, specify the filename, and click OK.

- *To delete a block of sound (or a block of silence),* position the insertion
  point before or after the block. Then choose Delete Before Current
  Position or Delete After Current Position on the Edit menu. Be sure
  to use these options before inserting other sounds.

Saving and Reverting

When you've finished modifying a sound file, use the Save or Save As
option on the File menu. However, if you don't want the changes you've made
since the last save, choose the Revert option. Save your file when you're
satisfied with its sound, then continue trying other modifications.

*When modifying the existing Windows sounds, be sure to save changes to a different
filename.*

Caution

When combining sounds, it's often necessary to make changes to a sound,
save it to disk, then open another sound file and insert the edited sound you've
just saved to disk. Using the disk in this way to store "intermediate" sounds
is slightly inconvenient, but more importantly, it can clutter your disk with
unwanted sound files. Be sure to remove these files when you're done with
your sound editing.

Opening more than one copy of Sound Recorder helps you work with multiple sounds.

Tip

Adding Special Effects

Sound Recorder lets you mix sounds together, increase or decrease the
volume of selected segments, change the speed of a sound, reverse a sound,
or add an echo effect to a sound. These options are added after a sound has
been recorded, or after you open a sound file from disk. Here are descriptions
of the special effects, which are available from the Effects pull-down menu:

- *Increase Volume* and *Decrease Volume* let you change the volume of
  the sound. To reverse the change, immediately choose the opposite
  option.

- *Increase Speed* and *Decrease Speed* let you slow down or speed up a sound by 100 percent. You can use this option to create new sounds. For example, load CHIMES.WAV, slow it down once, and then save it as CHIMES2.WAV.

- *Reverse* flips the sound horizontally in the windows and plays it backwards. For example, to create the Beatles' "Strawberry Fields" effect, load CHIMES.WAV, slow it down twice, and then choose Reverse.

- Use *Add Echo* to add an echo effect to a sound. Sounds that quickly rise and fall will benefit from the echo feature. For example, load DING.WAV, and choose Add Echo four or five times, clicking Play between each selection.

14

Playing with Sound Recorder

One of the best ways to learn Sound Recorder and create interesting sound files is to experiment with the Sound Recorder features. For example, try writing a little song by following these steps:

1. Open CHIMES.WAV.
2. Play the sound, or click the Fast-forward button to move the scroll button to the end of the sound.
3. Choose Insert File from the Edit menu, and select TADA.WAV.
4. Play the new combined sound. This places the pointer at the end of the file so you can insert another sound.
5. Choose Edit, choose Insert File again, and select CHORD.WAV.
6. Play the new sound.
7. Save the sound as SONG.WAV, or another descriptive name.

Now experiment—try slowing the song down, adding an echo, and reversing it. You get the idea. Working with sound is more fun than playing Solitaire. If you save the sound, be sure to use another filename.

You can attach a sound to one of your system messages by using the Sounds utility in the Windows Control Panel.

Tip

Here's how to create a sound like London's Big Ben:

1. Open DING.WAV.

2. On the Effects menu, choose Decrease Speed three times.

Notice that as you slow the sound down, its decay becomes quite long. To remove the extended decay,

3. Click the Rewind and Play buttons, and get ready to click the Stop button.

4. About halfway through the decay, click the Stop button. Don't worry if you don't get this right the first time—you can always choose File Revert and try again.

5. From the Edit menu, choose Delete After Current Position, and click OK to confirm the deletion.

6. Save the new sound as BIGBEN.WAV.

Now that the Big Ben sound is saved as a file, you can create a double-gong sound as follows:

7. With BIGBEN.WAV still loaded, click the Fast-forward button to get to the end of the sound.

8. Choose Edit, choose Insert File, and select BIGBEN.WAV.

9. Click the Rewind button, and then play the new combined sound.

There's only one problem with this sound. You probably heard a small gap of silence between the first and second gong. You can remove this gap by overlapping the second sound at the trailing edge of the first sound, using the Mix With File option.

10. Choose File, and choose Revert to remove your last change. Click OK to confirm the action.

11. Click either the Play or the Fast-forward button to move to the end of the sound.

12. Click the right-arrow button on the scroll bar twice. This moves the pointer into the trailing edge of the sound.

13. Choose Edit, choose Mix With File, and select BIGBEN.WAV.

14. Click the Rewind buttton and then the Play button to hear how mixing can cover up flaws in the sound.

15. Save the sound as BIGBEN2.WAV.

Continue mixing in more gongs as you like, or slow the sound down one time—does it sound more like a bell in your neighborhood? Want to make your windows vibrate? Choose Increase Volume.

Now try another mixing exercise—this next sound is built from three sounds. Start with CHIMES.WAV.

1. Open CHIMES.WAV.

2. Choose Effects, and choose Decrease Speed twice.

3. Play the sound, or click the Fast-forward button to get to the end of the sound.

4. Click the right-arrow button on the scroll bar to scroll into the trailing edge of the sound.

5. Choose Edit, choose Mix With File, and select CHIMES.WAV again.

6. Rewind and play the new sound.

7. Save this sound file using any name you like.

Now try mixing in another sound with the one you just created.

8. Rewind and play the new sound again.

9. Just as the first chime starts to fade, click the Stop button.

10. Choose Edit, choose Mix With File, and select CHORD.WAV.

11. Rewind and play your new mix.

If you don't like the mix, choose Revert and try again with another sound. You can continue the mixing process by adding as many new sounds as you like.

Feel free to work with the sound effects. Create a repertory of sounds by changing speeds and adding special effects. If you have a sound board, create new sounds with a microphone. You can also connect a cable from your stereo to the microphone input of the sound card, and record sounds from recordings such as sound libraries. Have fun!

14

Organizing the Accessory Files

The Windows accessories described in this chapter automatically store the files you create in the Windows directory. It's a good idea, however, to create special directories for the various accessory files, so your Windows directory doesn't become cluttered or disorganized. For example, you might create a directory called PERSONAL to store all your personal Notepad, Calendar, and Cardfile files. A directory called BUSINESS could be used to store your business files.

To ensure that your files are automatically saved in your special directories, you'll want to change the properties (path, and so on) of appropriate icons in the Accessories group in the Program Manager. Before doing so, make duplicates of icons in special groups, then change the properties of the icons in the groups. You can copy icons to other groups by holding down the CTRL key while dragging the Source icon.

Two customized groups are illustrated in Figure 14-11. In this figure, files created by applications in the Business group are stored in the BUSINESS directory, and files created by applications in the Personal group are stored in the PERSONAL directory. Note that each directory has its own set of three Notepad icons. Some of these Notepad icons open specific files in the Notepad accessory, such as Proposal and Timelog in the Business group. The icon specifically named Notepad is used to create new files.

Here is the Program Item Properties dialog box for defining the Notepad icon in the BUSINESS group:

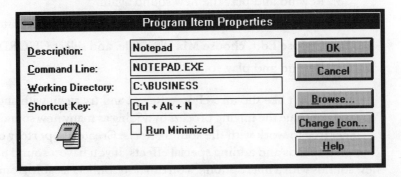

Figure 14-11.   *Organizing the Windows Accessories*

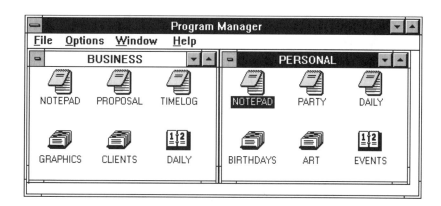

Notice that the Working Directory box specifies the BUSINESS directory. The other Notepad icons in the BUSINESS group also specify this working directory, but each has its own icon name (Proposal and Timelog) specified in the Description box, with a specific document named in the Command Line box.

To prevent any application from saving its files in the Windows directory, specify a different path in the Working Directory text box of the Program Item Properties dialog box.

Tip

15

Playing Games

When the boss is away, the game players will play...

Now that you've learned how to use Windows to streamline your workday and its tasks, it's time to relax and play a few games. Windows comes with Solitaire, a single-player card game similar to Klondike, and Minesweeper, a game in which you search for hidden mines.

To start the games included with Windows, double-click their icons in the Games group. The games open in their own windows that you can minimize, maximize, and resize.

Solitaire

Solitaire is a computerized version of the popular single-player card game. The object of the game is to rearrange a deck of shuffled cards into four stacks. Each stack must be a specific suit, in ascending order starting with the ace. You lose the game if you cannot achieve this arrangement.

A picture of the Solitaire window is shown in Figure 15-1. The Solitaire window is divided into three areas:

- The *deck* contains all cards that remain after the row stacks have been dealt. You draw cards from the deck and play them to the row stacks or the suit stacks.

- The *row stacks* consist of a row of seven stacks of cards; the number of cards in each stack increases from one on the left to seven on the right. The top card in each stack is face up and underlying cards are face down. When you can move the top card from a stack, you can then turn over the card under it and play it, too, if possible. Cards are played within the stacks in descending order and alternating colors.

- In the four *suit stacks*, cards are stacked in ascending order by suit, starting with the ace.

Figure 15-1.   *A Solitaire game in progress*

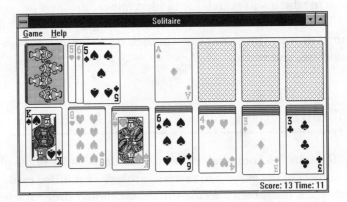

Rules and Techniques

When playing Solitaire, your objective is to uncover the cards that are face down in the row stacks and in the deck, and play them into the suit stacks. To play a card, click and drag it to a row stack or to a suit stack. If a card can be played on a suit stack, just double-click it; Solitaire will move the card for you.

Solitaire won't let you make illegal moves. A card moved illegally bounces back to its original location.

Note

To turn over the first hidden card of a stack, you must move the face-up card from the top of the stack to another stack, and then click the hidden card to turn it over.

Here are some guidelines:

- Cards can be moved to other row stacks only if you maintain alternating colors and descending numerical order. For example, in Figure 15-1, the red 3 can be played on the black 4, and the red queen can be played on the black king. The exposed face-down cards can then be turned face up, and played if possible.

- An entire sequence of face-up cards can be moved from one row stack to another. Figure 15-2 illustrates this event in a sample game. Here a sequence of three cards starting with the red 9 is being moved to the black 10.

- Empty row positions appear when all the cards in the stack have been moved elsewhere. You can then place a king in the empty position to start a new stack. No other card may be used for this play.

- In the suit stacks, cards in each suit must be played in ascending order. You must start the stack with an ace; then you can begin stacking other cards of the same suit, starting with the 2.

Once you've exhausted all possible plays within the stacks, you can begin drawing cards from the deck. Typically, three cards are drawn at a time, but

15

Figure 15-2.   *In this game, a sequence of three cards is being dragged to atop the row stack with the black 10*

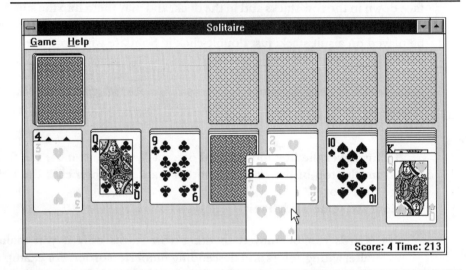

you can set Solitaire to draw one card at a time to increase your chances of winning. The deck is played as follows:

- Draw three cards (or one) from the deck. Play the top card if you can, then the second and the third, if possible.

- When the top card can't be played, click the deck to draw three more cards, and play as many cards as possible from that draw.

- Continue drawing cards until you reach the end of the stack; then click the empty stack to restack (not shuffle) the deck cards and continue playing. Note that the deck is never shuffled during the game, but when you play a card from the deck, you shift the order of the deck in relation to the draw, so it's possible to play every card if you're lucky.

 Choose Undo from the Game menu to undo your last move.

Tip

You win the game when all the cards are stacked in the suit stacks, or you lose when you've been through the deck several times and can't find any more cards to play. If you think you've lost the game, do one last check for overlooked plays. Look for groups of cards in the row stacks that can be shifted to other stacks, or individual cards you can move to the suit stacks.

Another trick when looking for "last-resort" plays is to see if part of a face-up row stack can be shifted to another stack to free up a card that is holding up movement of other cards into a suit stack. Alternatively, it may be possible to move a card out of a suit stack back into a row stack, to make a place for a card from the deck or for another row stack.

To start a new game, choose Deal from the Game menu.

Tip

You can change the design on the back of the cards by choosing Deck from the Game menu. A dialog box with several different card designs appears. Select a design, and then click the OK button. Watch the cards carefully. You'll see tricky animations and a "cool" sun.

15

Grandma Prullage's Playing Strategy

Solitaire is hard to win if you simply play the cards as they are pulled from the deck. To increase your chances of winning, it is sometimes beneficial *not* to play cards as they are drawn. Consider that there are initially eight three-card draws in the deck. Start by clicking the deck eight times to see what the last card is; you can safely play any card in this last set of three without changing the draw sequence for the preceding cards. In this way, you'll know what cards are playable in the deck before actually playing them. The next time through the deck, click seven times to reach the seventh draw and play those cards. Continue this routine with the sixth set, then the fifth, and so on.

As you click through the deck, also look for sets in which all three cards can be placed. You may want to play one, two, or all three; if you play all three, the draw sequence will not change.

You can also choose to play a card from the deck in order to make other cards accessible the next time through the deck. For example, let's say an ace

is the last card in the third draw, and there are several playable cards preceding
it in the first and second draw. To get to the ace, you can go through the deck
and play one of the cards from the first or second draw, but not more than
one. The next time through the deck, the ace will appear on top of the second
draw because its position in the deck shifts forward.

Is card counting a form of cheating or a form of strategy? Veteran players
count cards because they know it makes their investment of time in the game
pay off. For some people, playing strategy is better than playing the luck of
the draw.

The Solitaire Options Menu

The Solitaire Options menu offers some alternative features for the game.

- *Draw One*   Turn on this option if you want to draw one card at a
  time from the deck instead of three. Though a one-card draw
  increases your chances of winning, it is not considered "proper"
  Solitaire.

- *Draw Three*   This option reestablishes the default three-card draw
  method.

- *Scoring*   The scoring choices are Standard, Vegas, or None. For
  information on these scoring methods, choose Index from the Help
  menu, and click Scoring under the Procedures heading.

- *Timed Game*   Mark this option to time the length of your games.
  The time appears in the status bar at the lower-left of the Solitaire
  window.

- *Status Bar*   Click this option to turn the status bar on or off.

- *Outline Dragging*   When this option is on, an outline appears for
  cards as they are moved. As you drag over cards in the suit stack,
  Solitaire indicates valid moves by highlighting the underlying suit
  stack.

Figure 15-3.   *The Minesweeper playing board*

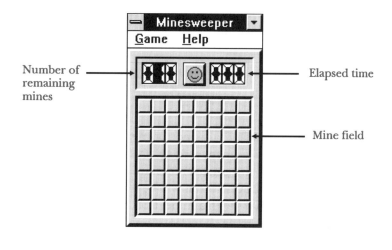

Number of remaining mines

Elapsed time

Mine field

Minesweeper

The Minesweeper playing board, shown in Figure 15-3, consists of a mine field, a timer, and an indicator of the number of mines remaining in the mine field. Your objective is to find all the mines without being blown up. You locate mines by *stepping* (clicking the left mouse button) on individual squares in the mine field. If you step on a mine, you're blown up and the game is over. If the square doesn't have a mine, a number appears in the safe square telling you how many mines are in the surrounding area.

Part of the Minesweeper game involves guessing, and part of it involves strategy. Your first few moves are guesses. If you don't get blown up right away, the safe squares you step on in the mine field tell you how many mines are in nearby squares. You can then put your playing strategy to work to determine which squares are mined and which are safe.

When you suspect a mine in a square, you can keep from accidentally stepping on it by clicking it with the right mouse button to mark it with a flag. As you mark mines, the counter at the upper-left of the mine field counts down. In the following illustration, two mines are marked:

If you click on a square that is not bordered by a mine, all the squares around the safe square are uncovered to reveal a blank space or a number. If you're lucky, some of the uncovered squares will also not have adjacent mines, and the squares around them will be uncovered as well.

Click on just one square with a mine, and the game ends. When you win, you can enter your name in the championship roster if you have the best score with the fastest time. Click the New option on the Game menu to start a new game. You can also choose one of the skill options. Choosing a more advanced skill presents a playing board with more squares, or you can choose Custom, and then define how many squares you want.

Playing Strategy

To locate mines, analyze the numbers that appear in uncovered squares. In the following example, the covered square in the upper-right must contain a mine, because the center square indicates that only one mine borders it and the other squares are already uncovered.

Your best strategy is to first locate any squares containing a 1 that are bordered by a single uncovered square, and then mark the square as a mine. Then you can start working the area around marked squares.

Tip

In the next illustration, you know the covered square indicated by the arrow does not contain a mine, because the 2 square to its upper-right is already bordered by two flagged mines.

Must be safe if flags are correct

Go ahead and click the safe square, but keep in mind that you might be wrong about the squares you've marked as having mines.

In the next illustration, you know that mines are in the two squares marked as such.

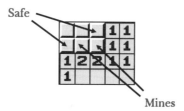

Note that the right square marked 2 is bordered by two uncovered squares, which therefore must contain mines. In addition, the squares marked as safe cannot contain mines because the 1 squares next to them must be detecting the same mines. You can click the safe squares with the left mouse button.

The last example demonstrates a mouse technique known as "clearing around a square." Notice in the following illustration that the two mines adjacent to the center square are already flagged.

The remaining squares must be safe. To uncover them, hold down both mouse buttons and click the center square.

16

Creating Compound Documents

Don't let the title of this chapter scare you off. It's about traditional Clipboard cut-and-paste techniques. It's also about *object linking and embedding* (OLE), a new Windows 3.1 feature that gives you additional power when you're copying pictures, text, and other information into your documents. Think about how you use the Clipboard to copy and paste between applications—you paint a picture in Paintbrush, for instance, then copy the picture to the Clipboard, and finally paste it into another document. Before OLE capabilities were developed, it was not possible to alter a picture pasted in a document; the picture became a static part of the document. You had to change the picture in Paintbrush and then copy and paste again to get the edited picture into your document.

OLE provides *dynamic data exchange* (DDE). Dynamic is the keyword here, as opposed to *static*; pictures, text, charts, and other information that you've pasted into other documents become objects that are updated automatically when you make changes to the original object in the application that created it (assuming you maintain the link).

Tip

Think of an object as a package of information (a graphic, a drawing, some text, or other data) that you paste into "containers" in other applications.

OLE frees you from having to think about the applications among which you are transferring the objects, and lets you focus on the information being manipulated. OLE lets you create *compound documents*—documents containing information that comes from many different applications, and that you can manipulate without having to jump back and forth between the creating applications. In a compound document environment, applications appear within each other. Compound documents are part of Microsoft's Information at Your Fingertips strategy.

Host applications that support compound documents will appear to have features they don't normally have. For example, you can copy sound files from Sound Recorder into a Write document and then double-click the pasted sound objects to play them back. Write thus appears to have this sound capability; in reality, however, the objects call the playback functions from the application used to originally create the sounds. Both Write and Sound Recorder have built-in OLE functions, as do Cardfile and Paintbrush. Check your applications to see if they are OLE compatible.

Understanding OLE Concepts

As the name implies, OLE provides linking and embedding of objects into one or more compound documents. You double-click an embedded object to open the application that originally created it, and edit the object as necessary. A *linked object* maintains an automatic link to the creating application, so any changes made to the original object affect the linked copies. Objects may consist of

- Text from word processors, text editors, and electronic mail packages
- Spreadsheet data from Microsoft Excel, Lotus 1-2-3, or other Windows 3.1-compatible spreadsheet applications
- Graphs and animations from presentation packages like Microsoft PowerPoint

- Pictures from drawing and painting programs
- Video and sound from multimedia applications

In some cases, objects look like icons similar to the ones you see in Program Manager. These icons contain a package of information related to the command or application that runs when you double-click the icon.

Embedding

In its simplest form, OLE provides *embedding*. An embedded object knows how to call the application that created it. When you double-click the object, the application opens so you can make needed changes, as shown in Figure 16-1. Then you close the application to add your changes to the embedded object.

The most obvious place to embed an object is in text documents such as those created by Write or Word for Windows, as illustrated in Figure 16-1.

Figure 16-1.   *An embedded object calls the application that created it*

16

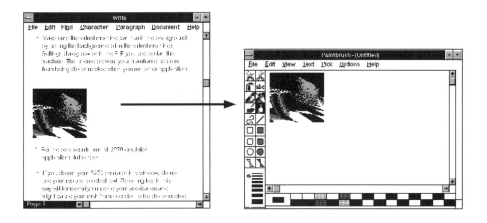

The Cardfile illustration in Figure 16-2 presents another example. Each card in the stack contains a graphic image for use as a slide in a presentation. Notice that the numbered index headers indicate the order the slides should appear in the presentation. Cardfile helps organize the slides for creating and editing the presentation. Simply double-click the image on a card, and the application used to create the image then opens with the graphic in its workspace. In this example, OLE serves as an advanced organizer, giving you a way to track multiple files.

Linking

Linking provides a sort of communication network between the original object and its pasted location in documents, as shown in Figure 16-3. The original object maintains these links to its pasted locations.

Figure 16-2.   *To edit this graphic embedded in Cardfile, just double-click it; the creating application opens so you can make changes*

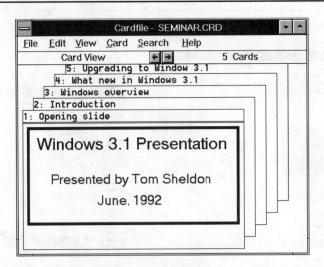

Figure 16-3. *Linking establishes a "communication" link between an object and its pasted copies in compound documents*

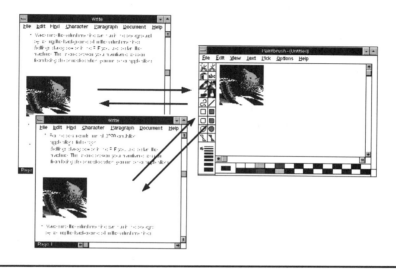

An Example of Linking and Embedding

Let's compare OLE with the cut-and-paste methods you already know. Imagine you're putting together a conference and trade show later in the year. You've created documents related to the conference using several different Windows applications—you used Windows Write to prepare press releases and other in-house documents, Microsoft Excel to create schedules, Paintbrush to draw a map of the conference rooms, and Cardfile to keep track of exhibitor and speaker information.

Let's say you need to piece all this information together into several compound documents: a general press release, a brochure for attendees, an in-house document to inform the rest of your company of the conference schedule and events, and a handout for the exhibitors and speakers. Each document will, of course, be designed for its intended audience, but all will contain some of the information described earlier, such as the map and the schedule of events.

16

Initially, you need to create, copy, and paste various objects into your four documents, so the amount of work is the same whether you're using OLE or not. The real savings in time begins when you start to make changes to your schedules, floor plans, and the other information you've pasted into the compound documents. In non-OLE applications, you would need to copy and paste the edited information into each of the four documents. In contrast, OLE makes this part easy, because the objects in the documents contain links to the applications that created them. Changing the originals also changes the linked objects in all four documents, automatically. For example, alter the floor plan in Paintbrush, and the floor plan changes in all four linked compound documents.

Icons as Objects

OLE extends the use of icons beyond the Program Manager to your applications. You can now create *packages* in your documents that start other applications. These packages use icons similar to those you see in the Program Manager. For example, look at the Cardfile illustration in Figure 16-4. This cardfile contains a stack of cards used to keep notes for writing the book you're reading now. Notice that the top card contains an icon. When you double-click this icon, you open another cardfile stack called FEA-TURES.CRD that contains notes about new Windows 3.1 features. So in this case, one cardfile tracks another cardfile, and provides a quick and easy way to open that card stack.

In Figure 16-5, notice that the Write document contains two embedded icons. You can double-click one icon to open a set of instructions in English and the other to open a set of instructions in Spanish. Using Sound Recorder, you could even include audible instructions.

The English and Spanish instruction files can also contain embedded icons providing access to other text files. In this way, a single file does not need to contain the bulk of the text. Instead, individual files can contain specific lessons or procedures that are easier to edit when necessary—and, moreover, easier to understand by the user. By double-clicking icons, readers can choose the exact topics they want to see. Figure 16-6 illustrates an instructional file for new employees.

Figure 16-4. *Double-click the embedded icon on a card in Cardfile to open another cardfile*

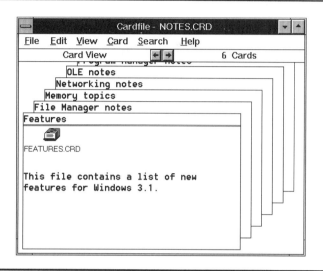

Figure 16-5. *These embedded icons let readers choose the document they want to see in the language they want to read*

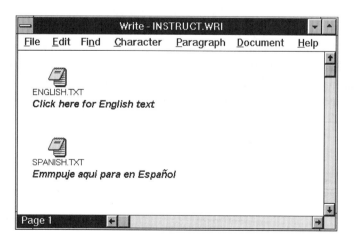

Figure 16-6. *This embedded icon lets authorized readers get to a special security procedure*

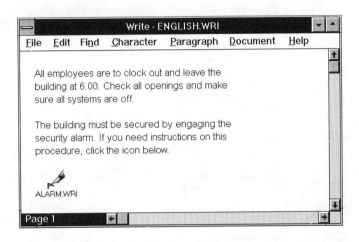

Special documents that provide security information should not be accessible to just anyone. By using OLE, you can lock certain files and restrict access to selected readers. In the foregoing example, and also in Figure 16-6, not all employees should know the security alarm procedure. To limit access to this document, just remove the linked file from the systems of restricted employees; on a network, you can put the file in a directory that has limited access.

Figure 16-7 shows how you can attach both sounds and pictures to a Write document. In this example, the ear with musical note is a sound package created with Sound Recorder. A young reader of the document could double-click the icon to hear a prerecorded sound for the animal pictured.

Embedding Objects

To embed an object from a source application to a destination document, use the copy-and-paste procedures with which you are already familiar. If both

Figure 16-7.   *Sounds and graphics can be combined to create true "multimedia" documents*

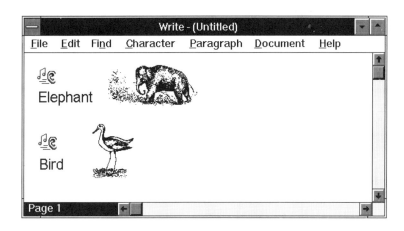

16

the source and destination applications support OLE, the pasted object will become embedded. If both source and destination applications don't support OLE, the pasted object becomes static.

Try the following exercise to see how embedding works:

1. Open Write and Paintbrush.

2. In the Paintbrush window, paint a picture to copy and paste, or open an existing picture file.

3. Use the Pick tool to surround part of the image; then choose Copy from the Edit menu to place the selection on the Clipboard.

4. Switch to the Write window, and choose the Paste command from the Edit menu.

Because both Paintbrush and Write support OLE, the selection is embedded in the Write document. Now try editing the image.

5. Double-click the image you have pasted into the Write document. The Paintbrush window becomes active, with the image in its workspace.

6. Change the image in any way.

7. Open the File menu. You will see the menu shown here:

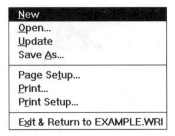

8. Notice the third (Update) and last (Exit & Return) options on the File menu. You can choose Update to store the changes you made to the image in Write, and leave Paintbrush open. For this exercise, however, choose the Exit & Return option. This updates the image in Write, closes Paintbrush, and returns you to the Write document. When the following dialog box appears, choose Yes to update the Write document.

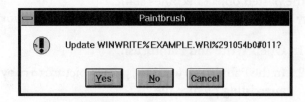

Tip

You can follow a procedure similar to the one just discussed to embed objects on Cardfile cards. Be sure to choose Picture from the Cardfile Edit menu before pasting.

Now try embedding a sound from Sound Recorder into the Write document. This exercise assumes that you have a sound board or speaker driver installed, as discussed in Chapter 14, "Using the Windows Accessories."

1. Start Sound Recorder.

2. Open any sound, or record a new sound.

3. Choose Copy from the Sound Recorder Edit menu.

4. Switch to your Write document.

5. Choose Paste from the Edit menu.

The sound is pasted into the document. Double-click the icon to hear the pasted sound.

Linking Objects

The procedure for creating a linked object is the same as the procedure for creating an embedded object, except that you choose Paste Link from the destination application's Edit menu to paste the image. This maintains the dynamic link between the object and its application. Try the following exercise with Paintbrush and Cardfile. Keep in mind that you can use this procedure to create a catalog of graphic images or sounds in Cardfile.

1. Open Cardfile and Paintbrush.

2. In Paintbrush, create an image. (You will paste this to a card in Cardfile.)

3. Save the image as a Paintbrush file. This is an important step, because the file of the source application contains the link information (explained in the next section) for a linked object.

4. Use the Pick tool to select part of the object to copy; then choose Copy from the Edit menu.

5. Switch to Cardfile, and choose Picture from the Cardfile Edit menu. (This is an important step.)

6. Choose Paste Link from the Edit menu to paste the object in the card.

Because the Cardfile object and the Paintbrush application are now linked, you can edit the Paintbrush file at any time to make changes to the Cardfile image, even when the Cardfile application is not open on the desktop. The next time you open Cardfile, it gets the latest version of the

16

Paintbrush image, including whatever edits you've made. To see how dynamic this link is, continue with the Paintbrush/Cardfile exercise and experiment with the sample image:

7. Double-click the linked and embedded image in Cardfile. The Paintbrush window becomes active, with the image in its workspace.

8. Arrange the Cardfile and Paintbrush windows side by side, so you can see both images at once.

9. Make some changes to the image in the Paintbrush file, such as altering the color or drawing some lines. Notice that as you edit the image in Paintbrush, the Cardfile image also changes.

If you wish, you can continue this example even further by opening Write and paste-linking the image from Paintbrush into the Write window. Then change the image in Paintbrush and watch how the linked objects in *both* Cardfile and Write change simultaneously.

Links specify the location of linked files. Moving a linked file may destroy the link. When you send or transfer documents that contain links, be sure to also send the linked files.

Caution

Viewing Link Information

You can view the *link information* for a linked object by first selecting the object, then choosing Links from the Edit menu. You'll see a dialog box similar to this one:

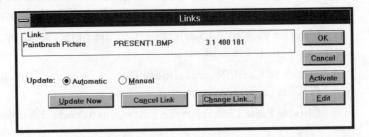

The type, name, and size information for the linked object appear in the Link display box.

The two Update options, Automatic and Manual, determine the current update method for the linked object; you can switch to Manual if you want changes to occur in the linked object only when you choose to make them. To update a link manually, choose the Update Now button after you've made your edits. Another way of editing the linked object is by clicking the Edit button and making your changes; this is the same as double-clicking the linked object.

For linked objects that play back a script or sounds, click the Activate button to play the objects.

To cancel a link, choose the Cancel Link button; or choose Change Link if you want to define a new file for the link.

Embedding Icons

As explained earlier in this chapter, embedded icons can execute commands, open other documents, or start other applications. These icons contain the set of instructions for accomplishing the icon's assigned task. To create embedded icons, you can click and drag icons from the File Manager to your documents. Or you can use the Packager accessory in the Program Manager Accessories group.

16

In the following example, you use the click-and-drag method to place an icon for a file on a card in Cardfile.

1. Open Cardfile and File Manager, and arrange the windows side by side.

2. Locate a file, say a Paintbrush .BMP file, in the Windows directory.

3. Click the filename and drag it over the top card in Cardfile; this embeds an icon for the file in the card. You can now double-click the icon in Cardfile to open the file you just pasted.

Try the same procedure with a Sound Recorder .WAV file, or even another Cardfile. Double-clicking the embedded icon will play the sound or start the application. Remember that you can use these techniques in Write or other OLE-compatible applications to create links to other documents. Try copying an icon for a text file into a Write document.

Using Packager

With Packager, you can create a *package* to embed as an icon into your documents. Packager is an alternative to the click-and-drag method just described for embedding an icon; Packager is also used when creating the document that will contain the embedded icon. This latter technique is special because it eliminates the need to open File Manager or another application—you can create the OLE links from the application you're working in. Packager also lets you define a different icon for the object. For example, you could use an envelope icon for a recording of your voice. Try the following exercise to see how this works:

1. Open Write.

2. Choose Insert Object from the Edit menu. The following dialog box appears, listing all the currently available applications that can supply OLE objects.

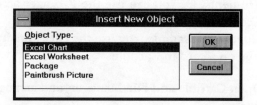

3. In the Object Type list box, choose Package, and click the OK button. You'll then see the following dialog box:

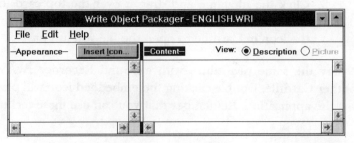

Packager contains all the tools you need to create your own embedded icons. In this case, Packager will insert the icon in the Write document when you're done. Let's create a link to another document, such as README.TXT in the Windows directory.

4. Select an icon for the new object. Click the Insert Icon button, and choose one of the suggested icons that appear. To see more icons to choose from, specify one of the following filenames in the File Name field:

    \WINDOWS\PROGMAN.EXE
    \WINDOWS\MORICONS.DLL

5. Create a label for the icon you have selected, by choosing Label from the Edit menu. Type **README.TXT** in the text box of the Label dialog box and click OK.

6. Define the command to be executed whenever this icon is double-clicked. Choose Command Line from the Edit menu and type **C:\WINDOWS\README.TXT**. (You may need to replace C with the drive letter for your Windows directory.)

7. To create the embedded icon in the document, you may elect to choose Update from the File menu. This keeps Packager open so you can create other objects. For this exercise, however, choose Exit from the File menu. Packager asks if you want to update the object; choose Yes.

Your Write document now contains the embedded icon, and you can double-click the icon to open the README.TXT file. Use this same procedure to add other icons to your documents as you create them.

Note

The preferred method for copying sound files is to drag their file icons from the File Manager to the destination document.

Editing a Packaged Object

If you need to change the properties of a packaged object in your linked documents, follow this procedure:

16

1. Click once on the object to highlight it.

2. Choose Package Object from the Edit menu, and then choose the Edit option.

3. When Packager opens, make the needed changes using the menu options described earlier in this chapter.

4. Choose the Update or Exit option on the File menu to complete the change.

This chapter has given you a broad overview of OLE concepts and techniques. A more thorough discussion is included in *Windows 3: The Complete Reference*, by Tom Sheldon, [Berkeley: Osborne/McGraw-Hill, 1991]. An edition of this book that covers Windows 3.1 is scheduled to be available in mid 1992.

A

Windows Modes and Memory

This appendix provides a basic discussion of memory and how it is used in the Windows standard and 386 enhanced modes. Its purpose is to help you determine which mode to use, and to show you how to overcome memory-related problems when running non-Windows applications in Windows. Non-Windows applications are DOS applications not specifically designed to work with Windows.

Products like Microsoft's MS-DOS 5.0, Digital Research's DR DOS 6.0, Quarterdeck's Expanded Memory Manager, and Qualitas's 386Max all help you use the memory in your system efficiently. Having the additional memory provided by these applications often makes the difference between successfully running an application and viewing an out-of-memory message. You will, however, need an 80386 or 80486 system to take advantage of some of these products.

When you run short of memory on an 80286 system, you can add more memory to your system and/or upgrade to an operating system that makes more memory available. Memory problems on 80386 systems are less severe, because you can use a Windows feature called *virtual memory* that makes hard disk space look like system memory. This gives applications all the memory they need.

Types of Memory

The random access memory (RAM) in your system holds program code and document data while you work. Programs are loaded from disk files into RAM, and are then executed by your computer.

RAM is volatile; data in it can be lost if your system loses power, so it is essential that you save your work to disk often.

Note

Memory is measured in bits and bytes. A bit is either 1 or 0 (on or off) in the binary number system, and is the smallest unit of information in RAM. A byte is a group of eight bits (in various on and off states) that is used to represent letters of the alphabet and numbers. Certain abbreviations are generally used in discussions about computer memory: KB is used to represent kilobytes; 1024 bytes equals a kilobyte, so a file with 1024 characters is 1KB in size. A million bytes of memory is referred to as one megabyte (abbreviated 1MB).

Systems that run DOS and Windows have three types of memory: *conventional memory, upper memory,* and *extended memory*. All systems come with some amount of conventional memory, usually 640KB, but upper memory and extended memory must be made available by using some of the techniques described in this appendix. Each memory type is illustrated in Figure A-1, and discussed in the paragraphs that follow.

Conventional Memory   Conventional memory is the lowest part of memory, starting at 0KB and going to 640KB. DOS uses this memory to load itself and to run DOS applications. Because conventional memory is often insufficient for these applications, newer versions of DOS—such as Microsoft's MS-DOS 5.0 and Digital Research's DR DOS 6.0—can load part of their operating code into other parts of memory, thus making more conventional memory available for applications.

Upper Memory   Upper memory blocks (UMB) make up the area of memory between 640KB and 1MB. This is the area sometimes called the adapter area. DOS uses this area to store program code (called *drivers*) for your video display, disk drives, and other hardware. Because the UMB often contain blocks of unused memory addresses, various strategies have been devised to

Figure A-1.   *A typical memory map for a DOS-based system*

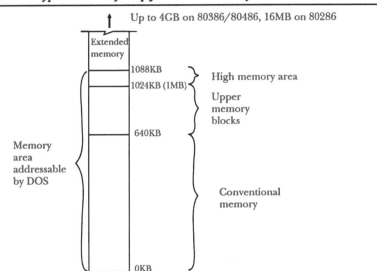

move program code from conventional memory to the UMB, thus freeing conventional memory, as discussed in the foregoing paragraph.

Extended Memory   Memory that extends beyond 1024KB (or 1MB) is called extended memory. An 80286 system can access up to 16MB of extended memory; 80386 processors can access up to 4 gigabytes (4000MB) of extended memory. Windows and Windows applications use extended memory extensively, so the more you have, the better. However, to maintain compatibility with 80286 systems and software, Windows addresses only 16MB of extended memory.

Note

Another type of memory is called expanded memory. It provides up to 8MB of additional memory to DOS applications that are written to take advantage of it. Expanded memory requires a special memory board and/or software. With the advent of Windows, expanded memory is falling into disuse, and many expanded memory applications have been converted to Windows applications.

Caution

The line DEVICE=HIMEM.SYS in your CONFIG.SYS file is the command that lets Windows access the high memory area (HMA) and extended memory. Do not remove this command unless you have an 80386 system and intend to use Quarterdeck QEMM, Qualitas 386Max, or another similar memory manager instead. The HMA is an extra 64KB of memory (located in extended memory) that DOS can address.

Windows Operating Modes

Windows starts in either *standard mode* or *386 enhanced mode*, depending on your processor type and the amount of memory in your system. During setup, Windows determines which mode your system can start in, but may be able to start in the other mode under certain circumstances.

Standard Mode   If you have an 80286-based system, or a 386 or 486 system with only 1MB of memory, Windows starts in standard mode. If you have a 386 or 486 system with more than 1MB of memory, you can "force" Windows to start in standard mode and gain some performance benefits. Doing so, however, precludes the use of features provided by the 386 enhanced mode. Standard mode is typically 10 to 20 percent faster than 386 enhanced mode and should be used whenever possible.

- To start Windows in standard mode, type **WIN /S** at the DOS prompt.

386 Enhanced Mode   The 386 enhanced mode is the normal operating mode for 386 and 486 systems with 2MB or more of memory, although you can force the mode if your system has only 1MB. While 386 enhanced mode is slower than standard mode, it provides virtual memory and other advanced features.

- To start Windows in 386 enhanced mode, type **WIN /3** at the DOS prompt.

Standard Mode and Memory

Standard mode uses extended memory to provide an optimal environment for running multiple Windows applications. You should add as much memory to your system as possible and configure it as extended memory.

Some of you may have systems with an expanded memory board for running DOS expanded memory applications. Windows does not use expanded memory, so if you no longer need the expanded memory application, reconfigure the memory on the board as extended memory, if possible. Your manual should provide details on how this is done. If you must run the expanded memory application, you can do the following:

- On a 386 or 486 system, start Windows in 386 enhanced mode when you need to run the expanded memory application. In this way you can configure all memory as extended memory, and Windows will emulate the expanded memory needed by the applications. The memory used in the emulation is taken from extended memory.

- On a 286 system, you need to configure some of the memory on an add-in memory board as expanded memory. The board must have built-in expanded memory support. Determine exactly how much expanded memory the application needs, and then configure only that much on the board. Configure the remaining memory as extended memory for use by Windows. You also need to load the expanded memory manager supplied with the board. Place its command in your CONFIG.SYS or AUTOEXEC.BAT file.

A

386 Enhanced Mode and Memory

Systems with 386 or 486 processors can run in the 386 enhanced mode. This mode provides several important features that standard mode does not, as described in the paragraphs that follow. Evaluate your need for these features; if you don't need them, run Windows in standard mode to improve performance.

- *Virtual Memory*   This lets Windows run more applications than will fit in RAM memory, by using part of your hard disk as if it were memory.
- *Multitasking*   This means DOS applications can be run in a separate window, simultaneously with Windows applications or other DOS applications.
- *Expanded Memory*   This can be emulated for DOS applications that need it, allowing you to configure all your system memory as more efficient extended memory.

Virtual Memory

Virtual memory techniques move information in RAM to a temporary or permanent *swap file* on your hard disk. Swap files can be used only on 80386 and 80486 systems. The type of swap file depends on the amount of free space on your disk.

- A temporary swap file is installed when Windows starts and is removed when you exit Windows. It only uses available disk space.
- A permanent swap file is set up on a hard drive and used every time you start Windows. Because the swap file occupies a contiguous area on the drive, it provides better performance.

If, during installation, Setup finds adequate contiguous disk space available, it sets up a permanent swap file that theoretically provides better performance. As a beginning Windows user, you need not be too concerned with the type of swap file—just know that it is there to provide you with more memory should you need it.

To check your system's virtual memory capabilities,

1. Start Windows in 386 enhanced mode by typing **WIN /3** at the DOS prompt.
2. Choose the About Program Manager option from the Program Manager Help menu. You'll see a dialog box similar to that in Figure A-2.

Figure A-2. *About Program Manager dialog box*

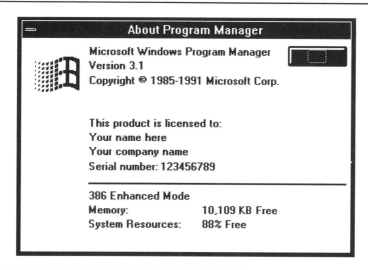

If a swap file is in use, the memory setting at the bottom of the dialog box will indicate more memory than your system has. Figure A-2 is from a system with 4MB of memory that thinks it has 10MB!

Virtual memory depends on the existence of a swap file. You can add, remove, or change the settings of a swap file by following these steps:

1. Double-click the 386 Enhanced Mode icon on the Control Panel.

2. Click the Virtual Memory button on the 386 Enhanced dialog box. You'll then see a dialog box like that in Figure A-3.

3. The current swap file settings are listed at the top of the dialog box. Note whether the Type field says Permanent or Temporary, and the drive location of the swap file.

4. In the Settings box, you can add a swap file, change a swap file's settings, or remove a swap file. Look at the number in the Space Available field, and

   • If you have large amounts of available disk space, use the dialog box to set up a permanent swap file if it doesn't already exist.

A

Figure A-3.   *Virtual Memory dialog box*

Virtual Memory

Current Settings
Drive: D:
Size: 7,794 KB
Type: Permanent (using 32-bit access)

OK
Cancel
Help

Settings
Drive: d: [drive-d]

Type: Permanent

Space Available: 33,624 KB
Maximum Size: 25,672 KB
Recommended Size: 7,794 KB

Approximate Size: 7794   KB

Optimal Size for Windows: 7,804 KB

- If you're running low on disk space, use the dialog box to set up a temporary swap file, or disable the swap file completely by choosing None in the Type field.

5. In the Drive field, choose the drive for the swap file.

6. In the Type field, choose Permanent, Temporary, or None. (Choosing None disables virtual memory and removes existing swap files.)

7. Windows recommends a size for the swap file in the Approximate Size field. Change this setting to reduce the size of a swap file. It's not recommended that you increase the size of the swap file beyond Windows's suggestions. If you're running low on disk space, reduce the value.

8. When you are finished, choose OK to activate the new settings.

9. Follow the instructions on the screen to restart Windows.

Do not use (CTRL)-(ALT)-(DEL) *to restart your system after changing swap file settings. Simply click the Restart Windows button.*

Caution

B

Running Non-Windows Applications

This appendix examines how non-Windows applications are used with Windows. Non-Windows applications are DOS programs that aren't specifically designed to work with Windows. They do not use the windows graphical interface, nor do they share memory in the same way as Windows applications. Certainly you should upgrade all your applications to newer Windows versions whenever possible, but many applications will never be designed to work under Windows.

When you do need to run a non-Windows application, there are good reasons to run it under Windows: you can quickly switch to a non-Windows application while other Windows applications stay loaded, and you can cut and paste information between Windows and non-Windows applications.

A primary topic in this chapter is the *Program Information File*, or *PIF*. Normally, Windows uses a standard set of parameters to start non-Windows applications. If you can't get the application to run properly in this way, however, or you need to specify other startup parameters, you can create a special Program Information File to supply Windows with specific information about the application. You can then double-click a PIF to start the program. Program Information Files are created and edited with the PIF Editor, found in the Program Manager Main group.

Even though non-Windows applications don't always need a PIF to run properly, some settings in the PIF can help the program run more efficiently; or you can designate startup parameters and data file locations.

Types of Applications

Here are the various types of applications that can run with Windows; they are discussed in the sections that follow.

- *Windows 3.0 Applications* are designed to run with Windows 3.0 and will probably run fine with Windows 3.1.

- *Windows 3.1 Applications* are designed to take advantage of new features in Windows 3.1, such as object linking and embedding (OLE), and Drag and Drop features.

- *Pre-Windows 3 Applications* are written for versions of Windows earlier than version 3.0. You need to upgrade these applications for use with Windows 3.1, or run them in Windows 3.0 real mode.

- *Non-Windows Applications* are normally run under DOS and were not designed for use with Windows. You can run them from Windows by switching into a full-screen or windowed DOS environment.

- *Memory-Resident Software Utilities (TSRs)* are small programs that load and stay resident in memory. Examples are pop-up programs such as Borland's Sidekick, or software drivers that provide the operating system with information to run special hardware or network support.

Non-Windows Applications

Non-Windows applications were written by programmers who did not have Windows in mind. These programs do not take advantage of the Windows graphical interface or memory access method. Think of Windows applications as being very generous with memory. They will give up a portion of their memory, if necessary, when another application needs it. Non-Windows applications, on the other hand, are selfish with memory. They do not share it with other applications and, in the process, limit the total number of applications you can run at once.

There are some other things to keep in mind regarding non-Windows applications. For instance, they normally run full screen in all Windows modes. In 386 enhanced mode it is possible to run them in a separate, resizable window.

Note

You must load MOUSE.COM to use a mouse in non-Windows applications when running in standard mode or 386 enhanced full-screen mode.

Processing in all other applications temporarily halts when you switch to a non-Windows application in standard mode. In 386 enhanced mode, non-Windows applications can be multitasked, which means they can continue processing in the background when you switch to other applications.

In standard mode, a full screen of information can be copied to the Clipboard. In 386 enhanced mode, specific sections of the screen can be copied to the Clipboard.

Non-Windows Applications Requiring Expanded Memory

Some non-Windows applications use expanded memory. If you have an 80286-based system, you need to add expanded memory on a memory expansion board, and then load the expanded memory manager that comes with the board in your system startup files. Instructions for doing this will be in the board's manual.

If you have an 80386 or 80486 system, run expanded-memory applications in the 386 enhanced mode to take advantage of its ability to emulate expanded memory. To run expanded-memory applications in DOS when your system does not have an expanded memory board, be sure to load the EMM386.SYS expanded-memory emulator by including the following command in your CONFIG.SYS file:

B

DEVICE=C:\WINDOWS\EMM386.SYS

If necessary, replace the C in this command with the letter of the drive that holds your Windows directory.

Up to 256K of memory will be set aside as expanded memory. You can specify a larger amount of expanded memory by including a parameter for it at the end of the DEVICE command. For example, the following command sets aside 512K of memory:

DEVICE=C:\WINDOWS\EMM386.SYS 512

If you use DOS 5, include the DOS=HIGH option in your CONFIG.SYS file. Also, refer to your DOS manual for a discussion of the LOADHIGH and DEVICEHIGH commands.

Note

Memory-Resident Software

Memory-resident utilities are programs that start and stay loaded in memory while other applications run. Commands in the CONFIG.SYS and AUTOEXEC.BAT files usually load this software when your system first starts. There are two types of memory-resident utilities:

- *Noninteractive memory-resident software* typically provides instructions to the operating system for handling peripheral equipment such as tape drives and optical disk drives. These programs may also provide support for connections to networks or electronic mail systems.

- *Interactive memory-resident software* is sometimes referred to as pop-up software because it appears on the screen when certain keys are pressed.

When you want a memory-resident utility to be available to applications when Windows is not running, start the utility in the CONFIG.SYS or AUTOEXEC.BAT file. If the utility takes up too much memory and prevents other non-Windows applications from running, try loading it after Windows starts since Windows allocates its use of memory more efficiently. (Note that some of these utilities can only be started with commands in the CONFIG.SYS file and never from within Windows.) If you still run out of memory when running non-Windows applications, exit Windows and run the utility and applications that use it from DOS.

Start pop-up programs after starting Windows. In this way, Windows can allocate memory for its own use first, and then provide the utility with the memory it needs. You may have to create a Program Information File to get the pop-up utility to run from Windows. In some cases, keys used by the pop-up program may be the same as those used by Windows. If so, reconfigure the keys in the pop-up utility as described in the utility's manual.

Working with Non-Windows Applications

To start a non-Windows application, do one of the following:

- Double-click the icon of the application in the Program Manager (you may have to create a startup icon first).

- If the application has special memory or startup requirements, you may have to create a PIF. You then double-click the PIF to start the application, or create a startup icon for the PIF in the Program Manager.

- Start the application from the File Manager by double-clicking its executable filename or its PIF.

- Double-click the DOS Prompt icon in the Program Manager Main group, and then run the application from the DOS command line.

Note

If an application locks up or you lose mouse control in 386 enhanced mode, Windows will let you terminate the faulty application without rebooting your entire system, by pressing (CTRL)-(ALT)-(DEL).

B

Running Non-Windows Applications in a Window

When a non-Windows application runs full screen, it has no window borders or menu options. A Control Menu exists, but can only be accessed

Figure B-1.   *A non-Windows application running in a window*

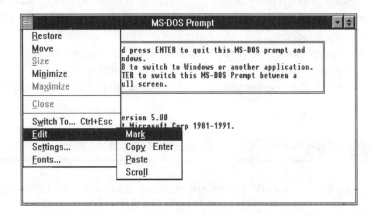

by pressing (ALT)-(ESC) to switch from the full-screen display back to Windows. You then click the application's icon on the desktop to display its Control Menu. The options on the Control Menu are limited—unless you're running in 386 enhanced mode, in which case the application can be run in a resizable window, as shown in Figure B-1.

If you're in 386 enhanced mode, there are two ways to get a non-Windows application to run in a window:

- Start the application as usual, and then press (ALT)-(ENTER). If this doesn't work, press (ALT)-(ESC) to return to Windows, and click the icon of the application. On its Control Menu, click Window in the Display Options box, and click the OK button.

- Create a PIF to specify that the application always start in a window.

Once your non-Windows application is in a resizable window, click its Control Menu button and choose a new font and screen size to fit your needs.

Choose the Fonts option to display the Fonts dialog box. Select any of the listed fonts and then click OK.

Tip

Copying and Pasting in Standard Mode

Copying and pasting to and from non-Windows applications in standard mode is somewhat limited, but workable. Only text can be copied and pasted; and when copying from a non-Windows application, you must copy a full screen of information.

Here are the steps for copying from a non-Windows application to a Windows application:

1. Switch to the non-Windows application. It appears full screen.

2. Press the (PRINT SCREEN) key to copy the entire screen to the Clipboard.

3. Press (ALT)-(ESC) to switch back to Windows.

4. Position the insertion point where you want to paste the information; then choose the Paste command from the Edit menu.

5. Delete any lines or characters that you did not wish to copy.

Here are the steps for copying from a Windows application to a non-Windows application:

1. In the Windows application, highlight the text to copy.

2. Choose Copy from the Edit menu.

3. Switch to the non-Windows application, and position the insertion point where you want the text pasted.

4. Switch back to Windows by pressing (ALT)-(ESC).

5. On the Windows desktop, click the non-Windows application icon to open its Control Menu.

6. Choose Paste on the Control Menu to paste the text into the document.

B

7. Switch back to the non-Windows application to continue working with the document.

Copying and Pasting in 386 Enhanced Mode

When running a non-Windows application in 386 enhanced mode, you can copy specific portions of the screen to the Clipboard using commands on the Control Menu. If the window is running full screen, run it in a window, as discussed earlier in this appendix. You can then open its Control Menu to access the Copy and Paste options, as illustrated in Figure B-1.

To copy information from a non-Windows application to the Clipboard,

1. Make sure the application is running in a window.
2. Highlight the area to copy by clicking and dragging with the mouse.
3. Choose Edit from the Control Menu, and then choose the Copy option; or choose the Mark option, highlight the text to copy by pressing the arrow keys, and then choose Copy.
4. Switch to another application, and choose Paste from its Edit menu.

To paste information to a non-Windows application running in a window,

1. In the Windows application, highlight the text to copy.
2. Choose the Copy command on the Edit menu to copy the text to the Clipboard.
3. Switch to the non-Windows application, and position the insertion point where you want the text to be pasted.
4. Choose the Edit option on the Control Menu, highlight Paste, and release the mouse.

Setting Options for 386 Enhanced Mode

To control how a non-Windows application runs in 386 enhanced mode, you can choose the Settings options on the Control menu of a running application, or you can set system-wide defaults in the Control Panel. You can also create or edit a PIF to designate permanent startup settings for the application. Each method is described in the paragraphs that follow.

Note

The following discussion assumes non-Windows applications are running in a resizable window.

Using the Settings Dialog Box

In the non-Windows application window, choose Settings from the Control menu to display the dialog box pictured in Figure B-2. The options in this dialog box are used to switch from full-screen display to window display, to change the way the application works with other Windows applications, and to change the way processing time is allocated to the non-Windows application. There is also a button you can use to "informally terminate" applications that have locked up. All these options are explained in the following paragraphs.

Display Options   Click Full-Screen for best performance, but click Window to perform copy and paste operations or to switch easily among applications.

Figure B-2.   *The Settings dialog box for a non-Windows application running in 386 enhanced mode*

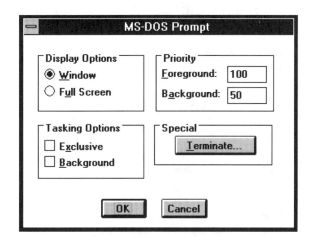

B

Tasking Options   Click Background to run the application in the background (inactive) window when working in other windows. Click Exclusive to give the application exclusive use of your system processor when the application is in the foreground (active) window.

Priority Options   Use the Priority options to specify how much processor time the application should receive in relation to other applications. Refer to your Windows manual for information on setting these options.

Terminate Button   Click the Terminate button to quit a non-Windows application when it has locked up. Use this option only as a last resort, because data may be lost. After terminating an application in this way, always save your other work and restart the computer, because the operating system could become unstable.

Setting Control Panel Options

Double-click the 386 Enhanced icon in the Windows Control Panel to display the dialog box pictured in Figure B-3. The options in this dialog box are used to set *default* multitasking options, which are used by any non-

Figure B-3.   *The Control Panel 386 Enhanced dialog box*

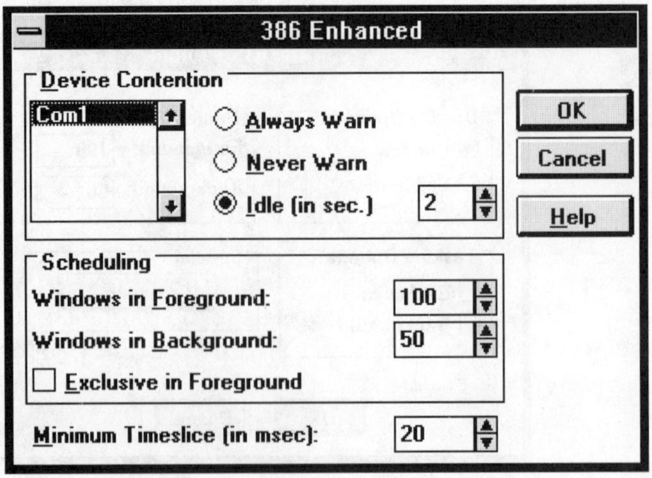

Windows application you may start. Note that the Scheduling options are used to set options for Windows, not DOS applications.

Note

To change startup options for individual applications, use PIF settings.

Device Contention Settings   Some non-Windows applications may try to use a COM or LPT port while it is in use by another application. To change the warning method for this situation, click a device name, and then click one of the option buttons. In most cases, choose Always Warn. If you select Never Warn, the non-Windows application can use the device at any time; select this option only when you're sure no other devices will be using the port. Select Idle when two devices may use the port, one after the other. Designate an idle time interval for the time that must elapse before the next application uses the port.

Scheduling Options   The Scheduling options let you divide the processor time between foreground and background operations for Windows applications, as discussed in the following section.

Multitasking Options

The microprocessor in your system can multitask by giving processing time to each running application, one after the other.

The *foreground application* is the currently active application, whether it is running in a window or full screen. *Background applications* may be running in a window, or full screen "behind" the active foreground window. *Exclusive processing* is when an application is given the full processing power of your system, and no other applications are processed.

In multitasking, the amount of processing time an application receives can be adjusted based on whether its window is currently active in the foreground or running in the background. Alternatively, processing can be stopped altogether when the application is in the background, or the application can be given exclusive processing when it is in the foreground.

In most cases, the default settings of the multitasking options are sufficient, but you can control them in special cases. For more information, refer to your Windows manual.

B

Using Program Information Files

Program Information Files (PIFs) are used to supply Windows with startup information for non-Windows applications. The files will normally have the same name as the program file, with the extension .PIF. PIFs are normally stored in the Windows directory. You create or edit existing PIFs using the PIF Editor, in the Windows Accessory group.

There is a difference between PIFs created for applications that run in standard mode and PIFs created for applications that run in 386 enhanced mode. A PIF for 386 enhanced mode contains multitasking options used to control how the application behaves when running with other applications.

Remember that you are not required to create a PIF for every non-Windows application. Windows will attempt to run the application using its own default values, but if the application doesn't run properly, you can try creating a PIF to specify custom parameters.

Note

You should always run the Setup utility after installing a non-Windows application. Choose Setup Applications from the Options menu. Windows will then find the application and attempt to create a PIF for it. Windows is aware of the required PIF settings of hundreds of non-Windows applications, so Setup is your best bet to get the application running properly under Windows.

Keep in mind these features and functions of Program Information Files. If a PIF already exists for an application, you can use the PIF editor to make some of the listed changes:

- PIFs are usually given the filename of their corresponding application, with the extension .PIF. For example, a PIF to start Microsoft Word would be named WORD.PIF.

- Information in PIFs is used to specify the path to the directory where the program is located, and the path to be used for retrieving and storing documents.

- Startup parameters for non-Windows applications can be specified in PIFs.

- You can start a non-Windows application by double-clicking its associated PIF file.

- An application can have several PIFs, each with different settings. One PIF could be created to use files from a business directory, and another to use files from a personal data directory. You might also want to change the memory settings of one PIF if you need to load documents or run programs that require full system memory.

- You can create PIFs for batch files. Commands in batch files are executed sequentially and can be used to run other commands before or after running a non-Windows application. For example, you might load a memory-resident package before starting an application.

Using the PIF Editor

To start the PIF Editor, double-click its icon in the Program Manager. In a moment the PIF Editor dialog box appears. The first four items in the PIF Editor dialog box are common for all Windows modes. Complete these four text boxes first, as described in the following paragraphs. Then refer to the Help option for information on setting the other options. To edit an existing PIF, choose Open from the File menu.

Program Filename

In the Program Filename text box, type the path and filename of the program you want to run. Files can be executable files with the extension .EXE or .COM, or batch files with the extension .BAT.

To avoid startup problems when Windows can't find a non-Windows program, specify the path to program directories in the AUTOEXEC.BAT file.

Tip

Window Title

The Window Title text box is optional. You can type a descriptive name for the PIF in this box. The name you type will appear under the application's icon on the desktop. Try to keep the name short so it doesn't overlap other names.

B

Optional Parameters

In the Optional Parameters box, type any additional startup parameters the application may require. For example, some versions of Microsoft Word for DOS can be started in graphics mode by typing **WORD /G**. To start Word in this way from a PIF, you would type **/G** in the Optional Parameters box. If you are creating a PIF to start a program and then load an existing file in its workspace, you can include the filename in the Optional Parameters box. Be sure to include the drive and path, if necessary.

If you want Windows to prompt you for a parameter whenever you start the application, type a question mark in the Optional Parameters box. This lets you start applications in a different way every time they are run.

Start-Up Directory

In the Start-up Directory field, type the name of the directory where files are to be opened and saved for this application. Typically, the directory where data files are stored is specified in this field. You can create several PIFs for a single application, each pointing to a different data directory. In this way, you can start applications with one PIF to access business files, and with another PIF to access personal files.

Other Settings

A complete explanation of the remaining settings in the PIF Editor dialog box is available on the PIF Editor help system.

Some applications don't need all the memory allocated to them in a PIF. You can reduce these allocations and provide more memory for your Windows applications. To do this, reduce the value in the KB Desired field in small increments until the application refuses to run; then return the setting to the last workable value.

If your application requires expanded memory, specify the amount of expanded memory it needs in the EMS Memory KB Required field of the 386 Enhanced version of this dialog box. If your application requires extended memory, specify the amount in the XMS Memory KB Required field.

If you're running low on memory, try setting the Video Memory to the Text option first; then switch to Low Graphics, and finally to High Graphics until you get the application to work.

In the 386 enhanced mode, applications will run faster if you choose the Full Screen option for the Display Usage setting, rather than the Windowed option. Then when you run the application, you can switch to a window when you need to by pressing (ALT)-(ENTER). Also, don't select the Background option for the Execution setting unless you really need to run the application while working in other windows. Background operation slows performance.

Be sure the Detect Idle Time option is marked in the Advanced Options dialog box. Windows will then borrow unused time allocated to your non-Windows application and give it to other applications.

B

C

Optimizing Windows's Performance

The best system configuration for Windows is an 80386 or 80486 system with 4 megabytes or more of memory. If you have an 80286 system, you'll be satisfied with Windows's performance—until you see it run on a 386 or 486. When you do, you'll probably want to upgrade your hardware, and the best way to do that is to add more memory. In fact, the majority of Windows performance problems are caused by insufficient memory. Once you've installed enough memory to keep your system running smoothly, you can achieve additional gains in performance by "tweaking" various system parameters, or changing the way you use Windows. This appendix offers some suggestions in these areas.

Choosing a Windows Mode

If you have a 386 or 486 system with more than 2MB of memory, Windows automatically starts in 386 enhanced mode. This mode lets you multitask non-Windows applications and use virtual memory. However, your system may operate faster if you start Windows in standard mode (by entering the command WIN /S at the DOS prompt). This is because in 386 enhanced mode your processor spends extra time maintaining the virtual environment used to multitask non-Windows applications and prevent them from conflicting with the memory and system resources of other applications.

Although there are definite advantages to using the 386 enhanced mode, speed is not usually one of them, unless you have the fastest system on the market. As mentioned before, the primary advantage of 386 enhanced mode is its ability to multitask non-Windows applications. But is multitasking essential for your needs? Is the slowdown in performance really worth it?

One of the first things you should do, if possible, is upgrade your DOS-based applications to Windows-compatible versions. Windows 3.0 was announced in early 1990, and by now most major applications are available in Windows versions at a typically small upgrade price. By upgrading all of your applications, you can work in the Windows environment most of the time and benefit from its graphical interface.

If you must run a non-Windows application, decide whether to run it in the multitasking environment of 386 enhanced mode. Remember that multitasking lets applications continue to process in the background while you work with other applications in the foreground. A non-Windows application can run in a resizable window in 386 enhanced mode, as well as full screen. Applications running in standard mode can only be displayed full screen.

Another aspect of this discussion is memory. If your system is low on memory, you may need the virtual memory capabilities of 386 enhanced mode. Because Windows applications share memory cooperatively, out-of-memory errors are more likely to occur when running non-Windows applications. Non-Windows applications run in conventional memory, so you need to take steps at the DOS level to increase conventional memory. You can do this by upgrading to Microsoft's MS-DOS 5.0 or Digital Research's DR DOS 6.0.

Tip

If you get out-of-memory problems when working with large graphic files and scanned images in a Windows application, start Windows in 386 enhanced mode. The swap file will make up for memory deficiencies. If you still have out-of-memory problems, try increasing the size of the swap file.

Improving the Performance of Non-Windows Applications

When running non-Windows applications in 386 enhanced mode, there are a few things you can do to improve performance. The options described in the following paragraphs are available from the Settings dialog box while an application is running in 386 enhanced mode, or you can specify them in a Program Information File, or PIF (see Appendix B) for the application. To open the Settings dialog box (Figure C-1), press (ALT)-(ESC), click the application's icon, and then choose Settings from its Control Menu.

Note

When the startup settings for 386 enhanced mode are established using a PIF, you can still change the settings when the application is running, using the options described here.

Window Versus Full-Screen Display Options   The best performance is realized when non-Windows applications run full screen, instead of in a window. So select Full Screen from the dialog box for the fastest mode, but select Window when you need to compare the contents of the non-Windows applications with other windows.

Exclusive Processing   Mark the Exclusive Processing check box under Tasking Options to give the non-Windows application exclusive use of the system processor.

Note

If you don't want the non-Windows application to process in the background or exclusively, leave both the Exclusive and Background check boxes unmarked. In this way, processing in the non-Windows application is suspended when you switch to Windows applications.

C

Figure C-1.   *The dialog box to edit the settings of a non-Windows application,*
                  available from its Control Menu in 386 enhanced mode

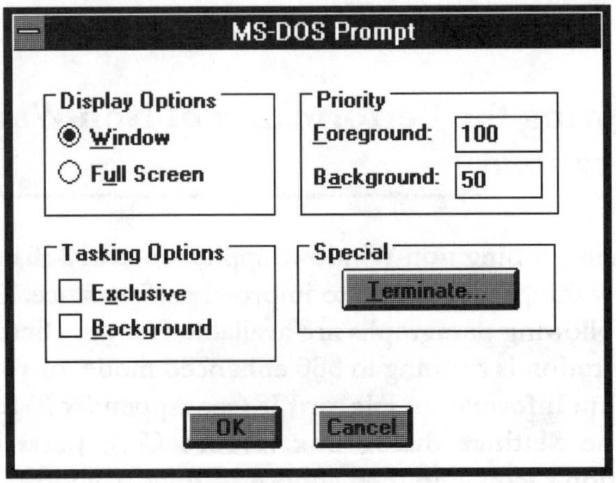

```
┌─────────────────────────────────────────────────┐
│ ─            MS-DOS Prompt                        │
├─────────────────────────────────────────────────┤
│  ┌─Display Options─┐  ┌─Priority──────────────┐   │
│  │ ⦿ Window        │  │ Foreground:  │ 100 │   │   │
│  │ ○ Full Screen   │  │ Background:  │ 50  │   │   │
│  └─────────────────┘  └───────────────────────┘   │
│                                                    │
│  ┌─Tasking Options─┐  ┌─Special───────────────┐   │
│  │ ☐ Exclusive     │  │    │ Terminate... │   │   │
│  │ ☐ Background    │  └───────────────────────┘   │
│  └─────────────────┘                               │
│                                                    │
│              │ OK │      │ Cancel │                │
└─────────────────────────────────────────────────┘
```

Optimizing System Startup

When your system does not have enough memory, no matter what type
of system it is or what type of applications you run, it will operate inefficiently,
or it will prevent you from running more than one or two applications at a
time. You can gain extra memory by running Windows in 386 enhanced mode
and using virtual memory, or by attempting to gain memory used by utilities
and applications at system startup. The second method is covered here.

Using Windows SYSEDIT

The SYSEDIT utility is a convenient tool for changing the contents of
your startup files. When you start SYSEDIT, the startup files are automatically
loaded into its workspace in separate document windows, as shown in Figure
C-2. You can thus quickly make changes to any file, save it, and exit SYSEDIT.

Figure C-2. *Use SYSEDIT to edit DOS and Windows startup files*

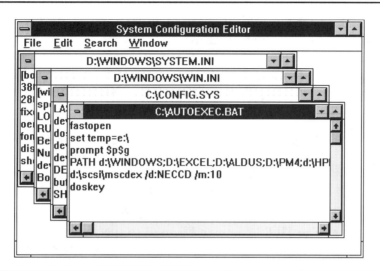

To start SYSEDIT, select Run from the Program Manager or File Manager File menu, and type **SYSEDIT** in the Command Line box. (Chapter 8, "Organizing Applications," tells you how to create a startup icon for SYS-EDIT.)

Tip

The following sections recommend disabling some commands in the startup files. Rather than deleting the command altogether, insert a REM statement before the command to disable. In this way, you can easily reinstate the command later. When your system boots, you'll see error messages for commands that start with REM statements in the CONFIG.SYS file, but you can ignore them.

Once you've made changes to the startup files, close the SYSEDIT window. SYSEDIT will ask if you want to save the changes you've made. Answer Yes to save changes in all four of the files that appear in the SYSEDIT window. Then reboot your system.

C

Note

Changes made to startup parameters do not take effect until you reboot your system.

Changing the CONFIG.SYS File

The CONFIG.SYS file is used to load device drivers for peripherals attached to your system, such as a mouse or special video equipment. The file may also hold DOS commands that configure the DOS operating parameters. For more information on these commands, refer to your DOS manual. To make the following changes, click the CONFIG.SYS document window in SYSEDIT.

- Remove any unnecessary device drivers for equipment that is no longer installed on your system. For example, if you use your mouse only with Windows applications, and not DOS applications, you can remove the command DEVICE=MOUSE.SYS, because mouse support is handled internally by Windows.

- The FILES command is used to specify the maximum number of files that can be open at once. Set its value at 30, using the following command:

   FILES = 30

Note

Set the FILES value higher only if you receive the error message "Insufficient file handles" when running an application.

- The BUFFERS command lets you specify the number of buffers used to improve disk access. If CONFIG.SYS contains a DEVICE= command that loads SMARTDrive, set BUFFERS to 10 with the following command:

   BUFFERS = 10

- The LASTDRIVE command is used to specify how many hard drives, RAM drives, and optical drives your system supports. This value is important if you are attached to network drives. For example, if you have an F drive, set LASTDRIVE to F with this command:

   LASTDRIVE = F

- The SHELL command uses the parameter /E to specify a larger amount of environment space. You may want to remove this value from the SHELL command to free up memory. If you receive an "Out of environment space" message, reinstate the command or increase its value.

- If you are using DOS 3.3 or higher, include this command in CONFIG.SYS:

    STACKS=9,256

- If your system has an EGA monitor, and you want to run non-Windows applications in standard mode, include this command in CONFIG.SYS:

    DEVICE=C:\WINDOWS\EGA.SYS

- *Do not remove* any lines that load the HIMEM.SYS extended memory manager or SMARTDRV.SYS cache program.

RAM Drives

Because the Windows SMARTDrive utility is very efficient at speeding up a system, RAM drives are usually not necessary under Windows. You may, however, gain some performance improvement by using a RAM drive for the storage of temporary files. Applications often create temporary files on disk to store information as you work with the application. These files are removed when you exit the application or Windows. Because these files are temporary, it makes sense to place them in a RAM drive. Moreover, access to a RAM drive is faster than to a disk drive. In addition, Print Manager queues its print files to a temporary directory; thus, its performance improves if the temporary directory is a RAM drive.

To install a RAM drive, include a command similar to the following in the CONFIG.SYS file. (Be sure to specify the correct drive and directory for your Windows directory.)

    DEVICE=C:\WINDOWS\RAMDRIVE.SYS 512 /E

The number at the end of the command specifies the size of the RAM drive. Here 512K is specified, but you can change this value based on the amount

C

of free memory you have. The /E parameter installs the RAM drive in extended memory; to install a RAM drive in expanded memory, use the /A parameter instead.

Once the RAM drive is installed, you direct temporary files to it by including a SET command in the AUTOEXEC.BAT file. For example, let's say the RAM drive will be drive E when your system reboots. You will need to include the following command in AUTOEXEC.BAT to direct temporary files to drive E:

SET TEMP=E:\

Some applications recognize the command TMP instead of TEMP. Therefore, include this command as well:

SET TMP=E:\

Note

If your system has many hard drives, network drives, and optical drives, you may need to also change the LASTDRIVE command to specify an additional drive letter for the RAM drive.

The AUTOEXEC.BAT File

The AUTOEXEC.BAT file automatically starts programs and utilities when your system is started. For example, commands you'll find in AUTO-EXEC.BAT are those that load terminate-and-stay-resident programs (TSRs). On a Windows system, TSRs should be loaded from within Windows, so you need to disable these commands in AUTOEXEC.BAT (using REM statements) and start them from within Windows. You can create startup icons for the TSRs, or start them using the Run command on the Program Manager File menu. TSRs started from within Windows are loaded into extended memory, leaving conventional memory free for non-Windows applications that need it.

If you installed a RAM drive, as discussed in the previous section, be sure to include in AUTOEXEC.BAT the SET command that directs temporary files to the RAM drive.

Improving Disk Performance

Performance diminishes if your system runs low on disk space. This section tells you how to periodically remove old files and optimize the way files are stored.

File fragmentation occurs when files are stored in several noncontiguous sectors on a disk. Reading fragmented files takes more time and causes the disk to work harder, since the read/write heads must jump to several different places to access the complete file. File fragmentation begins the first time you erase a file and save a new one in its place, because the old and new files are usually different in size. Each erased file leaves a blank area where a new file can be stored; however, if this area is not large enough to accommodate the new file, part of the new file is stored elsewhere. As more old files are erased and more new files are stored, fragmentation increases. Eventually, you must unfragment the disk.

Never run a disk fragmenting utility when a disk cache utility like SMARTDrive or DOS FASTOPEN is active. Temporarily disable the disk cache command in AU-TOEXEC.BAT and restart your system first.

Caution

Hard Disk Cleanup

To keep a hard drive running efficiently, you need to remove unnecessary files and *optimize* the drive to remove file fragmentation. Files you want to keep but that are not currently needed can be archived to disks or tape for future use.

You can use File Manager to archive and remove files, but you must close all other applications when doing so. To remove files in the Windows directories and subdirectories, use only the Setup utility, as described in "Removing Unnecessary Windows Files with Setup," later in this appendix.

Note

Deleting .BAK Files   Major candidates for deletion are .BAK files, which are the previous versions of files you've edited. These backup files are created

C

so you can quickly restore a file to the way it was before editing. When you're
sure you don't need them, you can delete these .BAK files.

One of the best ways to delete .BAK files is to use the File Manager Search
command. The Search dialog box is shown here:

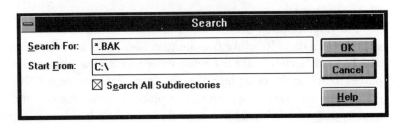

Type ***.BAK** in the Search For field, and in the Start From field specify the
drive to search. For this task, the Search All Subdirectories box should always
be marked. (The preceding example tells Windows to search all directories
on drive C for .BAK files.) When Windows displays the list of .BAK files,
highlight the files you want to remove and press the (DEL) key.

Removing Unnecessary Windows Files with Setup

When you really run short on disk space, it may be necessary to delete
some of the Windows files. You can do so by starting the Setup utility in the
Control Panel and choosing the Add/Remove Windows Components option.
You'll then see the dialog box shown in Figure C-3.

To remove an entire set of files, unmark one or more of the boxes in the
Windows Components column. To remove individual files, click the button
in the Customize column for the files you want to delete.

Disk Optimizing Techniques

After you've scanned your disk and removed unnecessary files, it's a good
idea to unfragment (optimize) the disk. You can use any of various third-party
utilities designed for this task, or the methods described here. In fact, it's wise
to put your disk on a regular optimizing schedule, say once every month, or
whenever you begin to see a slowdown in disk performance.

Figure C-3. *The Windows Setup dialog box that lets you add or remove Windows components*

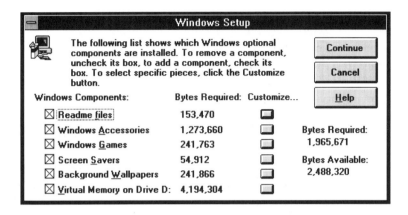

 Disk optimization can be conveniently scheduled to coincide with regularly scheduled disk backups.

Tip

Disk optimizing utilities automatically unfragment files by moving them around on the disk until they are all in a contiguous form. This shuffling method ensures that files are not lost should the system crash during the unfragmenting session. Popular disk optimizing programs are Speed Disk by Peter Norton Computing (now Symantec), and PC Tools by Central Point Software.

Backup-and-Restore Method

The backup-and-restore method of optimizing a disk can be done with the DOS BACKUP and RESTORE commands, or with a tape backup utility. The process involves first backing up your entire hard drive to disks or tape,

C

then formatting the hard disk, and finally restoring the data. When the files are restored, they are restored contiguously.

When you use the backup-and-restore method, it is important to do a file-by-file backup, not an image backup. An image backup-and-restore would copy the files exactly as they are on the hard drive, in fragmented form. On the other hand, the file-by-file method gathers together the fragmented portions of each file on the backup medium and restores them in that state (assuming the disk has been formatted).

Formatting the hard drive is an important step because it clears the table DOS uses to keep track of files and their location on the disk. This information includes the locations of the fragmented portions of the files. If you restore without removing this table, DOS could replace the files in their old locations, based on the table.

Another important step in the backup-and-restore process is to remove old files before you perform the backup. In this way, only the files you really want get restored to the drive, thus reducing clutter and increasing available disk space.

If you plan to unfragment the boot drive using this method, keep in mind that DOS won't let you format the drive from which you booted. You'll need to create a boot disk so you can restart your system from its floppy drive. Then you can format the hard disk. Be sure the FORMAT.COM command is on the disk.

Index

Windows Update Notes

The update notes provide the latest information on Windows and Windows products.
They are continually updated. The first update note will be available approximately
2 months after the release of Windows 3.1.

Send a $10 check or money order to the following address.
California residents add 72 cents sales tax.
Make checks payable to Tom Sheldon.

Tom Sheldon
P.O. Box 947
Cambria, CA 93428

Send the Windows Update Notes to:

Name: _____

Company/Phone: _____

Address: _____

City/State/Zip: _____

If you received previous update notes, write their date here: _____
There may be a slight delay as we prepare the next set.

Osborne McGraw-Hill

Tear off for Bookmark

Computer
Books

(800) 227-0900

Bookmarker Design — Lance Ravella

▼

You're important to us...

We'd like to know what you're interested in, what kinds of books you're looking for, and what you thought about this book in particular.

Please fill out the attached card and mail it in. We'll do our best to keep you informed about Osborne's newest books and special offers.

► *YES, Send Me a FREE Color Catalog of all Osborne computer books*
To Receive Catalog, Fill in Last 4 Digits of ISBN Number from Back of Book (see below bar code) 0-07-881 _ _ _ — _

Name: _____ Title: _____

Company: _____

Address: _____

City: _____ State: _____ Zip: _____

I'M PARTICULARLY INTERESTED IN THE FOLLOWING *(Check all that apply)*

I use this software
□ WordPerfect
□ Microsoft Word
□ WordStar
□ Lotus 1-2-3
□ Quattro
□ Others _____

I use this operating system
□ DOS
□ Windows
□ UNIX
□ Macintosh
□ Others _____

I rate this book:
□ Excellent □ Good □ Poor

I program in
□ C or C++
□ Pascal
□ BASIC
□ Others _____

I chose this book because
□ Recognized author's name
□ Osborne/McGraw-Hill's reputation
□ Read book review
□ Read Osborne catalog
□ Saw advertisement in store
□ Found/recommended in library
□ Required textbook
□ Price
□ Other _____

Comments _____

Topics I would like to see covered in future books by Osborne/McGraw-Hill include:

_____

IMPORTANT REMINDER
To get your FREE catalog, write in the last 4 digits of the ISBN number printed on the back cover (see below bar code) 0-07-881 _ _ _ — _

Osborne McGraw-Hill

Computer
Books

(800) 227-0900